DOCTOR
WITH TWO AUNTS

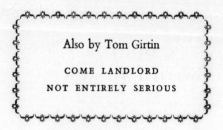

Also by Tom Girtin

COME LANDLORD
NOT ENTIRELY SERIOUS

Dr. John Wolcot by John Opie
By kind permission of
Sir John Seale, Bart.

DOCTOR
WITH TWO AUNTS

A biography of
PETER PINDAR

TOM GIRTIN

HUTCHINSON OF LONDON

HUTCHINSON & CO. (*Publishers*) LTD
178–202 Great Portland Street, London, W.1

London Melbourne Sydney
Auckland Bombay Toronto
Johannesburg New York

*

First published 1959

*This book has been set in Bembo type face. It has
been printed in Great Britain by The Anchor Press,
Ltd., in Tiptree, Essex, on Antique Wove paper and
bound by Taylor Garnett Evans & Co., Ltd., in
Watford, Herts*

DEDICATED
IN LOVE AND GRATITUDE
TO MY PARENTS

ACKNOWLEDGMENTS

My thanks must go, as always, to the Staffs of the Reading Room and the Print Room at the British Museum and of the London Library. Moreover, I am deeply indebted to all those in the West of England who by their friendliness as well as by their active co-operation and interest made my task more easy. Among many others are those in charge of the Maritime Museum at Falmouth and in the Town Clerk's office at Truro.

In particular I am most grateful to Miss Mary Peter of the Plymouth Art Gallery and to Mr H. L. Douch of the Royal Institution of Cornwall at Truro.

And to my wife, who for so long both suffered and encouraged John Wolcot, I owe—quite apart from all her help in research and criticism—the happy results of a number of positively inspired suggestions.

T. G.

ILLUSTRATIONS

UNSOLICITED TESTIMONIALS
ABOUT DR JOHN WOLCOT

How well he wrote, how original his style and talents; he understood character thoroughly, he played with human foibles.
—*William Beckford*

That desperately facetious Drawcansir.—*Dr Whalley*

The most unsparing calumniator of his time.
—*Sir Walter Scott*

This modern Aretin.—*Robert Chambers*

I swear to you that my flesh creeps at his name!
—*S. T. Coleridge*

The miscreant Peter Pindar.—*William Cobbett*

A delightful fellow and a first favourite of mine.
—*Robert Burns*

A man who possessed extraordinary powers, great acquisitions and an original genius . . . a man among those of the most distinguished talents that this country has produced and whose works ought and must be considered as compositions marked by extraordinary powers, inexhaustible humour, satire and imagination.—*John Taylor*

A venomous reptile . . . a vile compound of Blasphemy and Obscenity.—*John Agg*

Merry and Wise.—*William Hazlitt*

Old, obscene, beastly Peter Pindar.—*Charles Lamb*

That buffoon Peter Pindar.—*de Quincey*

Boileau and Pope and the redoubted Peter. These are great names.—*William Wordsworth*

Nature has seldom afforded a more original genius.
—*Gentleman's Magazine*

More original than any other poet since the days of Shakespeare.—*Ladies' Magazine*

This motley renegade, half Apothecary, half Parson.
—*The Times*

Ein potpourriartiger Charakter.—*Theo Reitterer*

'I SWEAR to you that my flesh creeps at his name,' Samuel Taylor Coleridge wrote to Perdita's daughter.

This became so common a sentiment that it is almost surprising that no violent portents were reported from the South Hams of Devonshire the day the Wolcots' fourth child was born. In after years there were so many people, including clergymen of the Established Church, who were ready and willing to contribute, without any excessive regard for strict accuracy, to the compilation of a horrid legend that anything might have been expected. The fact that John Wolcot was subsequently terrified of lightning they might well have adduced as evidence that a tempest had that day dropped fire, but they missed the opportunity. If any bird of night sat hooting and shrieking at noonday in Kingsbridge market-place they failed to notice it. Even the date on which Mary—before her marriage to Alexander Wolcot, the surgeon, she had been a Miss Ryder—gave birth to her second son went unrecorded. One descendant of the family put the year as early as 1737, but as John was not baptized until May 9th, 1738, the latter year, most usually given as that of his birth, seems more likely.

Kingsbridge at the head of the long, twisting inlet from Salcombe forms a twin parish with Dodbrooke, whose fifteenth-century church stands high above the town, and it was in Dodbrooke Church that the baptism took place. On another May day, three years earlier, William, the infant first-born son, had also been baptized there—only ten days before his burial.

Now John came as a brother for Mary, aged four, and Grace, aged two. In the ancient font where, as is rather sweepingly asserted, 'never a queerer Christian was baptized', his original sin was washed away, and the family returned with the new heir to their 'smart little mansion with a white front on a gentle verdant declivity extending to the water's edge at the flow of the tide'. Standing on the east side of the estuary, it was an old property that had belonged to them for several generations. Dodbrooke at that time consisted of no more than twenty or thirty houses; the narrow road to Dartmouth separated the Wolcots' home from its walled garden and barn. There were two or three large chestnut trees on the lawn, and the setting of grass and foliage sloping down on both sides of the narrow inlet to the waters' edge was one of great peace. Indeed it is hard to believe that so gentle a landscape could have produced a figure so bitterly controversial as John Wolcot was to become.

★   ★   ★   ★   ★

There were enemies who, in later years, adduced from apocryphal incidents in his early life reasons for the twists in his character. After more than half a century in 1800 when, under the *nom de plume* of 'Peter Pindar', John Wolcot was at the height of his fame, an anonymous correspondent declared in a letter to the Editor of the *Anti-Jacobin*:

> '. . . the cause of his disgusting propensity is not commonly understood. I therefore beg leave to lay before your readers the origin of this writer's fondness not for the sublime and beautiful but for "*the beastly*".

> Peter was but two days old
> When his nurse, old Cornish Dinah
> Let the ill-starr'd bantling fall
> Into vase of *Cloacina*.

> Peter was in such a pickle
> No one e'er could get him clean
> Though they rubb'd him, mopp'd and scrubb'd him
> Ev'ry effort vain has been.'

There was a good deal more in this vein—which surely anticipated the 'Ruthless Rhyme'—concluding:

From such a wretch his Theban title
The public voice indignant takes
No longer Peter Pindar call him
His *true* name's the Walking Jakes.

The writer signed himself 'Anti-Sordes'.

Another critic foisted upon him the Pindaric legend that, in his infancy, a swarm of bees alighted on his cradle and left honey on his lips—an invention clearly aimed at providing the opportunity for comment that the swarm must surely have been of wasps which left the caustic venom of their stings and not their honey. Nor were there lacking those who would imply that any bee settling on the infant Wolcot cradle was likely to have its wings torn off.

> His little tongue in blasphemies was loos'd
> His little hands in deeds of horror us'd
> While mangled insects strew'd his cradle o'er
> And limbs of birds distained his bib with gore

said William Gifford also in 1800—clearly a vintage year for invective—investing the baby with what must have been a remarkable agility.

Happily unaware of this literary jungle John Wolcot played under the chestnut trees.

*   *   *   *   *

The school in Kingsbridge to which at the age of six he was sent was already respectably old. Thomas Crispin, a Kingsbridge man who had prospered as a Fuller in Exeter, had not forgotten his old birthplace. In 1670 he had built and endowed the Free Grammar School that bore his name. Over the door he had rather pleasingly caused to be placed the inscription:

> Lord ^t_w I have was thou ^t_y gavest me
> And of thine owne this I return to thee.

It was a neatly turned couplet and no bad example in compression for young Wolcot: in all probability—for the standard of education in the West was high—quite early in his school career he found himself engaged in the task of translating it into Latin verse. Certainly the headmaster, John Morris the Quaker, in addition to being a young man, popular with the boys and of an amiable disposition, had the reputation of being a good scholar. He was only twenty-seven when John Wolcot first attended his school, and when he died at the age of seventy-one his epitaph gave almost as much praise to his early and still living pupil as to himself. The third and fourth stanzas point out:

> . . . From his instruction Wolcot caught
> The spark that kindled radiant thought
> Illumined paths that led to fame
> And with the Nine enrolled his name.
>
> Blest shade! That could the Muse inspire—
> The modern Pindar's sounding lyre;
> Harmonious lays that charm the heart
> And pleasures balmy zest impart.

It is almost with reluctance that the anonymous writer tears himself away to return to the subject of the epitaph:

> Such liv'd the man; interred he lies
> Expectant with the good to rise
> May those who read these lines as well
> Deserve among the just to dwell.

It is tempting, but unprofitable, to speculate on the authorship. Whoever the writer may have been, he saw Peter Pindar in a very different light from those whose verses have already been quoted. 'Pleasures balmy zest . . .'—it was not thus that 'Anti-Sordes' or William Gifford saw him.

*   *   *   *   *

Infant survival in the eighteenth century, even in a doctor's family, was a chancy business. In the Wolcot ménage the Lord gave and the Lord took away. When John was one year old a younger sister Amy had been born. When he was two his sister Grace had died. When he was three the last of the family, Ann, appeared. When he was five his oldest sister Mary died. Jacky, as he was called, was now the senior of three children. It would not be unnatural if he showed off before his two sisters, and there are indications that he was beginning to be known around Kingsbridge as a wild character. There was, for example, the incident with the cobbler. Jack's way to school lay along Fore Street, down which the town spills precipitously to the quayside, and each day, both coming and going, he had to pass a cobbler's shop. The snob, a man evidently of one idea, never failed to call out after him, 'Jacky, you've been *whipped* today!' This line, though it does not now seem particularly sparkling, he repeated *ad nauseam*, jovially rasping out the word 'whipped' over and over again in time to coincide with the whiz of his waxed thread as he drew it through sole and upper.

In time this performance began to pall on young Wolcot: he determined to silence the cobbler. One day, returning from school, as the fellow sat at the window of his shop repeating his parrot cry, John Wolcot produced a horse pistol and discharged it full in his tormentor's face. The man fell back, his features unrecognizable beneath a torrent of blood. The rattle of the explosion and the cries of the victim brought people running. The cobbler's son shouted out with a somewhat curious complacency that he was 'darned if Master Wolcot hadn't a scat vather's brains clean over the shop'. The miscreant was seized by passers-by. They sent for the constable. There were plenty of witnesses to agree darkly that they 'allays *had* said as how the young blackkurt would come to the gallies'. As it turned out they were proved wrong. The cobbler seemed, for one who has received from close range the contents of a horse-pistol, remarkably alive. The blood was sponged from his face and he was found, though no doubt suffering from shock, to be quite uninjured. The horse-pistol had been loaded with nothing more lethal than bullock's blood, but none the less it achieved its aim; henceforth the cobbler remained silent when Master Wolcot passed his window.

Such was the story. It is only after brief consideration that doubts begin to creep in. Without going too deeply into the subject of eighteenth-century fire-arms, certain technical objections present themselves. How was a horse-pistol full of blood secreted about a boy's person? When it was presented at the cobbler's head why did the blood not escape before the charge was exploded? How . . . but the tale is not for too close investigation. It is significant only because it has the appearance of being handed down by word of mouth in the town and not attached to him by enemies subsequently made in the great outside world. And, as a piece of folk-lore, it indicates the sort of thing that was expected of Dr Wolcot's son.

*   *   *   *   *

That Kingsbridge held happy memories for him is evident. Often in later years he spoke wistfully of returning there. He would rebuild the family house and escaping from the literary jungle he would live again in Arcadia. If he had made enemies in the South Hams it was clear that in retrospect they caused him no embarrassment. Kingsbridge and Dodbrooke, in their peaceful fertile landscape, represented the Golden Age that came to an end when, just after he had entered his teens, in 1751, his father Alexander Wolcot died. It is not absolutely clear why Jacky should have been sent away to live with his uncle John, the surgeon-apothecary, in Fowey. It is possible that his father's death coincided with the time when he had outgrown Crispin's Free School. If the story of the cobbler may be taken as symbolical it may well have been thought that his upbringing would prove too much for a widow with two young daughters to cope with. And although it seems likely that eventually they all moved to Fowey (for sister Amy married a Fowey man—yet another doctor in the family—and both sister Ann and his mother were buried there), seldom, if ever again, did Jacky live in his mother's house.

'Good old Doctor John Wolcot [wrote Edward Long, who as a schoolboy at Liskeard Grammar School sometimes spent his holidays with the doctor] was an old Bachelor and his Family consisted beside himself of an elderly sister named Roberts and Mr Joseph Fox, the Quaker, who was his apprentice. . . . The Doctor was one of the sweetest humoured souls in the world and I believe one of the most innocent and virtuous . . . very expert and judicious in the medical line and universally respected. . . . Mrs Roberts had a smattering of bad Latin and loved an argument but she governed her Bachelor Brother with an absolute Sway. During one of the last vacations I spent there there came an aunt of the Doctor's, from Bideford, I think, and brought with her a clumsy but arch-looking boy, since his manhood well-known by the name of Peter Pindar. He at this early period shewed a degree of quickness in repartee and sarcastic jokes which was the first dawning of that satiric humour he afterwards displayed. As he removed to Liskeard we soon became schoolfellows. I do not recollect he was remarkable there for anything so much as negligence of his dress and person. . . .'

From this it may be inferred that he was sent to Liskeard as a boarder. The school, at that time under the headmastership of a Mr Heyden, stood on a height overlooking the town. It appears to have consisted of nothing more than one long room, gabled at both ends and open to the rafters of the roof, with a smaller room at one side of it where there was a fireplace and where the boys said their lessons in winter. Built on the site of and using the materials from an old Roman fort—said to be a station of the Legio Augusti Victrix—and standing in three or four acres of playground surrounded by remains of Roman walls, it sounds, with its old rusty cannon outside the door, just a little bleak.

The fact that young Wolcot was allowed to be negligent in dress and person is unlikely to have pleased the redoubtable Aunt Amy Roberts: within a year Jack had been removed to Dr Fisher's Academy in Bodmin. Fisher, wrote one of Wolcot's Cornish obituarists, was

'a severe disciplinarian but considered as a sound classical scholar; and he was not only fond of poetry himself but cultivated a taste for it in his pupils. . . . It is therefore extremely probable that Wolcot was not wholly unindebted for his subsequent celebrity to the care of his old master. . . .'

Nor, though it was in a quite different way, was he wholly

unindebted for his subsequent notoriety to life in his uncle's house at Fowey.

On the face of it there was no reason why the time should not have passed pleasantly enough. In the holidays there was sailing and fishing on the River Fowey. There were mixed boating parties and walks through the woods, and drinking creamy coffee on the river banks to the sound of music and the 'triumph of the echoing horn'. In many ways, if the pilchards of which Fowey in those days reeked may be discounted, it was idyllic, but there was a worm—or, rather, two worms—i' the bud.

It is a pity that so little is known of Jack Wolcot's two aunts. Aunt Amy, the one who held absolute sway over Dr Wolcot, had been married to Jones Roberts an attorney at Fowey, and when, in 1745, she was widowed she went to keep house for her bachelor brother. Of the other aunt, the spinster Mary Wolcot, even less is known. Though she lived at Fowey, Edward Long does not mention her in her brother's household, but she must have been a constant caller at the house for there are a number of scattered references to the fact that the young Wolcot was brought up by two aunts. The *Penny Cyclopaedia*, for example, comments that 'he much annoyed his uncle and two aunts by cultivating his talents for versifying and painting'.

Spinsters and childless widows, though they often have an exaggerated confidence in their abilities, are not always best qualified to bring up other people's children. Male children, in particular, who are brought up by a number of managing women, are apt to develop strongly marked defence mechanisms. They acquire an imperviousness to constantly reiterated prohibitions. They, who are not permitted to shine at home, not infrequently seek, outside their family circle, to shock and to show by their unorthodox behaviour the independence that they feel has been denied to them. They demonstrate an increasing antipathy to authority (whether real or merely pompously apparent) that borders on the pathological. When they take pains to please they can be disarmingly lovable. To live with them is nerve-racking but at least they are seldom dull.

If this were true of John Wolcot it would explain much. The contrary elements in his character would be reconciled. And although a certain scepticism may be aroused when some canting sinner blames his behaviour on his early upbringing, yet a casual remark made upon some irrelevent occasion may provide the necessary clue to his delinquency.

And it was to respectable old John Taylor, the editor of the *Morning Post*, his friend of many years and his constant defender, that John Wolcot, one day late in his life, let slip a significant remark: he had been 'kept under rigid control by two aunts who cowed his spirit so much that though he had long been released from their tyranny he should never think himself a man'.

And as the eighteenth century clatters on, behind the man whom *The Times* called 'this motley renegade, half Apothecary half Parson' it becomes increasingly possible to sense the shadowy, incorporeal presence of Amy and Mary the two aunts.

2

At the age of seventeen young Wolcot left Bodmin School and became, rather later than usual with most boys but still as had always been intended, an apprentice to his uncle the surgeon-apothecary. The school had turned him out to be a very fair Latin scholar with an adequate knowledge of Greek and with an over-riding passion for verse. Somewhere, too, he had picked up an appreciation of, and a more than elementary skill in, art and music.

That a scientist should first be an all-round personality with a knowledge of the humanities was not then the fantastic idea that, two hundred years later, it seemed to the technocrat, with results that became depressingly apparent. Of course there is always the danger that acquaintance with the arts may arouse an antipathy to science: in Jack Wolcot's case this soon became obvious. Of his job he was later to write, in the form of directions to the pupils of country apothecaries:

> The lad who would as 'pothecary shine
> Should powder claws of crabs, and jalap, fine
> Keep the shop clean and watch it like a porter
> Learn to boil clysters; nay to give them too
> If blinking nurses can't the business do
> Write well the labels and wipe well the mortar.
>
> Before the boys can rise to master tanners
> Humble these boys must be and master *manners*
> Despising Pride whose wish it is to wreck 'em
> And mornings with a bucket and a stick
> Should never once disdain to pick
> From street to street rich lumps of *album graecum*.

The West Country at this time was putting out into the world some famous characters to spur the ambitions of a young man who had it in his head to be something more than an apothecary-surgeon in a sleepy Cornish village. Sir Joshua Reynolds from Plympton, Admiral Boscawen, Pitt the elder . . . these were names to conjure with and Wolcot was not very zealous, in his own words, to become a plodder:

> 'As my uncle was always averse to my shining I used to steal away to an old ruined tower, situate on a rock, close by the sea where many an early and late hour was devoted to the Muses.'

The old towers of Fowey were built as coastal defences, some by Edward IV, others by Henry VIII: as Turner's view of them clearly shows they are dramatically situated and ideal haunts for a young romantic, feeling himself misunderstood and already at odds with the adult world. There, safely removed from the ever-watchful gaze of his aunts 'who although women of solid intellects and literary acquirements could not overcome the common prejudice that poetry is a very dangerous interruption to business', he could give himself up to the pangs of love, inevitably unrequited.

Three girls, at least, he worshipped in poetic theory. In an Answer to a Faded Beauty's pertinent question

> 'Whither! Oh whither are my graces gone?'

he replied

> 'I'll tell thee, fair one, where thy charms are flown
> Flown to the nymphs where all perfection springs
> To peerless Coryton, to Pennington and Kings!'

Of these Miss Coryton seems to have affected him most seriously. His acquaintance with her had only lasted a short time but, as he said himself, to a man of tolerable discernment she was a mistress of such perfection as almost her entire sex were strangers to. Caught, as he admitted, by her natural, easy, innocent, unaffected

23

simplicity, he poured out to her from his romantic solitude verses addressed variously to Delia or to Flavia:

> . . . Flavia's cheek with beauty glows
> Fresher than the Damask Rose
> Flavia rolls the brightest eye
> Cause of many a thousand sigh
> See the trembling lightnings play
> Keener than the di'monds ray
> Flavia's pouting purple lip
> (Where the Loves soft Nectar sip)
> Sweeter than the flow'rs that blow
> Beats the coral's charming glow. . . .

Hardly had he finished than he heard from her that she loved another. Because he was hurt his sentiments had to be hidden behind a self-consciously dramatic façade.

'How think you [he wrote to her] did I receive the news of your being flown? Why it came like a clap of thunder. J. S. brought it with all the air of a triumph, hugging himself on his own good fortune and happy at my disappointment. I could have torn the brute to pieces for refusing to call me [out]. I abused him in the most severe language; and not the innocent Miss Coryton herself can condemn me for it on the smallest consideration of the circumstances. Your sending back by him your remembrance of me exasperated me to the last degree against him as it engaged me the more to you. His answers were paltry and equivocating. I am this instant in a rage to think on it. Good G—d! Miss Coryton such outrages are inexcusable for the philosophy of Job never met with so severe a trial. . . .'

All the same the verses were too good to waste:

> Flavia boasts a gentle breast
> Fair, inimitable chest. . . .

With the uncertain artist's desire for nothing so much as recognition he packed them off to Miss Coryton under the same cover

24

as the angry letter the penultimate sentence of which began, 'I am at this moment to be plagued with business very disagreeable to my present state of mind. . . .' He was wanted in the shop.

*　　*　　*　　*　　*

But the loss of Miss Coryton could be forgotten in the discovery of Miss Betsy Cranch. Of all the girls that Wolcot ever knew Betsy Cranch was the nonpareil. More than sixty years later he still spoke of her with affection. Now at the age of seventeen what were perhaps his first published verses appeared in *Martin's Magazine* addressed to her. More will be said of Betsy later—that she must have been of great personality and charm is apparent, and the knowledge that he loved her with a hopeless passion must have frequently come with its melancholy pleasure between himself and his work in his uncle's apothecary's shop. It was not work that he enjoyed. He disliked being at the beck and call of the public; he had tasted the pleasures of publication, and having once broken into the market in praise of Betsy Cranch he had followed up his success with another verse in *Martin's Magazine* in less romantic vein, *On the Recovery of Mr Pitt from an Attack of Gout.*

These few triumphs apart—triumphs which no doubt evoked a certain amount of sour comment from Aunt Amy and Aunt Mary—the years of his apprenticeship, the years of his adolescence, of his coming of age passed in the sort of obscurity from which he was determined to escape. He was twenty-four when his apprenticeship ended and he was still dependent upon his uncle and his aunts. Some time in 1761 they sent him for a year in France to learn the language which, although he brought back with him an aggressively British approach to the Continent, he did with some fluency.

> I hate the shrugging dogs
> I've lived among them, ate their frogs
> And vomited them up, thank God, again . . .

he was to write, recollecting, twenty-five years later though not in tranquillity, his emotions.

It is not surprising that in his first reaction to the temporary

25

escape from domestic control he should incline towards the more revolutionary philosophers. When he came back to England he took up residence in London where 'he walked the hospital and diligently attended the best medical, anatomical and chymical lectures'.

Another Cornish medical student, Thomas Giddy of Penzance, wrote to a friend:

> 'Mr John Wolcot who now lodges in the same house with me has very quick mental parts; but the component parts of his body are remarkably lazy and slow, except his fingers which applied to the fiddle or flute move very nimbly. *Entre nous* I am afraid he is too much acquainted with Shaftesbury and Voltair's notions. . . .'

Delille and Rousseau have also been mentioned as influences in his life but, in spite of this, the two young men became fast friends and eventually Giddy married Wolcot's cousin Mary. Nothing seems to be known of their life as medical students, other than that they lodged in the house of an asthmatic old landlady with a shadowy husband and a somewhat less shadowy daughter Nancy: it is unlikely to have been more edifying than the life of medical students anywhere or in any age. But for young Wolcot it meant for two years a further heady taste of freedom, and it can be imagined with what reluctance, his training completed, he returned in 1764 to Fowey and his uncle's house.

He was now twenty-six and still utterly dependent upon his family. His uncle was demanding that he should settle in Fowey and succeed him in his practice and shop. The constricted horizon of the small seaport town to a lover of the Fine Arts who had sampled what London could offer held no attraction. Moreover he was, once again, in love. Cousin Anna had married Benjamin Nankivell of Mithian the head of a family of nine brothers and sisters, and it was for sister Susan, then aged eighteen, that he yearned. In due course he proposed to her. The reply came in a letter from Mr Nankivell, and although it is not altogether possible to believe that Wolcot really sat down to his desk before unsealing the cover his reaction is not without interest as revealing his embryonic taste for the dramatic:

'Dear Mr Nankivell,

        I have just received yours which remains yet un-opened—now guess my sensations, all the blood up in my face, my ears tingling, my heart drumming against my ribs and my spirits in an uproar! What a thin partition betwixt me and despair or supreme felicity? Fortune has hitherto turned her back on me but let her now be kind and I will fairly for-give her all her former injurious treatment. . . . A confounded jilt! She has murdered me! . . . to be plain I have opened your letter, am acquainted with its contents and find my hopes blasted. . . . Blessed is he that expects nothing for he shall not be disappointed—had I followed the advice what a misfortune had I missed! Previous to your account of the amiable Sukey's determinations there is a profusion of unmerited com-pliments a sufficient indication of what was to follow—I im-mediately saw it in the light of a mother's giving sugar plums to her children to make their physic go down more glibly. . . .'

Susan's sister Joyce, it seemed, had extended her pity, but had refused her assistance—Wolcot hoped to see the day when her heart should 'be wringed like a dish-clout'. His own heart 'the mad rebellious rogue with a kick against my ribs as if he would burst them' cried as King David did over Jerusalem 'If I forget thee may my right hand forget its cunning'. He echoed Othello: 'perdition catch my soul but do I love her and when I love her not chaos is come again'. Though the letter resounds with a natural disappointment it is all just a shade too thoughtfully polished to seem entirely spontaneous.

However the force of the storm passes over:

'To whine over misfortune is both inconsistent with my nature and the idea of a character I am highly ambitious of—viz the philosopher—not the heathen philosopher but the man of wisdom! Now I am got upon self compliments let me add a more glaring instance of my vanity—'tis the opinion of a certain wise man (I have forgotten his name) that there is something in the object of our love similar to that we our-selves possess and which excited the passion—from these premises I draw this natural conclusion that the inexpressible sweetness of Sukey's disposition so perfectly corresponding with my own has laid such violent hands on my affections....'

Why, then, had Susan Nankivell rejected him? Her brother suggested it was due to a difference in religious opinions, but Wolcot, more deeply hurt than all his posturing seemed to indicate, knew better; it was due to the fact that Susan had taken him at his face value. It was because he had displayed 'a want of austerity in my manner which Nature never designed for me. . . .' Sukey had been misled, by the flippant barrier behind which he vainly sought to avoid being hurt. If only she would look deeper she would find her sentiments perfectly coincident with his own.

Certainly this apparent lack of austerity—some people remembered him later as having been, even at this period, 'exceedingly merry and droll' though 'not over nice in his person'—was continually showing itself in ways that seemed really quite indefensible and calculated to have a depressing effect on a serious-minded young girl.

There was the affair of the Cookworthy picnic, for example. Old William Cookworthy, the Quaker chemist who founded the Plymouth porcelain industry, was in the habit of going in the summer with his daughter Lydia who kept house for him and with his grandchildren and other assorted relatives to Fleet, a rural retreat near Plymouth. On one of these jaunts, which included among others Cookworthy's widowed daughter Mary Hobson who had been deformed by an accident in her childhood, Jack Wolcot accompanied the party. They arrived at the house fairly early in the day, opened it up, and while Molly King, their old servant, was getting the place ready and unpacking the picnic luncheon they had brought with them they decided to go for a ramble through the woods. They were quite unable to persuade Wolcot to accompany them on this walk: there was a good deal of bantering him about his laziness and lack of gallantry, but they were eventually forced to leave him behind.

'After some hours of enjoyment in the woods they found on reaching the house that all their food was in confusion, scarcely fit to be used and the servant in great dismay. She said that Mr Wolcot would pull it about and eat in spite of

28

all her endeavours to prevent him; that he had then gone away laughing and had left a piece of paper for them.'

They read it:

> Folks that are lean may hop like fleas
> And travel whereso'er they please
> But I who am so big's a tun
> Must find it hard to walk or run
> I therefore have compos'd this card
> To say that I have laboured hard
> To eat the beef and to devour
> The pie which was confounded sour
> And that I'm gone t'escape a rattling
> From Sukey and the widow waddling.

It was behaviour hardly excusable, especially with its cruel reference in the last line to Mary Hobson's infirmity, in a loutish boy: for a man of twenty-six there is nothing that can be said in its defence. In essence, of course, Wolcot, living at home in a sleepy fishing village, still under the control of his dominant relatives and engaged in work he did not like, was, even at the age of twenty-six, little better than a loutish boy.

'Coarse, indolent and selfish' he was called for his behaviour at the picnic. The comment was mild, and it is hardly surprising that there were other picnic parties to which he was not invited—at one of these, in spite of all precautions, those sitting down to the spread discovered the apple pie to be filled with stones instead of fruit, together with a mocking rhyme.

That a serious-minded young woman such as Susan Nankivell should have refused to marry him is understandable, and yet there must have been something about him, though it was not always immediately apparent, that was irresistible. His gaiety was infectious. Many of his victims—those, at any rate, who could see below the surface—continued to like him. He was, for example, always welcome at Cookworthy's house in Nut Street, Plymouth, where he entertained the old man with diverting stories about the natives of the Devonshire and Cornish countryside. As for the natives, for some reason, they referred to Jack Wolcot as 'Maister Ould Cat'.

*　　*　　*　　*　　*

To escape permanently from the constricting limits of Fowey and life as a surgeon-apothecary, life in which he could find no excitement other than in acting like the under-developed young man he was, became a matter of urgency. Temporary escapes were few and far between. Although Susan had failed to change her mind—his 'strongest assurance of being ready to resign' the offensive levity of which she complained had not been accepted—Wolcot was still a visitor to his cousins the Nankivells of Mithian and sometimes there were escapades to be enjoyed upon the way, especially if he ran into his old fellow medical-student Thomas Giddy, amid the comparative sophistications of Truro. Returning to Fowey from one such expedition he wrote:

'Dear Bengy,
            That all my bones are not broken thou mayst discover by my being able to write thee this epistle. That they ought to have been broken is a proposition that will gain a pretty general assent. . . . I should have reflected on the too agreeable sorceries of St Agnes that seduced me from my duty to my dearly beloved relations. . . . With a determined resolution—you know—of reaching Fowey the same day I set off—at Truro the villainous Thomas Giddy undermined it and glorified in the victory—how wicked to triumph in the overthrow of the righteous! From hence you may deduce the excellent moral (if there be any moral in it) that we cannot be too guarded against the allurements of vice and that the best of men are not for ever and for aye fortified against the attacks of the old man.
            On Tuesday morning in the midst of thick rain (what a pity there was not a little thunder mixt with it) I set out for Fowey; an outset on so gloomy and dismal a day you will easily conceive to be a circumstance greatly recommending me to the favour of my relations as it strongly indicated an anxiety for home. On my arrival at Fowey by the quantity of dirt splashed about me (accidentally on purpose) I looked a riding dunghill. On approaching our door I paused awhile and encouraged myself beginning with this pretty expression of Sukey's: Jan Gout stand thy ground, collect all thy assurance and put on a bold face. . . .'

With this picture of him plucking up courage to face his uncle and his two aunts after being absent for a few days it is necessary to remind oneself that he was nearly thirty years old.

More than ever he must have burned to achieve his inde-pendence; and to do this demanded better qualifications than he then possessed. His writing, carried out in the romantic ruined tower, might provide, together with music and drawing, a mental escape but it showed no signs of providing him with a living even though, to encourage him, to lure him on with a will-of-the-wisp attraction, his acrostic addressed to Sally Pomeroy was published in *Blackwood's Magazine*. But for the immediate future, to earn enough money for his escape, he must improve himself. He decided to seek a medical degree that would raise him above the rank of a mere surgeon-apothecary. He selected for his purpose the University of Aberdeen. This may seem a curiously distant choice, but in the punning phrase of the *Anti-Jacobin* the uni-versities in Scotland 'were trying to get rich by *degrees*' and atten-ance at the university was not regarded as, in any way, essential. However

'it would appear that the diploma was not transmitted until after the receipt of the proper certificates testifying the skill and respectability of the candidate. The celebrated Dr Huxham, then residing at Plymouth, was so conscientious on the present occasion that he would not affix his signature until after a strict examination by himself.'

In due course a splendid

DIPLOMA
Medicinae Doctoratus
datum in favorem
Domini Joannis Woolcot
a Collegio Regio Aberdonensi
8vo Septembris 1767

was received. In the light of his subsequent success as a doctor it is likely that Wolcot was, in all probability, a more worthy recipi-ent than many others. The aunts it may be imagined were de-lighted by this: here was evidence, at last, that their insistence on his paying attention to business and their discouragement of the Arts was paying dividends. They would not have been human if they had not boasted in Fowey that their nephew was now Dr John Wolcot, M.D.

Wolcot's own account of the method in which he acquired the honour with its lengthy citation in Latin was: 'Huxham likes flummery. I supplied it liberally—he ate it greedily and gave me my diploma readily.'

It must have given him the greatest satisfaction to take the edge off his aunts' pleasure.

*   *   *   *   *

Among his uncle's patients at this time—some say, even, among his uncle's distant relatives by marriage—were members of the Trelawney family. And when Sir William Trelawney was appointed Governor of Jamaica Dr Wolcot saw his chance. He asked his uncle to pull such strings as might be necessary to get him an appointment to the governor's suite. This request must certainly have been something of a shock to the old man who had hoped to see his nephew succeeding him in his practice. According to one report he 'fell into a great passion, abused his nephew for his ingratitude and threatened to cut him off with a shilling'.

Eventually however, after much altercation, the young man got his way. An approach was made through those with the necessary influence and in due course, the eighteenth-century system of patronage having done what was necessary, young John Wolcot became physician to the governor's household.

In all the disappointment of his uncle's plans for the future there must surely have been an element of relief that the tiresome, dilatory young man, with the unhealthy taste for the Fine Arts, was going to travel a very long way from those it was so easy to shock.

As for Wolcot—at long last he was going to be independent. He was going to be free to behave as he wished.

3

THE last months of 1767 and the first months of 1768 were filled with preparations for the great adventure. He wrote from Fowey on September 2nd to Giddy who had a friend in London who was a fiddlemaker asking him to procure a three-guinea instrument, adding that no doubt he had heard of

'my intended peregrination to a place characterised for being hot as h . . l and as wicked as the d . . . l; and hot it must be if it be true as I have heard that on some particular warm days people can hear themselves fry like so many fish in the frying pan. Before I shall have spent a twelvemonth on the island I shall cry out with Me'nheer Ovid: "O rus quando ego te aspiciam"—you are acquainted I suppose with the respectable footing on which I shall proceed—in quality of Physician in ordinary to his excellency the Governor of Jamaica, a govt. filled by the Duke of Albemarle, the Duke of Portland, the Earl of Inchquin and others. To the first no less a man than Sir Hans Sloane, President of the Royal Society and Physician to H.M. went out as Physician in ordinary. Medicinae Doctor! hem! think now with what ineffable contempt I look upon you fumpers of the pestle. "Odi profanum vulgus et arceo."

The intent of my western expedition is undoubtedly to get money for which beautiful acquaintance I leave friends, sweethearts and old England! What a sacrifice to independency? . . .'

He was at any rate sailing under no false pretences. His motive was unequivocally stated: his hope that after a few years under the patronage of Sir William Trelawney and as beneficiary of all the perquisites that patronage could bestow he would be free for ever from Fowey and from medicine and from the aunts. To achieve that dream even Jamaica, the lovely plague-spot to which regiments of soldiers were sent and within a few weeks or months utterly swallowed up in the fever-filled graves, would be tolerable. There was much to be done in London getting ready for the voyage but he found time to write again to Giddy even though the letter was composed under difficulties—'drays, coaches and broad-wheeled carts are thundering at my back, milk screaming on one side of my head and smoking hot ginger-bread on the other so that there seems to be a general combination of the worst sounds in nature to try whether the drums of my ears are composed of steel instead of vellum. . . .'

He had set out to pay a visit to the house where he and Giddy had lodged as students, but while walking through St Thomas's Hospital a sudden strong premonition told him that he was wasting his time and that the old asthmatic landlady had died eighteen months earlier. None the less he continued on his way to find out how her few possessions had been disposed of, and in a manner which makes a refreshingly different climax to the story found that his premonition was entirely false. So certain had he been that she was dead that he afterwards professed himself hardly able to believe his eyes even though a sudden burst of asthmatic coughing (which caused him hastily to divert his proffered kiss away from her lips) persuaded him of her material nature.

Nancy, her daughter, delighted to see their old lodger, joined them. Wolcot asked after her father. 'Poor Dadda!' Nancy said sadly. Dadda, it seemed, had left them. Dadda had drank up his drink; Dadda was dead. 'Poor Dadda, good lass a day! Well . . .' she said, changing the subject and overwhelming Wolcot with a spate of questions: '. . . and how is Mr Giddy? Is he married? Yes—*well!* And children? Yes—*well!* And how is Mr Cookesley? . . .' The questions flowed on until they were interrupted by the entry 'with a mock-consequential strut' of another old acquaintance, one Anthony Hubback who had recently come back from the East Indies. To their enquiry about his expedition he replied with an emphatic, vulgar oath; he blasphemed with an air and began boasting of his many successes in love. Wolcot's comment: 'What an age!! when gentleman and scoundrel are coincident ideas' is revealing and so is the fact that he was not deceived by Hubback's dashing exterior:

'From the general tenour of his conversation he appeared to be extremely unhappy. . . . I am inclined to think he is not so great a rogue as he would induce the world to believe he is.'

Almost exactly one hundred years later a writer in *Blackwood's Magazine* was to say the same of John Wolcot.

$$\star \qquad \star \qquad \star \qquad \star \qquad \star$$

The strutting transparent Mr Anthony Hubback might be unhappy but John Wolcot, with life opening out with infinite promise before his feet, was on the crest of the wave:

'My time in London has been agreeably spent [he wrote to Giddy]; buildings, statues, pictures, books, music and plays are bewitching affairs. Ask the feelings of your own heart if I lie? Barry and Mrs Dancer I think you never saw. They are fine acquisitions to old Drury; the first in my opinion equal to Garrick, the last superior to Mrs Cibber. Barry I have seen in Jaffier and Romeo; Mrs Dancer in Belvidera and Juliet; it would be needless to tell you how the characters were played after saying that this eminent actor and actress performed them: and yet, my friend, notwithstanding all their eminence I have the assurance to find a number of faults among their excellences; in passionate and pathetic parts they are equal to our most perfect idea of just playing because they are equal to nature; but in declamation they run into cant and bombast; not Garrick himself is free; I appeal to yourself who have seen the little Roscius. The other night he appeared in Ranger and was inimitable; about a week before in Sir John Brute and was equally excellent! It has been a disputed fact whether he succeeds in the sock or the buskin; in the first after the strictest scrutiny I seldom ever caught him tripping; in the latter many times.

Mrs Yates was not in her zenith when you were in town; she is now the great luminary of Covent Garden; see her in the last act of Shore and you see the real unfortunate Jane; it is impossible to fancy it a deception—and eye her (?). In declamatory parts she is also faulty. So is Powell—so are all— the most exquisite singer that ever appeared at the Opera is Garducci, superior even to Manzoli of last year; Tenducci is a dog under a door to him. Campolini a fine songstress is likewise at the Haymarket but more of this when we meet. . . .'

He attended the first night of a new farce. 'It was damned,' he said, 'so ought the Author [to be] for writing it—it was a glorious uproar.' He was in fact acquiring a critical taste for the theatre which was, improbably enough, to bring him eventually on to the same stage, though at suitably opposed ends of the programme, with Charles Lamb and he was enjoying every minute of it. There were other Cornishmen in town and Wolcot had a bantering conversation with one of them—Nicholas Crews—who was courting that same Joyce Nankivell whose heart Wolcot had wished might be wringed like a dishclout.

'So, Mr Crews,' said Wolcot, 'you were happy I presume, very happy lately with the Miss Nankivells at your house?'

' 'pon my soul, sir,' admitted Crews, blushing, 'they are very fine girls.'

'So they are, Mr Crews: Joyce has the character of a wit.'

'She is devilish sensible, hem!' said Mr Crews, coughing in embarrassment.

'I think Sukey the handsomest,' said Wolcot, teasing him.

' 'pon my soul,' exclaimed Nicholas with emphasis, 'Miss Joyce is a pretty girl.'

'I wonder,' said Wolcot innocently, 'if any overtures were ever made them.'

'I don't know upon my word,' said Mr Crews, as if the thought had never struck him before.

'Let who will apply,' said his friend, sadly thinking of the adored Sukey; 'if he is not a disciple of Wesley, a good rank Methodist, he stands no more chance with them than a cat in hell without claws. I dare say some paltry rogue with a grave phiz and a mouthful of damnation, without a grain of honesty in his heart or a farthing in his pocket, will run away with one of them.'

'The devil he will!' exclaimed Mr Crews with some alarm.

'I have reason to believe it,' said Wolcot reminiscently. Crews stared at him.

'Whence had you your intelligence?' he asked.

'From their own sweet lips.'

'Then I'll be damned.'

'With all my heart,' said John Wolcot.

If he was still hankering after the obdurate Sue (who, as it happened, never married) he had little time for repining.

As he wrote to cousin Benjamin Nankivell on December 3rd, 1767, using a theatrical simile:

> 'I am at last arrived in the great city to prepare for the new farce in which I am shortly to make my appearance; my wigs, my hats, my swords, my canes, my laced cloathes and last of all (which however from its importance demanded first place in the catalogue) my chariot are all bespoke!'

Yet, splendid though the idea of possessing his own equipage and taking it with him on the long sea voyage might seem, it was not the visions of grandeur that powerfully affected him. Again he stated his general aim in life and his particular reason for the current expedition:

> 'Ah, Benjy, it is not the idea of grandeur but of independence that seduces me from Great Britain or I should rather say from Old England; to hope of placing myself by the labour of a few years beyond the caprice of a mob.'

He felt constrained to amplify this statement in a sentence that will evoke a burst of spontaneous applause from all those who have ever in any way found themselves servants of the public:

> 'This last passage of my letter perhaps contains somewhat of the unintelligible—turn apothecary, my friend, and get a number of patients and it will need no illustration. Should I be so fortunate,' he added, 'as to return with something of independence it will not be the least of my happiness as to find myself empowered to converse more freely with my friends at Mithian.'

37

For the days of the previous January, when he had paid them a visit, had been among the happiest days of his life:

> '... to be with you at St Agnes, to shoot woodcocks, play the fiddle to your damsels, descend into mines, talk of lodes, gozzans and flukans, exceeds all the state and grandeur I can imagine so rot the West Indies with all my heart. ...'

But in the name of independence he was committed. No doubt in his rôle as a member of the suite of the Governor-elect he was presented, on St Andrew's Day, Monday, November 30th, at the Court of George III. Repressed young countryman that he was, he was determined to be impressed by none of the splendours that the Court could provide. Yet as a stranger and unknown and alone he had to pluck up courage to mingle with those to whom he referred satirically as 'the deities of the earth'. He called philosophy to his aid: as he dressed for the occasion in a smart suit of white and gold with a bag wig and a gilt sword he held

> 'a serious confabulation with myself on the subject of nobility; on a philosophical analysis of nobility of title I found it to be the vox et praeteria nihil, transferable from a duke to a dog and therefore beneath my regard. To be confounded by the glare of dress I deemed absurd as I should carry as good a suit as most in the Drawing Room with this difference, too, in my favour that mine was paid for and theirs not. . . . But then their consummate wisdom! for the world has always annexed great talents to great fortune as if sense, like an estate, was entailed! This I considered as a popular error and sat it down with myself as a general axiom that the greater the man the greater the fool. . . .'

Fortified by these reflections he took a sedan chair from Temple Bar to St James's. On arrival he was set down to run the gauntlet of a long line of guards and spectators, but determined to appear composed and blasé he strutted forward carrying his hat fashionably under his left arm:

> 'Unfortunately in my march the sword got between my

legs and set me running to the no small diversion of the mob and guards; thank God I recovered myself though it was an even bet for sometime whether I should nose the ground or not. . . .'

Eventually he reached the upstairs drawing-room

'to see the King and the Queen and the Prince and the Princesses and the Dukes and the Duchesses, etc etc etc and behold I saw them! And behold I never desire to see them more!!'

The most sophisticated man-about-town could hardly have affected a greater disdain.

★   ★   ★   ★   ★

At last, on August 7th, 1768, the party, which included a young naval lieutenant, William Glanville Boscawen, set sail for Jamaica and after a pleasant eleven-day voyage they reached Madeira. Wolcot was entranced by the beauty of everything he saw. The governor, Lady Trelawney (the cousin whom Sir William had married in spite of family opposition, secretly and by night—she being rather curiously disguised for the ceremony as a boy) and the governor's entourage were guests in the country house of a Portuguese hidalgo.

'. . . we are extremely happy [Wolcot wrote], sometimes fiddling and fluting; at other times forming parties of pleasure on the mountains etc, etc, to make Father Time move off agreeably. The Governor is all ease and affability endeavouring always to render those about him as happy as himself. . . .'

Sometimes mounted on a donkey, sometimes on foot, he explored the woody mountain sides: on one occasion he met a peasant girl followed by a little black pig 'scarce bigger than my fist' but his solitary attempt to tease the pig ended in his being chased ignominiously down the mountain path by the girl and bombarded with large stones.

39

'The Manufactures [he noted] of the Island are (as the man said of the Monkeys) Grapes, Oranges, Lemons, Melons, Figs, Limes, Bugs and Itch in the highest perfection; the last commodity indeed everybody deals in from the Peasant to the Don so that it is not at all uncommon to see a circle of Quality crowding on their wrists and fingers like a parcel of Scotchmen. . . .'

One fiesta they paid a visit to the crowded hillside shrine of Our Lady of the Mount, where they found the statue decked with jewels and wearing a fine white wig. They appear to have shewn a certain reverence not always noticeable amongst tourists, placed alms in the offertory box and in general behaved with a decorum which earned the applause of the worshippers.

At the end of a fortnight they set sail once more and came to Teneriffe where the Spanish grandees received them with an even warmer hospitality. 'Our time slides away most deliciously —nothing but pleasure.' Each evening they drove to the house of the Governor of Teneriffe, listened to music, danced and enjoyed ice-cream and cool draughts of snow water and lemonade. Once again Wolcot was delighted by everything that he saw. The Peak was too high for them to make the expedition in a single day so, instead, they visited the city of Laguna which he found 'beyond all conception beautiful and so awfully striking as to awaken all the nobler feelings of the mind!'

The inhabitants of Teneriffe he found 'mighty civil and adorers of the English whom they look upon as belonging to the greatest nation in the world'. The party visited another shrine of Our Lady where they found the statue wearing a grey bob-wig, 'seemingly fresh off the Pipes'. There were, it is true, in this island Paradise, a few disadvantages. After staying, in the company of young Boscawen, at the house of Mr Mackerrick, a merchant in Santa Cruz, Wolcot was able to write a feeling *Ode to the Fleas of Teneriffe*. In it he also described himself as

> . . . a Doctor of redoubted skill
> A Briton born that dauntless deals in death
> Who to the Western IND proceeds, to kill
> And probably of thousands stop the breath.

40

A Bard, whose wing of thought and verse of fire
Shall bid with wonder all Parnassus start
A Bard whose converse Monarchs shall admire
And happy learn his lofty Odes by heart.[1]

But, verminous though they might be, he was entranced by the young ladies of the island.

He had always supposed that Spanish women were the most reserved people on earth: now he found them 'as full of talk and vivacity as the French or English and . . . though not so handsome as the latter, altogether as engaging'. He wrote a *Spenserian Imitation* to Donna Antonietta while visiting her villa:

'Instead of talking of Miss Jenny, Miss Letty, Miss Sukey, etc, it is nothing but Signora Donna Maria, Signora Donna Catherina etc.'

He professed himself again in love:

'My poor heart is lost to the Signora Donna Catherina and I believe nothing but a firm attachment to our Holy Religion prevents my turning Papist and marrying her.'

But in this it is possible that he was not being entirely serious. Certainly if he had any attachment to the Church of England it can have been no more than nominal or political for, although he might have been called a Deist, for he had a lively belief in a Universal Creator, he was not, and, as he frequently told old Thomas Polwhele, 'could not (with every struggle) be a Christian'. And, indeed, in this state of suspended spiritual animation he was to remain all his life.

The party stayed a leisurely two weeks in Teneriffe and Wolcot wrote '. . . should I be disappointed in my Jamaica views I shall still think myself happy in having gone thus far.'

Late in October they arrived at their destination.

---

[1] In a footnote to the 1794 edition of his *Collected Works* Wolcot remarked, 'Part of this prophecy has been amply verified.'

4

THE party landed at Port Royal and proceeded to St Jago de la
Vega or Spanish Town, the seat of Government, which was
described as 'a very dull town being totally devoid of commerce'.
The population consisted for the most part of men of varying
shades of colour—Mestizes, Quadroons, Mulattoes, Samboes and
Negroes. To Wolcot who had heard, in England, the many true
and dreadful tales of conditions in the White Man's Grave of the
eighteenth century it seemed highly probably that he would
before long contract one of the fatal diseases for which the island
was notorious.

'In consequence of such a conclusion [he wrote early in
January, 1796] I was for the first week extravagantly pious,
said my prayers three times a day which was three times
oftener than I had ever said them before and grace before
Meat with extreme fervency a circumstance that never happened before (owing to too high attention to the good things
on the Table) and gave sixpences frequently to the poor. After
a few of these truly Christian like proceedings I sat myself
down in expectation of Death with as much fortitude as the
brave Senators of Rome when they every moment waited to
have their throats cut by the Barbarians. My terrors are however subsided and I am inclined to think the Old Gentleman
will take no notice of me now as He has neglected it for so
long, for it is a general rule with Him to pay his compliments
to people immediately on their arrival.'

Now that he was relieved of this possibly not very serious fear
he found the time, in the pleasant company of the Trelawneys,
of Sir William's sister Anne and of young Boscawen, passed 'with

the utmost cheerfulness, and what in no small degree contributes to this cheerfulness is the idea of being one day able to live according to the popular acceptation of the word "independent"'. Always his cry was for independence. Never could he return to the days of family domination. He was thirty-one years old, but the fears of dependence were dying hard. Under the friendly patronage of Sir William there were all sorts of posts with their appropriate perquisites that might be his. There was the secretary-ship of the island, there might even be the governorship of the territory of the Mosquitoes, an Indian tribe on the Spanish main who owed allegiance to the British crown. Life was full of possibility: no wonder he was happy.

'The Governor [he wrote] is exceedingly liked, he adopts a different system of politics from those of his predecessors whose maxim it was to be attached to a party. Sir William declares against it and I believe will find the advantages: indeed I am pleased with such a determination for two reasons; in the first place for the Governor's repose; in the next for the power he will have for providing for his more intimate connections; you know what I mean. A Party would be full of eternal solicitations and devour every emolument. The King's House is a princely one and the state is kept up in great stile. . . .'

The King's House had been newly built in 1762, but it was fast falling into decay. New sash-cords were wanted for many of the windows, there were many windows broken and new panes of glass had been ordered to be sent from England. Under the influence of the West Indian climate the roof was rapidly reaching a precarious state, the outside offices were in a decrepit condition and the piazzas of the old buildings of the King's House were falling down. In this rather shabby splendour, amid the mahogany chairs with their fan backs and leather seats, the brass-gilt girandoles and the bronze busts of the Long Parlour, Trelawney dispensed a somewhat profuse hospitality. Wolcot the boon-companion, a splendid raconteur, well read, musical and a tolerable amateur artist, was much in demand.

Since the calls on his medical services were not extensive he performed a number of functions including what appears to have been that of grand master of ceremonies for the governor. The entertainment of visiting magnificos was entrusted to him and among these may be numbered the King of the Mosquitoes: on the arrival of every new governor their chief travelled to Jamaica for the express purpose not of giving, but receiving a present such as a tawdry lace coat or something of equivalent value.

Wolcot reported, on the occasion of the King of the Mosquitoes coming to visit Sir William Trelawney, that

> 'His Majesty was a very stout black man, exceedingly ignorant, nevertheless possessed of the sublimest ideas of royalty; very riotous and grieviously inclined to get drunk.'

This formidable figure came lurching up to Wolcot roaring out: 'Mo' drink for King! Mo' drink for King!'

'King, you are drunk already,' expostulated Wolcot.

'No, no; King no drunk. Mo' drink for King! Broder George love drink!'

'Broder George does not love drink; he is a sober man,' said Wolcot reprovingly. It must have been one of the last occasions on which he defended George III in public.

*   *   *   *   *

The arrival of Sir William Trelawney and his suite in Jamaica had coincided with the outbreak of a disastrous drought that was to last for nearly twenty months. In the sweltering heat of the island bathing parties must have been more than ever a desirable activity of social life. And on April 21st, 1769, a tragedy occurred that, unlikely as it must have seemed at the sad moment of its happening, was to have, years later, a most fortunate effect on John Wolcot's affairs. While swimming in a pond at the house of Sir Charles Price young Boscawen, the Admiral's son, was drowned. Wolcot in due course was moved, seated near the graveside of his friend, to produce an *Elegy*.

In its eighteenth-century conventional formality it is difficult to sense today any very deep emotion: Wolcot, however greatly he might be affected, was never really capable of conveying his

44

more serious feelings. To use the same sort of language in which he had criticized Garrick to Thomas Giddy, he excelled in the sock rather than the buskin—with what effects on his matrimonial chances has already been seen.

> Forlorn from shade to shade I rove
> By friendship's sacred spirit led
> Where Horror wraps the twilight grove
> That glooming seems to mourn the dead.
>
> Dear youth! tho' hence I wander far
> Thy fate will cloud each rising morn
> And lo! with evening's dewy star
> My tears shall bathe thy distant urn. . . .
>
> . . . With Sculpture let the marble groan
> Where Flatt'ry mocks the lifeless ear—
> How nobler far thy nameless stone
> Embalm'd by Pity's simple tear.

He read the verses through: they seemed at any rate competent enough for publication. He shipped them off to an editor in England. And there for some twelve years the matter rested; the influence the event was to have upon his affairs quietly germinating in the dusty files of a publisher's office.

In the meantime the life of a general factotum and court jester may have been entertaining, but there was little in it of the rich stuff of which preferment was made. It is probably true to say that the Governor of Jamaica had very little in the way of further patronage to bestow. From the point of view of a remunerative private medical practice there were not only too few white settlers, but also the whole island had been too much impoverished by a war with the runaway Maroons to offer many hopes in that direction.

To add to the difficulties that lay in Wolcot's path towards the goal of independence the death in England of Lord Shelburne placed administrative difficulties in the way of his preferment.

'You know, my dear Wolcot,' said the governor one day, 'that I am eager to serve you; but you must also be convinced of the insufficiency of my means. What a pity you were not bred a parson!'

45

The immediate reason for this comment lay in the fact that the rector of the rich Parish of St Anne, a living in the gift of the governor, was seriously ill and was unlikely to survive. Wolcot, pondering the situation, came to the conclusion that the implied suggestion that he should seek Holy Orders was not without its possibilities. The living, even though it might not make him a rich man, would make him comfortably well-off. It was worth some £1,200–£1,500 a year which, by the monetary standards of the time, was not inconsiderable. Moreover the job was one that was in the nature of a sinecure. Sunday was the market day, the negroes' holiday, and the planters, settling their accounts and adjusting their affairs, were more busy than on any other day of the week. The white people were, on the whole, lax in their morals; the clergy were inattentive of their duty. Attendance at church was negligible.

Wolcot expressed these thoughts to the governor.

'Away then to England!' exclaimed the genial Sir William. 'Get yourself japanned. But remember not to return with the hypocritical solemnity of a priest. I have just bestowed a good living on a parson who believes not all he preaches and what he really believes he is afraid to preach. You may very conscientiously declare that you have an internal call, for the same expression will equally suit a hungry stomach and the soul.'

It was to this state that the system of advowsons had brought the Established Church in the middle of the eighteenth century. Dr John Wolcot, the Deist who could not bring himself to believe in Christianity, armed with letters of recommendation couched in the warmest terms, set sail for England to seek ordination.

* * * * *

Richard Terry, the Bishop of London in whose Diocese Jamaica fell, was a man of whom Horace Walpole is reported to have remarked that his only episcopal qualifications were a sonorous delivery and an assiduity of backstairs address.

On June 24th, 1769, John Wolcot appeared before him and became without any apparent difficulty a deacon of the Church of England. The following day he became a priest, the news being promulgated in a manner that though, no doubt, standard and

46

formal must have raised an answering secret hilarity in Wolcot himself who, with all his faults, was neither a hypocrite nor suffering from illusions about his own nature:

'Be it known unto all men by these presents that we Richard by divine permission Bishop of London holding by the assistance of Almighty God a Special Ordination . . . did admit our beloved in Christ John Wolcot MD of the University of Aberdeen (of whose virtuous and pious Life and Conversation and competent Learning and Knowledge in the Holy Scriptures We were well assured) . . .'

The doctor thereupon declared that he would conform to the liturgy of the Church of England as it was by law established and in return for this promise was issued by the easy-going Divine with a licence addressed 'to you in whose Fidelity, Morals, Learning, Sound Doctrine and Diligence We do fully confide . . .'

His old roistering friend Thomas Giddy wrote in November 1769 to William Cookesley:

'I suppose you have heard of Dr Wolcot's going abroad as Physician in Ordinary to the Governour of Jamaica, of his returning to be ordained a Parson, and of his going out again to take Possession of a Living of £1500 a year. He still retains his singularities and is an exception to the received maxim "Honores mutant mores". Have you seen the last set of Jackson's Songs? The greater part of the Poetry is Doctor Wolcot's.'

To this Cookesley replied: '. . . I am very glad to hear of Dr Wolcot's good fortune but methinks he must make the D—l of a Parson.'

In spite of the rich living that now seemed within his reach the Parson dallied in England. What excuses he made to the governor are not known: perhaps even the cynical Sir William had not expected Wolcot to be so speedily japanned. In the welcome interval he no doubt renewed his acquaintance with the fascinating London world of music and the other arts. Between

47

the end of June and October there is no news of his activities and it is hardly to be thought that the new priest was indulging in a spiritual withdrawal from the world. He was perhaps preparing his lyrics for their setting by William Jackson the celebrated organist of Exeter. In October his uncle, the kind old surgeon-apothecary of Fowey, who had so dearly hoped to have his nephew succeed to his practice, died. He left John Wolcot £2,000. There were, no doubt, then as now, many long-drawn-out formalities to be complied with before he could come into his inheritance. There were the aunts to be settled in new circumstances in Fowey. Whatever may have been the reasons for his long delay it was not until March 1770 that he arrived back in Jamaica to take up the promised living of St Anne's. It became however immediately apparent that there was one great obstacle in the way of his preferment; the rector of St Anne's had quite recovered from his illness and showed absolutely no inclination to retire in favour of the Reverend Doctor Wolcot.

* * * * *

The long voyage to England, with all its attendant expense, had been in vain, and Sir William Trelawney undoubtedly must have felt in duty bound to do something tangible for his protégé whose hopes had been so sadly dashed. He therefore, according to one source, 'made him lay by his Gown and Cassock and resume his Gold-headed Cane and Wig'. To be more precise he created him on May 21st, 1770, 'Physician-General to all the Horse and Foot Militia raised or to be raised throughout the Island'—an appointment that 'took place just twelve months after he had been admitted into Holy Orders, an anomaly unparalleled perhaps in the history of the Established Church'.

This is accurate only in part: though it is certain that the governor gave him the lay appointment, at a salary that seems nowhere to be stated, there is ample evidence that John Wolcot also took up a clerical appointment at some £800 per annum to the minor living of Vere and actually officiated there.

William Gifford, whose graphic description of the infant Wolcot's blood-stained cradle has already been noted, later exclaimed:

How shook the altar when he first drew near
Hot from debauch and with a shameless leer
Pour'd stammering forth the yet unhallow'd prayers
Mix'd with convulsive sobs and noisome airs. . . .

But there is, no doubt, a more than permissible element of exaggeration in this picture. From rather less biassed reports it appears that Wolcot entered upon his sacred duties with a certain degree of reluctance. The younger Polwhele once said: 'As to his clerical pretensions he was always reserved. He once, I remember, was asked to repeat grace before dinner which he did with some hesitation: but in another company, very soon after, he declined saying grace so that at first he was a sort of amphibious being.'

As a parish priest his opportunities were limited. Vere, on the landlocked bay which made so good an anchorage for shipping, was primarily a sugar-producing parish. The population consisted of some 6000 negroes who provided labour for the nineteen sugar-works which together produced about 2000 hogsheads of sugar every year.

Such was the living to which Wolcot was presented. He was an excellent reader and an emphatic speaker. And at first, so it is said, he 'both preached and prayed occasionally, when a congregation could be found, but he at length relaxed into apathy and indolence. The truth is that he seldom saw a *white* man, and as a consequence in a country [which], cursed with slavery, depends solely on colour, his hearers were not deemed very reputable.'

The size of the congregation, as seems only proper in a Church in such a state of decadence, was never likely to be large. On one occasion, according to Wolcot, it consisted of a cow, a jackass, an old soldier and two negroes, but this exceptionally numerous attendance was undoubtedly due to the fact that it was raining.

It was moreover possible to please his congregation in ways other than the entirely spiritual. A respectable planter, who knew him well, used to tell how Wolcot and his parish clerk, both of whom were fond of shooting ring-tailed doves on the edge of the bay, managed to secure an uninterrupted Sunday's sport: if no member of the congregation presented himself within ten minutes of opening the doors of the church Parson and clerk proceeded with a clear conscience towards the sea-shore.

This device soon became apparent to an old negro who saw in it a means of raising a small weekly toll from the rector. Accordingly he would each Sunday present himself and his wife and children punctually at the door of the church.

'What do you come here for, Blackee?' said Wolcot, the first time this happened.

'Why, massa, to hear your good sermon and all the prayers of the Church.'

'Would not a *bit* or two do you more good?' suggested Wolcot, feeling in his pocket.

'Yes, Massa Doctor, me love your prayers much, but me love your money, too!'

Having pocketed the coins, worth about 5*d*. each, the negro and his family would withdraw leaving the coast clear for the doctor's pastime with the doves.

In after years it was cited by his enemies as evidence of Wolcot's appalling blasphemy that he used jokingly to say that he offered up prayers to the Holy Trinity in the morning and amused himself by shooting at the Holy Ghost in the afternoon. Blasphemy may be found only in the ear of the listener: certainly those who have enjoyed that early Italian 'St Jerome' in which the Lion, more *felis* than *leo*, hungrily contemplates the Holy Ghost descending are unlikely to be greatly shocked by Wolcot's frivolity.

But there were many occasions on which he had to officiate in his clerical capacity: on one of them the church was, as though by Divine disapproval, melodramatically shaken by an earthquake, and Wolcot, wearing on that occasion a surplice that was both too long and too narrow, was hard put to it to run out after the terrified congregation. It was only by seizing the fleeing clerk and refusing to let him go until he had helped him out of the constricting garment that, eventually, both men got clear of the swaying building. Earthquakes were, however, almost as good for the business of the Established Church as international crises of the twentieth century were to prove. In later years Wolcot shewed a realistic awareness of this fact:

Thus when an earthquake bids Jamaica tremble
On Sunday all the folks to Church assemble
To soothe Jehovah so devoutly studying—
Prostrate, they vow to keep his holy laws. . . .

. . . 'Ere Sunday comes again their hearts recover
The tempest of their fears blown over
Fled ev'ry terror of the burning lake
They think they have no business now with Church
So calmly leave th'Almighty in the lurch
And sin it—till he gives a *second* shake.

As parish priest, and as one of the few white men in the district, he was, of course, expected to take part in a certain amount of social activity. Pusey Manning of Vere asked him to a dinner party one night and introduced him, jocularly, to a stranger as 'Doctor Wolcot, the unworthy incumbrance of this Parish.' 'And this, sir,' countered Wolcot, 'is Pusey Manning Esquire, the scabbiest sheep in my flock.'

'I was invited,' he reported of another social occasion, 'to sup with a rich planter and his wife. During the repast my friend desired a female slave in waiting to mix some toddy on which the black girl in her peculiar way asked him if it was to be "drinkey for dry or drinkey for drunkey". When our supper was ended and our water being exhausted the planter sent his wife from the house for a fresh supply. The thunder and lightning being excessive during her absence I said to him, "Why did you not send that girl (the slave) for water on such a night as this instead of exposing your wife to the storm?" "Oh, no," replied he, "that would never do. That slave cost me forty pounds."'

In spite of the largely non-sectarian nature of his post the appointment of parish priest sat so ill upon him that it was not long before he withdrew from Vere to the governor's palace, and although he continued, according to the Parish records, to be nominally the rector until 1772, there seems little doubt that the cure of souls was in fact administered in his absence by a curate.

His short career as a clergyman of the Church of England as by law established was, to all intents and purposes, at an end.

*   *   *   *   *

Almost three years had gone since the path to fortune had opened so promisingly before him and he had still taken hardly more than a single pace along it. Though the salary attached to the living of Vere was one that many an envious twentieth-century rector might think adequate it was not to Wolcot, paying *in absentia* for the services of his curate, of a size that would ensure the independence for which he had shut himself away in the deadly climate of the West Indies.

Life with the governor, dancing attendance on the ladies of the household, was entertaining if unlucrative. Sir William's sister Anne was inclined to be credulous, and Wolcot could not resist the pleasure of pandering to her simple nature.

One day when she asked Wolcot what news there might be he told her that a cherub had been caught in the Blue Mountains and brought into the town.

'What did they do with it, my dear Doctor?'

'Put it in a cage with a parrot.'

'And what then, Doctor?'

'In the morning the parrot had pecked out both its eyes.'

'You don't say so!'

This story became one of Wolcot's standard tests of credulity: he repeated it with slight variations, and generally with a gratifying success, to a number of people including his aunts.

But he was fond of Anne Trelawney, and when shortly after he had returned from Vere to almost permanent residence at the King's House she unexpectedly died, Wolcot wrote to her memory an elegy entitled the *Nymph of Tauris*. This poem, which was evidently suggested by Collin's Oriental Eclogues, attained a fairly wide circulation and was published together with *Persian Love Elegies* in a work printed by Joseph Thompson of Kingston. The volume was an example of fine typography, and in fact appears to have been one of the earliest literary works to be published in the island. It was dedicated to Lady Trelawney.

There was nearly another death in the governor's house. Wolcot himself was taken desperately ill 'with the dreadful malady of the country'. Both he and his attendants had given up all hopes of his recovery. The night nurse was asleep on her couch and in the words of the anonymous author of *Physic and Physicians* the doctor 'was lying in that torpid state which is generally considered a fatal symptom when he was roused by two negroes who *sans ceremonie* began to place him in a straight position.

'The doctor enquired as well as he could do what they wanted and how they dared to disturb him. The fellows begged pardon and with an unmeaning grin replied:

' "Only to measure you for your coffin, massa."

'The doctor was so enraged that passion literally gave a turn to his disorder. When he recovered he determined to use his own words "to play the devil a trick and, if he despatched any more of his emissaries for him, not to be found in the same place!"

'Consequently,' the report continues with a splendid over-simplification of the facts, 'Wolcot returned to England with Lady Trelawney.'

*   *   *   *   *

The truth was, in fact, more tragic and far more disruptive of Wolcot's career.

On December 11th, 'after a long and tedious illness', Sir William Trelawney died. During the four years the governor, in the words of an obituarist, had 'so wisely guided and steadily held the reins of power and maintained such an inflexible integrity of conduct (altogether unbiassed by private attachments of selfish considerations), that PARTY herself forgot her resentment.'

Certainly he was sufficiently popular for the Legislature to vote £1,000 towards the cost of a public funeral. In a lead coffin, its outer shell covered with crimson velvet and richly furnished, the governor lay in state in a Council Chamber hung with black and illumined by large tapers of wax.

At seven o'clock in the evening of December 13th, 1772, the minute guns began mournfully to sound and the funeral procession set out from the King's House. It was headed by a mixed band, collected from various regiments and from a battalion that had recently arrived in the island, playing the 'Dead March in Saul'. Behind the bandsmen marched with arms reversed the Spanish Town Regiment of Foot Militia and the 36th Regiment of Foot, under the command of Colonel Campbell.

They were followed by eight mutes, the governor's secretary and household, the public officers, the Provost Marshal General,

53

the physicians and the clergy. Behind them rode the coffin that held not only all that was mortal of Sir William Trelawney but the shattered remnants of John Wolcot's hopes.

*　　*　　*　　*　　*

The protégé of one governor could not expect favours from the next. There is an isolated and tantalizing reference that states that Wolcot became 'captain of a band of Jews in the island'. If so it must have been a short-lived leadership for on February 20th, 1773, he was given twelve months' leave of absence by the new governor and, at the express request, so it was said, of the widowed Lady Trelawney, travelled back to London with her in His Majesty's frigate *Lowestoft* under the command of Captain Cartrett. With them in a coffin of a curious shape they took the body of young Boscawen.

His enemies in after years made the most of this return. William Gifford wrote that so disgusted were the residents of Jamaica at the way in which Wolcot

. . . took, O Heavens! the sacerdotal stole

that finally

> . . . rose the people passive now no more
> And from his limbs the sacred vestments tore
> Dragg'd him with groans, shouts, hisses to the main
> And sent him to annoy these realms again. . . .

Another attributed the credit for his departure to one Bryan Edwards who 'exercised his literary talents in a remarkable way in Jamaica: for by the strokes of his pen he drove Peter Pindar from the island and the bitter satirist never dared to attack his character while he remained in the country. . . .'

The basis on which this paragraph was founded is obscure. There seems to be no evidence at this period that Wolcot was indulging in any form of satire, bitter or otherwise. His extant verse is full of the solemn formal expression of eighteenth-century romantic feeling. But, since in after years any stick was good enough to beat him with, a strict adherence to the truth of his departure was not regarded as either necessary or desirable.

The voyage home took them to the Gulf of Florida and the Grand Caymans, on one of which they landed. Wolcot roamed the little island, noting the saltwater pens in which five or six hundred turtles were kept at a time, meeting the shoe-maker who acted as governor, and entering a miserable negro hut which had been converted into the residence of the commander-in-chief.

'But what delighted him still more was to behold a lovely Anglo-American, most unexpectedly inhabiting a humble dwelling, who recounted part of her adventure to him and added that she and her lover had been wrecked here.'

At this Wolcot rose to his feet and exclaimed with some emotion:

'I hope to God, madam, he lost his life.'

It was a sentiment that might have been expressed otherwise. But, happily 'the fair *incognita*' recognized that this was an unfortunate attempt at gallantry and 'relieved him from his embarrassment by calmly observing that the gentleman in question had gone out to shoot doves for her dinner'.

In fact he very soon returned and they had a long and cordial conversation together. It appeared that the couple had suffered at the hands of their parents who opposed their marriage; they had fled from America and had been saved from the wreck, and they found 'the little island on which they were thrown to be in the possession of a few inhabitants of the most perfect simplicity of manners and the most lively friendship; pleased also with the salubrity as well as beauty and fertility of the spot, they adopted the resolution of passing their days in this remote corner of the globe convinced that the most perfect happiness resides oftener in simplicity than in splendour. Their opinion soon became realized; fond of the innocent natives and equally beloved again, the delightful little republic flourished under their auspices and restored the golden age.'

By the time Wolcot met them their ménage had been increased by four beautiful children. He was delighted by everything he saw and when the time came for parting 'they all kissed and cried'.

The *Lowestoft* set sail once more and, leaving the Island of Innocence—of which more than a quarter of a century later Wolcot was to write—he came again at last to the England from which with such high and illusory hopes he had four years earlier set sail.

5

LADY TRELAWNEY and the Reverend Dr John Wolcot returned together to Cornwall. There was nothing more
natural than that they should do so: they were Cornish folk returning home, and they were bringing with them the body of
young Boscawen which was placed on top of that of the huge
coffin of the second Lord of Falmouth in a vault at Tregothnan.
But the fact that they journeyed together was quite sufficient to
account for the rumour that they were in love and, even, that a
day had been fixed for the marriage to take place.

If this was, indeed, so, then another bitter disappointment was
in store for Wolcot. Letitia Trelawney died in London on May
28th, 1775.

It might have seemed likely that he who had written verses
on the death of her sister-in-law and on the death of Boscawen
might, unless his grief were too deep to be publicly paraded,
have produced some verses on the death of his fiancée. But there
is no trace of any such work. In the absence of this evidence an
open, though possibly a slightly sceptical, mind may be kept on
the subject.

Certainly from this time can be dated the first budding of his
satirical verse—jejune though it might be—and it is tempting to
attribute his growing bitterness and his twisted smile to the twin
failures of love and fortune. On the other hand he himself declared
frankly that the reason he turned to satire was that there existed
more popular demand for that form of writing than for the
formal pastoral verses which had previously constituted his poetic
output. Songs set by Jackson of Exeter, elegies published in
Kingston, Jamaica, these might achieve a limited artistic acclaim
but they would never bring financial success. And Wolcot was
unashamedly seeking the latter. He was now thirty-five, he had

returned from the graveyard of the West Indies weakened both in health (for he had developed asthma in the tropics) and in pocket; half his expected span of life was gone with nothing to show for it. To return to Fowey and his aunts was unthinkable. On his way to Truro he paid them a fleeting visit during which he told them that he had brought them two angels, Seraphim and Cherubim, from his travels.

They were delighted.

'But alas!' he added, 'a melancholy accident has happened. We had a terrible storm at sea. There was a great uproar among the crew and the passengers. The angels quarrelled, took to fighting and pulled out one another's eyes. I could not offer you the dilapidated relics.'

Not for the first time the aunts must have reflected that they had a disappointing nephew.

*   *   *   *   *

Fortunately for his immediate future he could still fall back upon the profession of medicine for which he was well qualified. He obtained from Mr Daniell a house (later to become the Britannia Inn) on Truro Green overlooking the quay. It has been suggested that the old man allowed him to live in this house rent-free, and if this is indeed so it can be taken to indicate the uneasy state of the doctor's finances at this time. Certainly, it seems, he lived very simply: he dined seldom at home and when he did so his only servant, an old woman, prepared his favourite and frugal meal which consisted of a basin of 'girty milk'.

He soon achieved a growing reputation as a doctor although he always maintained that he did not like the practice of medicine as an art; whether the patient was cured by *vis medicatrix naturae* or by the administration of a little pill which was either directly or indirectly to reach the part affected, he professed to be unable to say, and in fact in after years, looking back on the days of his country practice, he once remarked:

'Physic is half of it humbug—at best a very uncertain affair. People's pockets are often picked by it. I could not in many idle cases go away without leaving a prescription. I took care to leave what would do no harm. A physician can do little more than watch nature and, if he sees her inclined to go right, give her a shove in the back.'

He was certainly ahead of his time in giving his fever patients long draughts of cold water—a treatment which, then described as 'peculiar', was admitted by his patients, if not by rival doctors, to be 'uncommonly successful'. 'Moreover from consumption many were rescued by his hand who had been given up as irrecoverable,' and 'to Wolcot's bold prescription of calomel' (not then in fashion) 'the elder Polwhele had to attribute a temporary escape from the gout that had attacked his stomach.'

He had conceived, too, a new and ingenious theory of such diseases as rheumatism:

'I consider the joints as blocks, the nerves as ropes and the whole system as a ship full-rigged; in fine weather all is lax and agreeable—in wet everything being tight and uncomfortable disease is superinduced: this on the other hand is alleviated by warmth or in other words by relaxation, which restores the body to its original tone.'

Above all things he dreaded wet feet and damp air. 'I keep a fire every day throughout the year. I must have dry air. I wear a flannel shirt—it is needful, and I take a little brandy or rum. Fire, flannel and brandy are required in our climate.'

Armed with these maxims and beliefs, he made his professional rounds of the Truro countryside between 1773 and 1778. 'Even when vacant from business the wit and pleasantry of Wolcot's conversation would always render him a welcome visitor at the house of all his acquaintances. . . .'

When attending the Reddings, if he arrived too late for dinner he would go into the kitchen and cook his own beefsteak because, so he said, servants never knew how to do a steak as it should be done; indeed, unless he prepared it himself he never in his life ate a beefsteak properly cooked in the West of England. As far as his patient's diet was concerned he seems to have inclined to the theory expressed later in the sentiment 'A little of what you fancy does you good'. One satisfied patient wrote that Wolcot 'indulged me in fever . . . with a piece of roasted pig for which I had expressed a strong desire and it brought me to myself again.'

The hard-living, hunting squire, Thomas Mitchel, too, he found one day very low and ill though he was naturally of a tough disposition:

'For some time I was puzzled to know what was the matter with him. It struck me at last that he might have taken something that had driven in a species of eruption that he had always on one arm. "Tom!" said I, "let me see your arm," and shewing it to me I perceived at once that the eruption, constitutional with him, had been driven in by the blockhead whom he had employed and who, besides, had kept him miserably low in diet. I rang the bell for Mrs Mitchel. "What had you for dinner, today—anything well-seasoned?"

' "Why, yes, Doctor, there was a highly seasoned beef-steak pie sent away untouched. Mr Mitchel was to eat nothing seasoned."

' "You will kill Tom. Let the cloth be laid again; bring up the pie. We'll cut it open, put a bottle of good Madeira by it and let him eat and drink as much as he likes."

'The patient was ready enough to sit down to it and by this plan in a day or two I got the eruption out again and Tom was as well as he ever was in his life without physic.'

Tom Mitchel, at whose house, Croftwest, Wolcot was always welcome, lived to an advanced old age and could certainly be reckoned among one of the doctor's livelier triumphs.

Perhaps the most striking of these cases was that of Miss Daniell who, with her fever coming to a crisis, said that nothing would do her good but lobster:

'A lobster was not to be had but the remnant of a lobster which had been thrown out on a dung hill was brought to her by Wolcot's own order in almost a putrid state: its very smell revived her—its flavour more and from that moment she fast recovered.'

It is hardly surprising that Wolcot used to exclaim, 'If the sword has slain its thousands the lancet has put to death its tens of thousands.'

Almost enough instances from Dr John Wolcot's case-book have now been cited to indicate his capacities as a medical practitioner. The inescapable fact remains that he was eminently successful both in actual fact and in the estimation of his patients, although they were not always as ready to pay his bill as they were to call him to their aid. One patient whom he had cured of deafness in fact affected to be still hard of hearing in order to avoid paying the fee: but Wolcot sat quietly abusing him and calling him terrible names in a normal conversational tone 'which so stung the patient that he forgot his deafness and replied heatedly'.

None the less, anxious though he might be to make money and make a great amount of it, with those who genuinely were unable to afford his fees he was capable of a great generosity that caused young Polwhele (whom he now met for the first time) to exclaim regretfully in later years:

> 'Alas! when he dispensed his medicines with such anxious attention to the sick—when he gave his bread to the hungry (for he would go dinnerless rather than send a poor man empty away) how much is it to be lamented that in his generous feelings and his exertions in consequence of those feelings there was no Christian principle.'

But young Polwhele, as will be seen, was always a little inclined to be pompous.

*   *   *   *   *

Richard Polwhele was a pupil at Truro School under the head-mastership of Cardew and aged fifteen when Wolcot met him first, and although the friendship which sprang up between the boy and the man twenty-two years older would in the twentieth century be regarded with some reserve, it is possible that it was founded upon nothing more sinister than a genuine desire on the part of the doctor, with the memories of his own frustrated youth always in his mind, to encourage youthful genius wherever it might be found. Certainly no contemporary, even among his

60

many enemies, in an age when homosexuality was common, seems to have expressed any suspicions about the relationship.

In Cardew's day the Saturday evening exercise of Polwhele's class was either to translate a Latin Classic into English verse or to render the Psalms into metrical Latin or to perform some similar boyish intellectual feat. 'By the assistance of Wolcot,' wrote Polwhele, who pious though he might be was evidently without any sense of indulging in sharp practice, 'I was enabled to excel my fellows in English. In the Latin versions Wolcot sometimes tried his hand but preferred the English.' None the less they together translated part of Gray's Elegy into Latin and, according to Richard, 'accompanying me from Truro to Polwhele he would often applaud the facility with which I perfected my task and at the same time approve the execution of it'.

An example of their collaboration has survived in Wolcot's effective translation of Warton's well-known Latin epigram 'Somme levis'. Young Polwhele had paraphrased the verse for a school exercise:

> Come gentle sleep with all thy balm
> And lull me to repose;
> The very image, thou, of death
> Yet soother of our woes!
>
> Kind to thy votary's wish, O come
> Companion of his bed
> How sweet to live thus void of life
> To die and not be dead.

'I showed it to Wolcot who liked it well enough and said it was "much better than any other of Cardews's boys could produce" but seized a pen and instantly translated the lines in this superior manner:

> Come gentle sleep, attend thy votary's prayer
> And, though death's image, to my couch repair
> How sweet, thus living, without life to lie,
> Thus, without dying, O, how sweet to die.

'He read poetry extremely well and these lines, I remember,

61

he repeated to me two or three times with a voice so plaintively soft, so musical in its cadences that his whole soul would seem to have been attuned to sensibility and virtue. But what a medley is man of good and evil!'

Polwhele was, it should be noted, reporting the incident some fifty years later at a time when it was accepted almost without question that Wolcot was in the words of John Agg 'A venomous reptile . . . a vile compound of Obscenity and Blasphemy', and the idea that he should have had a sensible side to his character was one that called for comment.

At this time, however, his reputation was still comparatively unsullied and to old Thomas Polwhele, Richard's father, 'he was not unacceptable as an accidental visitor'; all the same, 'tremblingly alive as that honoured parent was to every insinuation of an irreligious tendency' their meetings were generally marked by an uneasy air of constraint, the old man becoming increasingly nervous as the doctor's vivacity grew; from past experience he suspected that this might lead to something being said that would shock him. 'Yet Wolcot was fond of my father's company,' said Richard; 'from frequenting it he was induced to think seriously and had he more frequented it he would have become, perhaps, not only almost but altogether a Christian.'

He continued, however, to frequent young Richard's company and to direct his poetic talents. Even after Polwhele, who was in later years to be accused more than once of plagiarism, had taken a stanza from Wolcot's *Ode to the Genius of Great Britain* and had adapted it to his own poem, the *Genius of Karnbre*, their friendship continued and Wolcot introduced the boy to the notice of the printer of the *Sherborne Mercury* by sending him a copy of his verses on *The Fate of Llewellyn* which

'by a young gentleman still at school will be no discredit to your entertaining paper. They possess a strength seldom discoverable in a muse so young and a colouring which would not disgrace the pencil of a master. Elfinda after an address to Llewellyn is alarmed at the shout of a battle in which her father the Earl of Radnor is engaged. At length she discovers him a prisoner. The spectacle of a father in chains, too powerful for her sensibility, deprives her of her life. But let the young poet speak for himself:

> She ceas'd: when lo! the shouts of war
> Re-echoed thro' the trembling gloom
> Elfinda hears the rattling car,
> Pale horror warns her of her doom. . . .'

There was more, much more, of this. And, if young Polwhele had a fault poetically it was, in Wolcot's words, that he was too epithetish.

'You will acquire nerve every hour if you can get rid entirely of these damned epithets,' he wrote in February, 1777. 'Go on and conquer. You will descend to posterity with honour if you write like this.'

But the shape that Polwhele's poetry was to take will be discussed in a more appropriate place.

At the time that these approving lines were written Wolcot was working upon a new protégé and in a different field of endeavour.

*   *   *   *   *

John Wolcot's fondness for painting and drawing had continued unabated alongside his practice of poetry and music. During his visits to London, perhaps during the Anglican interlude between the years in Jamaica, he had made the acquaintance of a number of artists including James Northcote, Ozias Humphry and Richard Wilson. The first of these lodged in the house, in Leicester Fields, of Sir Joshua Reynolds whose work Wolcot always admired and the doctor used to spend whole mornings in Northcote's room there.

From Truro he wrote in 1774 seeking to add a portrait to his collection:

'Dear Northcote—Come out of that d-mn'd p-Hole or by G— you'll die, —much obliged t'ye for your compliments on my poetical talent, and yet, my friend, I have received a letter from a very great critic containing the opinions of other

63

brother critics which I *blush* to relate—when we meet I may shew 'em t'ye. I long for a head, I want to improve by it. Take my word for it, Jem, and I do not mean to flatter, the Devil fetch me if I do, you'll be the first of your profession. Let me mortifie you so far, however, as to say you'll never make a learned painter but for correctness and colouring, so far as relates to a head (for I can guess at no more of your powers) you will certainly be, notwithstanding that rusty head of hair, lousy blue surtout and ragged breeches which you carry about you, a very great man. In consequence of that idea I shall from time to time present you to the public in a couplet and arrogate to myself the merit of the first discovery of the talent which will amaze the world. This last speech looks as if I was laughing at you but seriously I admire your powers! I have sent you a compliment on your picture at the Royal Academy —send it by the Penny Post in a cover to the *St James's Chronicle* or the *London* or both, that I may see it in print; if you don't I shall be forced to employ somebody else, therefore I beg it as a favour for I like 'em.

You could not steal a little bit of Sir Joshua and send it with the head you have designed for me, could you? Has he no head of merit lying amongst some old spiders?

My pen has been riding post over the paper; indeed I am wanted out as we are pleased to express ourselves.

Therefore, Dear Northcote,

Adieu.

The flattering quatrain signed 'Pictor' that accompanied this letter was of indifferent merit and Northcote in his Memoirs wrote: 'Perhaps it may be unnecessary to observe that I did not send those lines either to the *St. James's Chronicle* or to the *London* or to any other.'

It has been suggested that the subsequent estrangement of the two men arose from Northcote's failure to comply with Wolcot's suggestion that he should steal a sketch from Sir Joshua. But it is difficult to believe that such a request was in any way a serious one: the coolness seems much more likely to have arisen (if it arose from this incident at all) from Northcote's failure to forward the verses for publication.

John Opie
Self-Portrait in 1785

For when a *Man is past his sense*,
There's no Way to reduce him thence,
But twinging him by *th'Ears or Nose*,
Or laying on of *heavy Blows*: *Hudibras*.

Mr. Rosewarne pulling Peter by the nose

Wolcot, in fact, tried in 1777 the same tactics on Ozias Humphry to whom he sent congratulations on his safe return from Italy. In a rather fulsome letter comparing Humphry's status to that of Claude he said:

'As I am myself a Dabler I want a Head in water-colours and in oil finished in your highest manner, not only for my Instruction but for the Vanity of being possessed of the finest paintings in the world. Will you please tell me in your next your Price? Your present of 'Mrs Collier' is still in my possession and held sacred. I have sent you a few stanzas, long since penned, which, if you do not disapprove I will print in some of the Papers. They are the Effusions of a real regard for yourself and your art carried to its highest perfection.'

Ozias Humphry, the verses maintained, combined all the excellences of Guido, Corregio and Titian combined and it must be suspected that they were, in their outrageous flattery, intended less as a serious statement of Wolcot's critical opinion than an attempt to get a Head at a lower price or, even, as another gift. For the fact is that Wolcot was an extremely shrewd judge of art and this shrewdness was made manifest in an encounter that eventually altered the whole of his life.

He was on a visit to the Nankivells at Mithian when he met John Opie.

★   ★   ★   ★   ★

John Opie, the son of a mine carpenter of St Agnes and apprenticed to a house carpenter named Wheeler, had been sent to Mithian to do some repairs for Benjamin Nankivell. In the parlour he had seen hanging a picture of a farmyard at Ellenglaze which had immensely attracted him. His sister Betty was working in service at Mithian and John had used this as an excuse for calling time and again at the house to have another look at the painting. From memory he began to transfer the details of it to a canvas that he had somehow acquired. It was inevitable that, eventually, Mrs Nankivell should have heard what was going on; she reacted by lending the boy the picture so that he might make a proper copy of it. When he subsequently sold this copy to Mrs Walker of Winnow for five shillings he presented in gratitude to Mrs Nankivell a portrait he had painted of her cat.

John Wolcot was on a visit one day to his cousin—the adored Sukey was still unmarried and, alas, destined to remain so—when he took notice of the original of the farmyard scene now hanging again on the Nankivells' wall. He remarked casually that it was a busy scene but ill-executed. Mrs Nankivell flew at once to the defence of the picture. It was one she said that was admired by many good judges of painting, very good judges, indeed, in particular by a lad of great genius—here, no doubt, she told Wolcot the whole story. Wolcot was intrigued. Here was a boy after his own heart, a boy in whom he could feel, in his devotion to an art discouraged by his parents, an echo of the young Wolcot who had retired to his romantic tower upon the cliff's edge to escape his aunts and to indulge his forbidden taste for verse.

He made enquiries and found John Opie, then fifteen years old, working as the bottom sawyer in Wheeler's sawpit. Wolcot called down to him and 'having enquired in the dialect of the county "Con you paient?" I was instantly answered from below in a similar accent and language that he could paint Queen Charlotte, and Duke William, and Mrs Nankivell's Cat.

'Well, my lad, can you go and bring me your very best pictures?'

The boy ran away and Wolcot in after years told John Taylor that, 'he should always have in his ears the sound of the boy's leather apron clattering between his knees as he ran eagerly to bring proofs of his graphic skill'. He brought back under his arm the cat, two other ferocious monsters and a 'portrait of the devil sketched out in strict conformity to vulgar tradition being provided with a monstrous pair of horns, two goggle eyes and a long tail'.

The way in which Wolcot received this exhibition has been variously described. One source says, a little improbably, that he instantly exclaimed, 'Eureka.' Hazlitt maintains that there was a very long pause, broken by the anxious Opie exclaiming:

'Well, what do you think of it?'

'Think of it? Why I think you ought to be ashamed of it—that you who might do so well do no better.'

According to Wolcot himself:

'A specimen was . . . shewn me which was rude, incorrect and incomplete. But when I learned that he was such an enthusiast in his art that he got up by three o'clock of a summer's morning to draw with chalk and charcoal I instantly conceived that he must possess all that zeal necessary for obtaining eminence. A gleam of hope then darted through my bosom and I felt it possible to raise the price of his labours from eightpence or a shilling to a guinea a day. . . .' He asked the boy to dine with him on the following Sunday. Although his manners were naturally coarse he was intellectually much above the average of his class. Wolcot made him a present of paints and brushes and began to instruct him in their use. One lesson led to another. On his visits to St Agnes, Wolcot continued to instruct John Opie in the art he had himself acquired in part from Richard Wilson. In the same manner as he had befriended young Polwhele he befriended Opie. Once again there was a difference of some twenty-two years in their ages; once again modern allegations of motives other than the purely altruistic must be considered and once again it must be, in fairness, recorded that there seems to have been no contemporary breath of scandal even though on this occasion Wolcot bought him out of his apprenticeship and took him into his own house on Truro Green. His father, Edward Opie, was quite willing for him to go.

'The boy was good for naught—could never make a wheelbarrow, was always gazing upon cats and staring volks in the vace.'

★   ★   ★   ★   ★

Whatever else may have gone on behind the plain Georgian front of the house backing on to the Quay at Truro, Wolcot, in the intervals of carrying on his now extensive medical practice, was trying to educate the boy above the limitations imposed upon him by his class. In addition to art lessons he taught him French, endeavoured to interest him in the Classics, instructed him how to play the German flute and, generally, to learn the rudiments of society manners. Patronage in the eighteenth century was prepared to go to considerable lengths to achieve an ideal.

It was, no doubt, in an effort to rationalize this relationship that the story gained credence that he had taken him into his house as a servant: in fact Wolcot seems to have treated Opie from the start as a companion and a friend.

He was at first unable to decide in what branch of art to encourage the boy: in later years after Opie had achieved his first blazing success Wolcot is known to have expressed the opinion that he would have made an even greater name in landscape painting than he did in portraiture. Sometimes the lessons would begin at three in the morning when Wolcot, 'used to take him into the fields; to give him an idea of landscape and of the aerial perspective'.

On one evening jaunt to Falmouth they walked to Pendennis Castle:

'It was a calm summer's evening, the sea at a distance added to the beauty and the majesty of the scene; the youthful artist contemplated it in silence, he listened to the instructions of his friend and the next day he drew the whole from memory. The piece is said to have been finely coloured and equal to any of our first masters in composition.'

In spite of this, however, Wolcot had decided in favour of portrait painting as a career for young Opie. 'The pecuniary advantages . . . had determined the doctor in favour of that branch of the art.' Wolcot himself, in spite of his flourishing practice, was almost without resources and it was clearly important that Opie should at any rate be capable of supporting himself. Under Wolcot's instruction the boy was soon capable 'of pencilling out a decent head for five shillings and, at the end of a twelvemonth he undertook small half-lengths'.

Wolcot's own portrait by Opie was exhibited in Truro. That it was not universally appreciated is indicated by the story of Wolcot taking a party of children to see it. One of them was asked of whom he thought it was a portrait: he replied confidently, 'A bear in a blanket. . . .'

68

Wolcot wrote on October 25th, 1777, to Ozias Humphry telling of the 'uncouth, raw-boned country lad' with whom he had encumbered himself and who had 'run mad with paint'. He suggested that Humphry might like someone to clean his brushes and his palette and generally make himself useful around the house, a boy moreover who 'wanted no wages for that if he would give him his food and a little money to keep the devil out of his pocket he would be perfectly contented'. The answer was, presumably, unsatisfactory.

At Wolcot's suggestion Opie, armed with letters of introduction, wandered from house to house painting the portraits of the leading Cornish families. The doctor asked his friends to treat the boy as a parlour-guest. 'I want to polish him. He is an unlicked cub yet; I want to make him learn to respect himself.'

Almost without exception and in a gratifyingly democratic spirit the Cornish gentry complied with this request.

The most notable exception was young Polwhele.

'We were much entertained [he wrote] by that unlicked cub of a carpenter Opie who was now most ludicrously exhibited by his keeper Wolcot—a wild animal of St Agnes, caught among the tin-works. . . .

To a lady of our party on whom he first tried his hand "Shaaant I draa ye as ye be?" was a question not soon to be forgotten. He had hit her likeness but had lost all the fine expression of her countenance.'

He added that 'the manners of every servants' hall in Cornwall were infinitely superior to Opie's'. There was no receiving the boy at the Polwhele table. He 'was the guest of our servants and it was the task of a faithful servant to entertain him'.

It may occur to the observer that perhaps young Polwhele was jealous of the place Opie had assumed in the doctor's favour. But whether this is more revealing of Polwhele's character than of Wolcot's cannot at this moment be determined.

And in any case passions even more disruptive than jealousy were beginning to be aroused against the doctor in Truro.

6

JUST at first, perhaps until he had taken the measure of Truro
society, something of the old elegiac Wolcot remained. He
was generous, travelled and a good raconteur—attributes which,
coupled with his reputation for being a kindly and successful
doctor, still ensured him a welcome in many homes. Some of
his songs were set to music by Charles Bennet, the local organist.
He was still given to the somewhat Gothick tastes that were
fashionable. His 'Christmas Hymn', for instance, which was
written about 1775, opened:

> The weeping world in anguish lay
> Despair to madness lent her sighs;
> In blood went down the orb of day
> And death-like horror dimm'd the skies. . . .

After this description of Christmas Eve he is prepared to
concede that on Christmas Day:

> The fiend of death shall hide his head
> Abash'd with all his spectre train
> And war, so long with carnage red,
> Shall glut no more the blushing plain. . . . .

But he was nearing the end of this phase. He was in love again
—or still in love, as perhaps he always would be, with the
fascinating Betsy Cranch. She was not the acknowledged beauty
of the town: that title was conceded to Miss Dickenson whose
father was saved in fever by Wolcot's draughts of cold water.
But her charm must have been immense. Even the staid Polwhele
took her to gather leaves from his mulberry trees to feed her silk-
worms. Wolcot himself proposed marriage to her and was, in

his own words, recollected in tranquillity when she died forty years later, 'dismissed with the most comfortable assurance that a man in love ever received. . . . She was a sweet creature. "Betsy!" said I , "will you take me for better or worse?"

' "Impossible, dear Doctor, unless you will wait. I am in six deep already!" '

She made, in fact, the 'match of the season' for she became engaged to John Vivian of Truro with the result that a Doctor Hopson, already a married man, shot himself in despair and might perhaps have shot Vivian too, had not the latter been warned of his intention. The marriage took place on August 24th, 1776. Betsy was now certainly the leading lady in Truro society, and became, in due course, the mother of the first Lord Vivian.

In those days Truro was a thriving little community, isolated and self-contained. It returned two Members to Parliament. About a dozen of its citizens were worth at least £10,000 per annum each. Because the journey to London or to Bath was too difficult to be taken for pleasure the inhabitants had, in their own local 'Season', to make their own entertainment centring around the Assembly Rooms. As in every country town the local leaders of society were clearly defined. It is possible that some of them, particularly those engaged in the Local Government of the Borough, the Mayor and Aldermen, were inclined with their narrow horizon to have an undue sense of their own importance. Such a thing is not entirely unknown in Local Government even today. To Wolcot with his hatred of pretentious people in authority, with his desire to shock and deflate pomposity, they presented a series of natural targets.

He had certainly turned his attention to satirical verse as soon as he returned from Jamaica for at the end of the same year he was sufficiently confident in his performance, when supping with the Cardew family, to read to the company his satire, no longer extant, upon the Duke of Dorset. And it seems almost more than a coincidence that shortly after his arrival in Truro the Mayor and Corporation were making angry resolutions in the Council Chamber for the Town Clerk to write to the *Sherborne Mercury* to deny the truth of a scandalous piece of verse, describing an imaginary funeral, which had been written in Truro by some person unknown. Whether or not the writer was, in fact, Wolcot, the members of the Town Council of Truro became increasingly the objects of his satire. Among the Aldermen was one Warrick, a surgeon-apothecary who had frequently been opposed to Wolcot's methods as a physician and the case of the putrid lobster was one in which he had been forced to stand helplessly by and see his gloomiest forecasts confounded. Wolcot was a great disbeliever in the use of drugs: he used to say that physic, with the exception of a few powerful medicines, was 'poison'. Warrick on the other hand was apparently over-ready to dispense drugs from the stocks in his apothecary's shop. There was another member of the Council of the same profession: Wolcot had thrown a bolus prescribed by him out of the patient's window. Apothecaries who, as a class, were apt to substitute less expensive ingredients for those specified in Wolcot's prescriptions were his natural enemies, and when they were in the proud position of law-givers they were more than ever to be attacked. The mayor, James Kemp, though not an apothecary, could not escape the general ridicule, but it was for Henry Rosewarne that Wolcot reserved his real hatred.

'It was unfortunate that he had such an antipathy,' said E. C. Giddy, 'but Rosewarne was a tyrant.'

He was also a self-made *nouveau riche*, the son of a small publican, who had been returned as one of the Members of Parliament for the Borough, and to Wolcot his unforgivable sin was that he seemed to ignore his less fortunate relatives in the apparent hope that his humble origins might be forgotten.

One of these poor relations whom he was too proud to notice was his cousin Mrs Incledon, who went from town to town selling quack medicines for a living. Wolcot, ever on the watch for an occasion to humiliate, seized his opportunity one day when Rosewarne was giving a party at which, according to Polwhele, he was 'encircled by lords and baronets and ladies gay and glittering'. Meeting poor old Mrs Incledon in the street, the doctor seized her, dragged her upstairs and pushed her, clothed in rags and bespattered as she was, into the drawing-room.

'Henry!' he called out as he bowed to Rosewarne, 'your cousin Incledon: Mrs Incledon! your cousin Henry.'

Henry Rosewarne's parties must, in time, have become uneasy affairs for no one could ever be certain what surprise

Wolcot was going to produce for the occasion. There was the dinner party, for example, which was long talked about in Truro. Henry had certainly boasted about it long in advance—quite long enough to give Wolcot time to forge a letter to another of Rosewarne's near relations, a woman of a very low character and gigantic stature who as a notorious drunkard and virago was dreaded throughout the district. The letter invited her to come to the dinner that same day and to come in her finest dress. She accordingly decked herself out in finery, some of it borrowed and many years behind the fashion, and, gaunt and grotesque, set out for the party. On the way to Rosewarne's house she fortified herself with some nips of Nantz brandy, and her appearance on arrival was such as to cause all the guests to stare in pale astonishment. Mrs. Rosewarne fainted. A footman made a feeble attempt to remove the gate-crasher: she levelled him to the floor with a single blow. She overturned and smashed a tea-table, threw down the letter that had been sent to her and stalked into another room where she started to commit further attacks on the furniture. One of the musicians who happened to cross her path had his fiddle snatched from him and broken across his head. The whole house was in an uproar, and since the servants were unwilling to tackle her they made a great show of running about, but in fact avoided any direct encounter. Almost an hour of chaos ensued before she could be got out into the street.

According to the writer in the *Anti-Jacobin* who reported this scene, 'Matters now grew disagreeable to the doctor. . . .'

*　　　*　　　*　　　*　　　*

He was, in fact, making a wide range of enemies. Among other doctors, deep-rooted amid their traditional cures, he was disliked for the novelty of his treatments, by the apothecaries whose prescriptions he analysed and found to be wanting in some expensive ingredient for which they had been paid he was both disliked and feared. The members of the Corporation who were accused of mismanagement of the municipal affairs were outraged at his attack upon their dignity. And among private citizens, too, the sharpness of his tongue made itself felt against humbug and pretentiousness. A good example of the way he could sting when he felt it necessary to do so occurred on one of the many evenings he spent at Croftwest, the home of Thomas Mitchel whose cure has already been mentioned. Amongst the company was a lady named Spencer who had a high opinion of her own attractiveness and who was continually importuning John Wolcot to write some verses about her: she was in no doubt, it seems, that the poem would do nothing but flatter. There is no means of judging her appearance except that it is known that although she had a complexion which is described as brilliant, her eyes were 'very indifferent'. Over dessert Miss Spencer leaned across the table and again importuned the doctor for some verses. This time, to her delight, the request was granted. Wolcot took a pencil and rapidly scrawled some lines. He handed them to her:

> O sweet Nancy Spencer those beautiful eyes
> Were made for the downfall of man
> At the sight of their fire, thy true lover fries
> And whizzes like fish in a pan
> Oh gemini father! How nature would quake
> Were you gifted with every perfection
> I tremble to think what a havoc you'd make
> Were you blest with my air and complexion.

Miss Spencer not unnaturally never forgave Wolcot for this. In fact she never spoke to him again. To her friends she exclaimed angrily:

'His filthy complexion, too! Only think what an insult!'

As a result of his stay in the tropics, Wolcot's complexion was a 'good, lasting mahogany colour': as he pointed out to his friends, a few lines of light praise would have been useless in curbing the importunity that arose from her vanity.

There were, of course, victims who were perfectly capable of defending themselves. There was General William McCarmick, for instance, who succeeded to his father's business as a wine merchant in Truro. He was an old friend of Wolcot's, but that did not spare him from a remark which the doctor afterwards conceded was more severe than just. The general retorted hotly. Wolcot became still more caustic. One thing led to another. The general issued a challenge to Wolcot to meet him without

74

seconds on the Green at six in the morning. Wolcot got up as a chilly dawn was breaking. The window of his bedroom overlooked the Green and while he was dressing he caught sight of the general already striding impatiently up and down by the side of the water although it was still some time before six o'clock. In his hands he carried a brace of duelling pistols. It was not a comforting sight in the grey light of dawn. Wolcot's anger the night before had been momentary, his jibe ill-considered. It now seemed to him a ridiculous reason for two old friends to do their best to kill one another. He rang for his servant, ordered her to make a fire and prepare breakfast and toast immediately. At six o'clock he opened the door that looked on to the Green and walked out. With an assurance that he was far from feeling he strode up to McCarmick:

'Good morning, General.'

The general bowed stiffly.

'This is too chilly a morning for fighting,' observed Wolcot.

'That is the alternative, sir, in case I have no other satisfaction.'

'What you soldiers call an apology, I suppose? My dear General, I would rather make twenty when I was so much in the wrong as I was last night. I will apologize—but on one condition alone.'

'I cannot talk of conditions,' said the general sternly, but with signs of weakening.

'Why then, I will consider the conditions accepted. They are that you will come in and take a hearty breakfast with me—it is ready. I own myself exceedingly sorry if I hurt your feelings yesterday. I did not intend it and no one was privy to our difference.'

The general held out his hand and the two men, friends again, went in to have tea and toast beside a blazing fire.

Wolcot then had to sit and listen to the general's views on his favourite subject of Johnson's *Idler*, and anecdotes about its production in which he claimed to have played a not inconsiderable part.

'The general is a liar and a fool,' Wolcot told Polwhele later.

'Take care, Doctor,' cried Polwhele, looking nervously round him, 'a second challenge may not end in smoke.'

However, all was well that ended well. Wolcot used to say,

'I believe many duels might end as harmlessly could the combatants view the field as I did from my window, and on such a cold morning, too!'

*   *   *   *   *

The number of Wolcot's friends was slowly but inevitably declining. Polwhele was still a constant visitor to the house on the Green, particularly on Sunday evenings, and presumably on occasions when Opie was away on his painting tours, for he makes no mention of the three of them forgathering at any time. On one of these Sunday evenings when Wolcot was helping Polwhele to translate a Psalm into Latin a violent thunderstorm interrupted them. Seeing the doctor in a state of terror young Polwhele could not but think, so he said, on the quotation, *hi sunt qui trepidant et ad omnia fulgura pallent,* and if he indeed did so he must have been an even more priggish young man than has already appeared. Aloud he expressed surprise at the doctor's alarm—after all, at the other end of the Green there lived a lady who was a native of St Helena and sat unshaken amongst her friends, although it was the first time she had ever heard thunder. And had not Wolcot been used in Jamaica to lightning at the end of nearly every day?

'Yes,' Wolcot agreed, 'Evening after evening I have seen the Blue Mountains in a blaze! But such lightning as this would have killed all upon the island. . . .'

He was still accepted, too, by the Dickenson family and often together with young Polwhele spent many evenings there. Miss Dickenson was a girl who as well as being beautiful was witty and spirited. At the Jubilee Party she and Captain Croker led cotillions dancing through the streets of Truro in the light of the moon, until James Kemp sent for the constables and threatened to commit them. Miss Dickenson was elegant in manner and had a gentle musical voice. 'Is it possible,' cried Polwhele, 'that any human being, much less a poet, could be insensible to such perfections?'

Certainly Wolcot was not insensible, although the lines which he wrote about her on a blank page in Polwhele's copy of Beattie's *Minstrel* really failed to do justice to its subject.

They were happy parties. Wolcot, when there was no occasion to be shocking, could be a delightful companion. Miss Giddy, an accomplished amateur pianist, was also frequently among the company and Wolcot wrote lines to her, too, in which he compared her to Cecilia, the patron saint of music, a piece of flattery which delighted her although she was puzzled by the reference to Cecilia of whose saintship she had never heard: Wolcot explain the allusion to her with apparent seriousness. What in fact he told her appears from a letter he wrote later (to Polwhele), anxious that Miss Giddy should not suffer for his joke:

'Bullsbeef will have a musical evening, this evening. His very sensible niece I fear will expose herself there. She literally believes that St Cecilia was the mother of Kirkman the harpsichord maker. Hasten to undeceive her.'

But these pleasant social contacts became increasingly touched with acerbity. Although he was still welcomed at many parties there were always amongst those present a greater number who were scared of his tongue than relished his humour. At every such party there was increasingly likely to be someone present who had suffered from his satires. Opportunities arose for revenge. At Penkalenick no amount of rather humiliating apologies could produce the same happy result as had attended the encounter with General McCarmick: Wolcot received a severe thrashing. At a bathing party, too, at Piranzabulo the doctor was ducked and his wig sent out to sea: there was an unpleasantly hostile feeling underlying the apparently humorous horse-play.

'In short,' said Polwhele, 'Wolcot was daily losing ground in our little world.'

★   ★   ★   ★   ★

His most violent enemy was, not unnaturally, Henry Rosewarne. The other members of the Corporation, it seems, were prepared to forgive and, in some cases, even to laugh at the outrageous libels upon them which were calculated more to create laughter than resentment. But Rosewarne was implacable:

His swelling gills were all on fire
Red-hot indeed was he with ire
Red as a turkey-cock so proud
That gabbles at his feather'd crowd
At length what for a speech was meant
(Like sour small beer long wanting vent)
Breaks furious spurting up its froth. . . .

He had suffered much from Wolcot. Quite apart from the un-forgivable interference with Rosewarne's social occasions there had been lampoon after lampoon which, bad verse though they were and deservedly excluded from Wolcot's collected works, had achieved a more than local circulation. As early as 1777 William Cookesley had written from Ashburton to Thomas Giddy asking for copies of Wolcot's verse. He enclosed a frank as he expected a whole bundle of Wolcot's poetry which he was prepared to exchange—with a certain irony as it was to turn out in the light of the later consuming hatred between the two poets —for some verses by the shoemaker William Gifford.

By this early date—although Wolcot was nearly forty his verses still cannot be classed as much more than juvenilia—the poems sent to Cookesley can hardly have been very memorable. His *Epistle to Benjamin Nankivell*, written in 1774 was a pedes-trian account of a day's outing on horseback with Sukey. The *Dame of Fowey* dating from the same year was a political squib, written during the contested election for Cornwall, vulgar in tone and over-lavishly sprinkled with asterisks. *An Epistle from Matilda Queen of Denmark* to George III, *Truro Pork*, a satire on Kemp and Warrick—there were many more besides those given in E. C. Giddy's manuscript volumes which oblivion has claimed.

But there and then in Truro they drew, as Wolcot intended, blood.

By 1778 his apprenticeship to satire was nearly at an end. '*The Noble Cricketers:* a poetical and familiar epistle addressed to two of the idlest Lords in His Majesty's three Kingdoms' was published in Truro. The moralizing Polwhele had acted as midwife to a piece of verse that in his own words 'dropped as it were still-born from the press and was soon forgotten, I believe, even by its author'. Certainly it had bad reviews and it was not thought worthy of inclusion in any edition of his Collected Works even though Polwhele, who was responsible during the period of its composition for the omission of one or two passages to which he took exception on account of their vulgarity, thought it contained some passages superior for beauty and sublimity to most of Wolcot's poetry. But the passages he quotes show merely that Wolcot's taste for the Gothick was not yet extinguished.

His *Poetical, supplicating, modest and affecting Epistle to those Literary Colossuses, the Reviewers*, written the same year, was better and it may be considered to be his first work of a professional standard. It provides a momentary anticipation of the writer Wolcot was to become but it was an exception to the general run of his provincial lampoons with their limited target of which the bull was Rosewarne.

The objects of Wolcot's attacks were not without the will and the means to hit back at their critic. There are confusing accounts of litigation and actions taken at law against Wolcot. The Book of Orders of the Corporation of Truro contains references to one such instance when on December 4th, 1778, notice was taken of 'a malicious and scandalous libel lately sent to Mr Buckland, the Overseer of Truro, reflecting on the Mayor and Deputy Recorder in their official capacities as Magistrates of this Borough by Dr John Wolcot'. The Town Clerk was ordered to take Counsel's opinion about it. On January 2nd, 1779, a resolution was passed that the libel was

> 'likely to make the Magistrates of this Borough disrespected and that [since] it leads to the subversion of good order in the Borough . . . they hope he will see the impropriety of such insult and apologise within four days or else a Bill of Indictment will be brought at the next Quarter Sessions.'

It seems likely that this apology was not forthcoming for from another source there is a report that a prosecution was begun that same January in the Court of King's Bench against Wolcot and that although the affair was at last made up by the mediation of friends it cost the doctor considerably above an hundred pounds.

Wolcot was only momentarily dashed. Some time in the

79

summer of 1779 he seems to have written a letter to Mr Rose-warne 'of such a nature that it occasioned his being taken into custody; and being obliged to give Security for his good be-haviour in £500 himself and his friend in another £500'. But whether this was the occasion on which Wolcot was apprehended upon a warrant from Mr Gregor of Trewarthennick and igno-miniously escorted through the town between two constables in consequence of Rosewarne's 'swearing the peace of him', or whether this was a third counter-attack by his victims, is not at this time entirely clear. In any case he was not to be intimidated. 1779 saw the publication first of *A Christmas Carol* ostensibly by Atty White the Town Crier of Truro but, in fact, yet another attack by Wolcot on his enemies and then of *The Hall*, a satire in the same genre.

But there can be no doubt that what with his public enemies and his private feuds Truro was fast becoming far from comfort-able for Wolcot. There is a frontispiece to a later satire against Wolcot of which the title is *Mr Rosewarne, Member for Truro, pulling Peter by the Nose*. It was alleged that Mr Rosewarne carried out this action in the Market Place and cried out, according to the satirist:

> Hold, good Master Wolcot, hold!
> I have not half my story told.
> Then with his cane he so did thwack
> Poor Peter Pindar's brawny back. . . .

There followed a simile to the beating of a carpet at the end of which

> He Peter left and cry'd 'tis said
> 'Now write another pasquinade!'

For a man who, according to Polwhele, for all his ferociousness in print was really of a very timid disposition in conversation, soon overawed by a superior character, or checked by the dread of corporal correction from the person he despised, the position must have become increasingly untenable. And at last the moment arrived when it could be endured no longer.

Authority with its ability to strike and wound in a number of

Satan in all his Glory
By James Gillray

Dec. 21.st 1794

John Taylor
By George Dance

ways not on the face of them connected with any personal animosities provided the decisive factor.

On November 23rd, 1779, Wolcot received a letter from John Buckland the Overseer of Truro:

'Sir,
    I'm ordered by the Mayor and Deputy Recorder of this Borough to acquaint you that there will be a regular drawing for apprentices tomorrow morning by ten o'clock in the Vestry Room within the said Borough where you are desired to shew cause if any why you should not have an apprentice.'

It was the beginning of the end. Wolcot replied:

'Sir,
    I have just received your official note. Be so good as to present my humble and respectful compliments to his Worship the Mayor and also to the Deputy Recorder of this honourable Borough and to inform them that their blunderbusses have missed fire. . . . As my house is taken by another tenant the furniture except a few immaterial articles removed to Helston and the servant discharged I'm tolerably certain that I do not come within the description of a person entitled to that good fortune. I must therefore desire them to transfer their Favour to some dearer friend. . . .'

In a manner common to the writers of twentieth-century war communiqués he contrived to pluck from defeat the semblance of victory. He had withdrawn to a previously prepared position, he had retreated to strengthen his line. His withdrawal had been a voluntary one made to outsmart the enemy and make him appear at a disadvantage. Wolcot was nothing if not entirely human in his reactions. He withdrew from Truro in good order leaving the enemy, it was to be presumed, discomfited by the unexpected turn of events.

Into the house on Truro Bowling Green, overlooking the Quay, eventually moved young Polwhele. What Truro gained in respectability must have been sadly offset by the loss of the generous vitality that, in the intervals of tilting publicly at the windmills of complacent and pompous bureaucracy, had selflessly tended in private the sick and the poor.

*   *   *   *   *

His life was now divided between Helston and Falmouth in both of which towns he seems fleetingly to have lived. Though he might morally have been defeated it is clear that, *pace* Polwhele, he was not on occasion lacking in physical courage for while he was at Falmouth the house of his Quaker friend, Charles Fox, caught fire. The better to enjoy the spectacle Fox climbed to the roof of a neighbouring house and watched the conflagration with the calmness of the philosopher: it was Wolcot who was the man of action and rescued the horses from the stables by muffling their heads in blankets and leading them from the flames.

He subscribed, as a substantial citizen should, to the works of local authors. *Life Review'd*, a poem by the Reverend Mr Samuel Walker, Curate of Truro, was one such work and of John Goodridge's *The Phoenix: an Essay being an Attempt to prove from History and astronomical Calculations that the Comet is the real Phoenix of the Ancients*, he ordered six copies.

His own work was beginning to take on a new authority. From 1780 for the next forty years hardly a month went by without one or more publications such as the *Monthly Review* or the *European Magazine* printing his verses. The work of his protégé Opie was also flourishing, and the boy was now on such terms with his patron that when Wolcot introduced him to a lady to whom he was making love Opie, thinking that being twenty years younger than the doctor his advances might be more welcome, also made love to her. Moreover, to make sure that he should not be interrupted by his elder rival he took the elementary precaution of borrowing Wolcot's horse to visit her.

'Jan had much youthful vanity even before he knew the great world,' said Wolcot ruefully.

The great world was beckoning to them both. Wolcot was not content to remain buried for ever in the Cornish countryside where he increasingly often encountered those who had reason to dislike him. Medicine had been the means to the end of escaping

82

from Fowey and from his aunts. Now one of those formidable women, Aunt Mary, was dead and buried at Fowey in March 1780, but, successful though he was, Wolcot still did not enjoy his profession. He would rather, he said, live happily on one guinea than miserably on ten. And at the age of forty-three he suddenly and spectacularly abandoned everything for which he had been trained, threw over his profession, and with it all but the tiny income from his property at Kingsbridge and in the company of John Opie left to seek in London the fortune and the full independence that had so long eluded him.

7

THE move to London for all its apparent suddenness must have been carefully planned. Stated in its most simple form the arrangement was that Wolcot and Opie should set up house together on a profit-sharing basis, pooling the proceeds of their writing and painting. But in fact Wolcot was something more than an artistic partner in the enterprise. With his superior knowledge of the world in general and the artistic jungle of London in particular he acted most skilfully as impresario for the younger man. Moreover his conduct of the campaign to launch Opie was so carefully conceived and so calculated that it becomes a question for conjecture at what early stage in the artist's development was Wolcot seized with the inspiration for the London adventure that was to be the turning point in the careers of both of them. For how many months, for how many years had Wolcot, as he rode from village to village practising medicine in a countryside so backward that the water of a boiled thunderbolt was considered a cure for rheumatism, planned this moment of an escape for which Opie was the necessary instrument?

In the words of Professor Waterhouse Wolcot's

'aim was to bring him on the London stage as "the Cornish wonder" an untrained and self-taught prodigy. . . . He fed him on Rembrandt and the Tenebrists, no doubt through the medium of prints. This was done with something of the secrecy that now attends the training of a racehorse and Wolcot established himself with the young Opie in London in 1781 and pretended that the young prodigy had never seen an Old Master or had any serious training. . . . Opie was sprung on the world as a sort of modern Ribera.'

84

He was also sprung on the world in the same manner that a fairground showman might have presented a Wild Man from Borneo. Uncouth and with green feathers in his hair—though that was an eccentricity that was soon abandoned—he was made to appear an artistic freak. To Hearne, who suggested cleaning him up a little, Wolcot replied, 'No, no! You may depend upon it in this wonder-gaping town that all curiosity would cease if his hair were dressed and he looked like any other man; I shall keep him in this state for the next two years at least. . . .'

In view of the letters that Opie was writing home to his family at this moment, which are very far from illiterate and, indeed, evince a certain sophistication, it is impossible to believe that he, too, did not enter into the amiable deception. The move to London must indeed have been well rehearsed.

*   *   *   *   *

They had come to London via Exeter where Opie had painted the portraits of some of the local nobility and gentry. They had taken rooms near Leicester Fields at Riccard's house in Orange Court where the raree-show of Opie's rustic genius was established. Their success was immediate for all fashionable London flocked to see the boy-wonder and to have their portraits painted by the untutored genius. In his single-mindedness of purpose Wolcot shewed a surprisingly ruthless side to his character. Being joined in self-interest with his protégé anybody who stood in his way was trampled underfoot. His old friend James Northcote felt, particularly, that he had been sacrificed to the young Opie. He had gone away to Italy to study the works of the great Italian Masters and on his return to England had been shattered by the news from the great Sir Joshua Reynolds himself that he might as well have stayed abroad for there was now in London a young boy who surpassed in genius even Caravaggio himself. To poor Northcote it seemed that

'Wolcot immediately considered everything as inimical to his good which might in any degree thwart his schemes towards Opie's benefit and for these reasons only became my enemy as I was struggling to make my way in the world,

85

and not only affected to despise my powers as an artist to the private friends of both but also wrote anonymous critiques against me in the public newspapers and never ceased doing me ill offices until such time as he and Opie had a violent quarrel on the score of dividing Opie's gains which at that time were very great. But that which made me particularly the object of Wolcot's hatred was this. Opie and I came both of us from the West Country and consequently were both well known to the same persons whose patronage might be of use to us on our entrance into public life; therefore this enmity which would have been of little consequence to one whose reputation was already established yet at such a critical moment certainly much increased my difficulties which were already too numerous for me to encounter.'

Certainly fashionable London was flocking to see the extraordinary exhibition of native, rustic genius that Wolcot was exhibiting in Orange Court. The great world, in fact, so flocked about him that the street was scarcely passable: Opie himself used to laugh with pleasure and say that he should really be obliged to plant cannon at his door to keep them all off. 'During this time,' said poor little Northcote sadly, 'my knocker might have been made of Glass. Opie was a dreadful hurt to me. . . .' Yet when he ventured to complain about it Wolcot unkindly coupled Northcote's diminutive stature and his natural bitterness in the descriptive epithet 'a walking thumb-bottle of aqua-fortis' and wrote him a furious letter saying that it was 'high time that little whippersnapper gentleman your tongue should be stopped in his career; he may possibly bring a disgrace to his neighbour nose by his licentiousness'.

But this popular success could hardly have been achieved without the patronage of Court circles and here the couple had been favoured by an entirely fortuitous stroke of luck. There came suddenly out of the blue a letter:

'Sir,
    I cannot forbear writing to you on a subject now doubtless forgotten to you, tho' your sweet verses on it have awakened that painful (yet pleasing) Remembrance that occasions you

86

this trouble. A Mother must always remember such a son! few indeed have had such a one to delight in or lament. . . .'

His elegy on the death of young Boscawen which for eleven years had been gathering dust on some editor's desk appeared in the Annual Register for 1779. Here Mrs Boscawen, the bereaved mother, had by accident stumbled upon it. She wrote instantly to Dodsley the bookseller and editor to enquire about its author. Dodsley replied that the verses came from Jamaica where he supposed, though he did not know, the author might reside. Mrs Boscawen spoke to Captain Wallis of Truro—it was he who had been one of the first to break the terrible news to her—and he gave her Wolcot's address:

'. . . You knew my lovely Child—it is plain you did—you describe him so well! I have a melancholy Curiosity . . .'

Mrs Boscawen wanted to know all the sad details:

'Quite at your leisure (and not sooner) you will answer. . . .'

It was an invaluable contact to have made. With this introduction, the likelihood of success of their adventure must have been greatly increased. It had been essential, too, that success should come quickly. Wolcot was almost without funds. He had abandoned a practice that brought him between £300 and £400 a year and litigation in Truro had proved expensive: there is a report that a final libel against the Mayor and Corporation had cost him some £200 that he could ill afford.

It was with Opie's forty pounds that the lodgings in Orange Court had been furnished, but it was Wolcot's introduction to Mrs Boscawen that proved the more valuable asset. After he had recommended young Opie to her patronage, said Wolcot, 'she made it a point to oblige me and immediately introduced him to Lord and Lady Bute, the Honble Mr and Mrs Walsingham, Lord and Lady Edgcumbe, Mrs Delany, a chief favourite of their Majesties, etc. etc. . . .'

As a result Opie was able to write home, 'I have all the quality at my lodgings every day, nothing but Lords, Ladies, Dukes,

Duchesses, etc.' But it was his portrait of Mrs Delany that caused him to be sent for by George III. According to Wolcot the greater part of the night before the visit was spent in instructing Opie how to bow ceremoniously to the Royal Family, in reminding him to keep his hands out of his breeches pockets and blow his nose before he got into Buckingham House, in beseeching him not to scratch his head as their Majesties approached, not to spit on the carpet or twist his hat nervously on his thumb. But there were those who maintain that the doctor fancied that the more of a savage he represented his protégé to be the greater wonder he would appear as a painter. And since it is from Wolcot that comes the account of Opie's visit to the king this too may be treated with slight reserve.

The pictures that Opie took with him were *An Old Jew*, *A Beggar and his Dog*, *Old Kneebone of Helston* and *Mat Trevenen*. As he was carrying the pictures into a room at the palace he was followed by the queen who treated him with great kindness,

'so much indeed that he is now turned Quixote and is ready to fight up to his knees in blood for Her Majesty. The King came in after with a skip (not a very proper pace, I think, for Majesty). West was with him—I mean West the famous painter, a monstrous favourite of George's—George asked Jan a number of questions which (from Jan's history of himself after his return) he answered with a St Agnes intrepidity. The pictures were placed in order and the British Monarch applauded the artist. The Queen turned up the whites of her eyes, marvelling, the little Princes lisped praises and Jan to be sure was in ecstasy. He remained nearly an hour and a half with 'em and then took his leave.'

The king bought *A Beggar and his Dog* and the money was paid to Opie by West who was commanded to tell the young artist that George III wished him every success. Back in their lodgings he boasted to Wolcot that he had been paid £10 for the picture.

'Why, John,' exclaimed the doctor, 'thou hast only got £8 for thy picture.'

'Indeed but I have, though, for I have got the £10 safe in my pocket.'

'Aye but dost thou know that His Majesty has got the frame for nothing and that was worth £2.'

'Damn it!' cried Opie. 'So he has! I'll go back and knack at his door and ask for the frame: damn it I will!'

Wolcot dissuaded his protégé from taking an action that would really have been quite typical of his business methods. 'I make them all, or most of them, pay half as soon as I begin the pictures which is a very good method,' he told his mother. Wolcot was less certain that this was a good idea. 'His damned democratic principles spoiled all,' he used to say in later years. 'Being ignorant how to get on he disobliged everybody . . . during the first year he actually took out writs against several of his sitters who were rather tardy in their payments.'

None the less his investment in Opie was proving a great success. Money was flowing into the common purse. Wolcot was indefatigable. He called on Sir Joshua Reynolds with two of Opie's portraits and reported the great man's surprise at the excellence of a boy whose knowledge of chiaroscura had been achieved, so Wolcot still maintained, without ever having seen a picture by the dark masters.

'It strikes me [added the doctor] 'that Reynolds expects Opie to be as perfect in the delineation of the graces as in the heads of vulgar nature and in consequence become a formidable rival. But here I am sorry to say he will be fortunately mistaken; Opie I fear is too fond of imitating coarse expression . . . to him at present elegance appears affectation and the form of Raphael unnatural. He too much resembles a country farmer who having never tasted anything beyond rough cider cannot feel the flavour of burgundy or champagne.'

That this was a sentiment echoed by others is shewn by Fuseli's scornful comment, gleefully reported by Wolcot, 'Dere is dat poo-re dogue Opee—de fellow can paint notin' but teeves and morderers—and wen de dogue paints a teef or a morderer he lookes in de glass.' Certainly Wolcot was under no illusions about the limitations of his pupil's work, but he exercised with great gusto all the functions of a publicity agent. The deflated Northcote, writing with an apparent decay of literacy in May 1782 to Sir William Elford, reported after decrying Opie's work:

> 'However he has powerfull and indefaticable friends who leave no stone unturned to do him service [so] he is yet in high credit and employment. Wolcot is allways with him and is as conceited vulgar and jawing as ever writing poetry for ever songs verses on the painters and things in the Newspapers on his addopted and takes all the merit on himself. Wanting to make Opie as a mere machine which he has inspired with this power but Opie himself seems to have great simplicity good sense and no conceit that I see.'

For Opie Northcote evidently could preserve a critical detachment that did him credit. But for his erstwhile friend Wolcot he had nothing good to say.

★   ★   ★   ★   ★

'Writing . . . for ever songs verses . . . and things in the Newspapers on his addopted . . .' The time has come to consider the literary contribution to the partnership in Orange Court.

The two men had arrived in London in the autumn of 1781, and his activities as impresario must have made any sustained effort at writing difficult for Wolcot. The first major work, for which he adopted for the first time the pseudonym 'Peter Pindar', was written the following year. Wolcot's eye for a painting was both intelligent and well informed. He was heavily involved in the art world. That he should have exercised his gifts on the then entirely novel enterprise of criticizing in verse the Exhibition of the Royal Academy was a happy inspiration. In *Lyric Odes to the Royal Academicians for 1782* he treated that Exhibition in a manner which has since become, not altogether unjustifiably, traditional. He looked, for example, at Benjamin West's religious canvases with a certain dismay:

> O West, what hath thy pencil done?
> Why, painted God Almighty's Son
> Like an old-clothes-man. . . .

90

But he was fair-minded enough to admit:

> To give the dev'l his due, thou dost inherit
> Some pigmy portion of the painting spirit
> But what is this compar'd to loftier things
> Thine is the fortune (making rivals groan)
> Of wink and nod familiar from the throne
> And sweetest whispers from the best of kings.

Mason Chamberlain, a painter now quite forgotten, was told in a particularly happy phrase that:

> . . . when it so shall please the Lord
> To make his people out of board
> Thy pictures will be tolerable nature.

And De Loutherbourg received praise of the same sort:

> . . . when Heav'n so wills
> To make brass skies and golden hills
> With marble bullocks in glass pastures grazing
> Thy reputation too will rise.

Of Serres and Zoffany (in what must surely be considered a moment of critical blindness) he said, 'I hope that you'll improve as you grow older,' a sentiment which in view of the fact that Serres was then already seventy years old and Zoffany sixty-four was perhaps not entirely serious.

Nor did their sex spare the luckless artists for Wolcot professed to sympathize with Cosway if his wife could look after his shirts no better than she painted. And of Angelica Kauffman he commented that:

> Were she married to such gentle males
> As figure in her painted tales
> I fear she'd find a stupid wedding night. . . .

One by one the public favourites of the Academy were demolished and the public themselves with their inconstancy in art did not escape the lash. One year, as Wolcot pointed out, drawing was everything to the fashionable gallery-goer and Raphael and Poussin the rage; next year colour was the criterion and Rubens and Vandyke the exemplars of modishness to those who 'pictures judge by other people's eyes'. And he attacked amusingly the gossiping female visitors to the Exhibition who admired only the way that dresses and complexions were painted:

> Whilst, unobserv'd, the glory of our nation
> Close by them hung—Sir Joshua's matchless pieces—
> Works that a Titian's hand could form alone
> Works that Corregio had been proud to own . . .

To Wolcot Reynolds could do almost no wrong ('Compared to other painting men Thou art an eagle to a wren') and in this appreciation, and in his much more unorthodox championship of the neglected Richard Wilson, he shewed himself to be an art critic of stature and sensibility. Poor 'red-nosed Dick', starving and ignored by the public, had been asked by Sir William Chambers to paint a picture for George the Third. The King inspected it, laughed at it and returned it with contempt to the painter from whom Wolcot acquired it for his own collection.

> But honest Wilson, never mind
> Immortal praises thou shalt find
> And for a dinner have no cause to fear—
> Thou start'st at my prophetic rhymes
> Don't be impatient for those times
> Wait till thou hast been dead a hundred year.

Enough has been said to shew the form that John Wolcot's satire was taking. The work received good notices from the critics but failed to make any money: indeed Wolcot claimed that he had lost some £40 on the production. Whatever other assets he may have contributed to the partnership, financially the doctor was a burden on the economy. And barely a year after they had arrived in London a breach between the two friends took place.

*   *   *   *   *

As in so many of the incidents of Wolcot's life his enemies have made it difficult to determine the exact truth of the estrangement. They were so eager to make much out of little, to see behind trifling disputes great and scandalous quarrels, to impute motives where none existed, that the facts disappeared behind a positive sepia ink-cloud of malevolence. One writer, for example, alleged that not only did Wolcot squander away on whores the money that Opie earned, but that he did not even leave him sufficient for his everyday needs.

Wolcot's own account of the whole transaction was simple:

'Having lost an income of £300 or £400 by the change of scene I entered into a written engagement by which we should share the joint profits in equal divisions. We actually did so for a year but at the end of that time my pupil told me I might return to the country as he could now do for himself.'

This account was perhaps just a trifle over-simplified, for it made no mention of the root of the trouble which was that Opie was getting married. Young brides as a class are apt to have a distaste at sharing their home with strangers, and when they are strangers such as John Wolcot, never a great favourite with women, this distaste becomes most marked. It is quite possible, too, that Mary Bunn, Opie's fiancée, considered that Wolcot was a bad influence: almost certainly, if she was in love with Opie, she must have resented the fact that he was being exhibited by Wolcot, however successfully, as a freak. Moreover Mary Bunn's father, to whom Wolcot's failure to contribute to the household expenses on the same scale as his future son-in-law was a source of annoyance, was no doubt at some pains to point out to his daughter that if she wished to lead a happy married life the doctor must be got out of the house.

John Taylor, who knew both Opie and Wolcot well, states quite unequivocally that 'the compact was dissolved by the interference of the father of Opie's first wife which induced the doctor in anger and disgust to relinquish all claims upon the successful artist'. One of the claims consisted of a note from Opie saying:

'I promise to paint for Doctor Wolcot any picture or pictures he may demand as long as I live; otherwise I desire the world will consider me a damned ungrateful son of a bitch.'

It was an obligation from which Opie never swerved even though he made his friend pay 1s. 6d. for each canvas.

But John Wolcot would have been less than human if he had not resented the way in which the whole rather shabby business of his dismissal was carried out. According to Polwhele the first that the doctor knew of Opie's intended marriage was when some friend pointed out the announcement in a newspaper. As for his removal from the ménage in Orange Court, it seems that Opie could not bring himself to cast off his old friend, to whom he owed everything, in a personal interview and face to face. He sent the ultimatum to Wolcot in a letter while the doctor was away from London.

If ever there was a man who had reason to complain of ingratitude it must have been John Wolcot and it must be adduced in evidence of the essential generosity of his spirit that so far from allowing this treatment to embitter him permanently against Opie he remained on terms of friendship, though perhaps not of the same intimacy, and always wrote generously of Opie's talent for the rest of the artist's life. Only those who could not or would not understand the doctor's attitude magnified this parting of the ways into the bitter quarrel that it was not.

Certainly Wolcot in moments of sadness was apt to complain of Opie's lack of gratitude: someone who had heard this complaint said to Opie, 'What ails Wolcot at you—once I thought he had been a friendly and kind-hearted man?' to which all Opie could reply was, 'Aye, in time you will know him.'

But Wolcot, essentially uncertain of himself, with the long years of subservience to female domination so close behind him, became ever less and less easy to know and less willing to be known.

★　　★　　★　　★　　★

Financially the break could not have come at a more unfortunate time for John Wolcot. His first *Lyric Odes to the Royal Academicians* had been a *succès d'estime* and nothing else. He had

94

abandoned his career as a doctor. He was almost without income. In a manner not sufficiently explained he attached himself, evidently intending to act in the same capacity of impresario and Press agent as he had done to Opie, to an artist named Paye. E. C. Giddy says:

> 'Wolcot took Mr Paye, an artist of much promise under his protection, lodged in his house, advised and praised him in public. But Paye never rose to the discarded Opie and the connexion between them was soon dissolved.'

According to the *Gentleman's Magazine* Paye, Wolcot's protégé and host, who lived in Broad Street, Great Marlborough Street,

> 'was like Opie, his predecessor and like the doctor himself a man of peculiar character and not likely to bend long to the humours of another. His pictures of domestic life, of children and, in particular, of a woman sitting at a window, had acquired him a celebrity as an artist not inferior in finish to the principal Flemish painters.'

Understandably these pictures took, in all their attention to detail, a great deal of painting.

'Damn it, sir,' said Wolcot, 'you will paint yourself into the King's Bench.'

Because of this criticism Paye took to working less carefully and became 'wooly and indifferent' and fell, as well he might do, into a decline.

A break with Wolcot was inevitable. Cyrus Redding, writing in the *Athenaeum*, reported that Paye 'misconducting himself the Doctor cast him off'. But although Wolcot may have removed his services which seem to have been, as far as Paye was concerned, little short of disastrous, he can hardly have been in a position to cast anybody off.

Paye, understandably piqued by the effect that the doctor had had upon his work, poured out his resentment in a portrait in which 'he ridiculed the poet's parsimonious disposition (though a lover of eating and drinking Wolcot was at home a very strict economist) by exhibiting him as a bear with the doctor's wig on, painting by the fire and putting kneaded clods of Thames mud upon it from a bucket'—an expedient that Wolcot, apparently, employed in place of expensive coals or Cornish turf.

Wolcot was, in fact, in no position to be anything but a strict economist. He retired in not very good order to a lodging in the attics of Number 13 Tavistock Row, alone and almost penniless.

8

JOHN WOLCOT had reached the nadir of his career. But even in failure Tavistock Street had the exhilarating aura of fame clinging to it. The house in the attics of which he lived frugally had formerly been occupied by Zincke the enamellist and later Nathaniel Dance had also lived there. A few doors away from Wolcot, where Vandervelde had once had rooms, there still lived 'Irish' Johnstone the actor. It was, in fact, a centre for the sort of people amongst whom Wolcot was happiest to be. Literary society was still dominated by Dr Johnson whom Wolcot frequently encountered at Sir Joshua Reynolds' table.

According to the *Anti-Jacobin* Johnson, due to his dislike for ribald discourse, repelled rather than encouraged advances by Peter Pindar. Wolcot himself admitted that, no less than the rest of the world, he went in awe of the great moralist. Once he asked Sir Joshua how the club to which he belonged could so patiently suffer the overbearing tyranny of Dr Johnson, to which Reynolds replied with a smile that the members often hazarded sentiments merely to try his powers of contradiction.

On at least two occasions Wolcot tried this himself. He observed to Johnson that his portrait by Reynolds was not sufficiently dignified and got the reply 'in a kind of bull-dog growl':

'No, sir! the pencil of Reynolds never wanted dignity or the Graces.'

Later he laid a trap for Johnson. 'I think, Doctor,' he observed, 'that picture of Sir Joshua's'—he named the work—'is one of the best he ever painted.'

'I differ from you, sir,' said Johnson emphatically. 'I think it is one of his worst.' Wolcot made no other attempt at conversation with the Grand Cham; the picture was in his opinion really one of Sir Joshua's best. It is unfortunate that, since the name of the painting has not survived, it is not possible to make an assessment of Johnson's worth as an art critic.

'Traps are good things to bring out character,' commented Wolcot, complacently confident of the rightness of his own judgment. 'The idea of a discussion with Johnson never entered my head. I had too great an apprehension of his powers of conversation to attempt disputing with the giant of the day.'

Dispute with him he might not but in those first *Lyric Odes to the Royal Academicians* he had dared to refer to Johnson:

> Who, surly, bore his tommy-hawk about
> And glorying in a Despot's rude dominion
> Scalp'd without mercy ev'ry man's opinion
> Which from his mouth should dare to venture out.
>
> Where JOHNSON sat (which Candour sore bewails)
> Men stole forth words so cautious!—just like snails
> So fearful putting forth their tender horns
> Shrinking and drawing in. . . .

And he once observed to Reynolds that:

> 'Johnson too frequently acts the reverse of gipsies. The gipsies when they steal the children of gentlefolks conceal the theft by beggarly disguises whereas Johnson often steals common thoughts disguising the theft by pomp of language.'

Wolcot was, in fact, almost certainly the first to be able to see through the dazzling majesty of Johnson's prose and analyse it to a degree in which he could achieve what must surely be parody of a high order.

> 'As Mr Boswell's Journal [wrote Peter Pindar] hath afforded such universal pleasure by the relation of minute incidents, and the great Moralist's opinion of men and things, during his northern tour; it will be adding greatly to the anecdotal treasury, as well as making Mr B. happy, to communicate part of a Dialogue that took place between Dr Johnson and the Author . . . a few months before the Doctor paid the great debt of nature. The Doctor was very cheerful

that day; he had on a black coat and waistcoat, a black plush pair of breeches, and black worsted stockings, a handsome grey wig, a shirt, a muslin neckcloth, a black pair of buttons in his shirt sleeves, a pair of shoes ornamented with the very identical little buckles that accompanied the philosopher to the Hebrides; his nails were very neatly pared and his beard fresh shaved with a razor fabricated by the ingenious Mr Savigny.

PETER PINDAR: Pray Doctor, what is your opinion of Mr Boswell's literary powers?

JOHNSON: Sir, my opinion is, that whenever Bozzy expires, he will create no *vacuum* in the region of literature—he seems strongly affected by the *cacoethes scribendi*; wishes to be thought a *rara avis*, and in truth so he is—your knowledge in ornithology, Sir, will easily discover to what species of bird I allude.

Here the Doctor shook his head and laughed.

PETER PINDAR: What think you, Sir, of his account of Corsica? —of his character of Paoli?

JOHNSON: Sir, he hath made a mountain of a wart. But Paoli has virtues. The account is a farrago of disgusting egotism and pompous inanity.

PETER PINDAR: I have heard it whispered, Doctor, that should you die before him, Mr B. means to write your life.

JOHNSON: Sir, he cannot mean me so irreparable an injury.— Which of us shall die first is only known to the Great Disposer of events; but were I sure that James Boswell would write *my* life, I do not know whether I would not anticipate the measure by taking *his*.

(Here he made three or four strides across the room and returned to his chair with violent emotion.)

PETER PINDAR: I am afraid that he means to do you the favour.

JOHNSON: He dares not—he would make a scarecrow of me. I give him liberty to fire his blunderbuss in *his own* face, but not murder *me*. Sir, I heed not his ᾽αυτος εφα—BOSWELL write my life! Why the fellow possesses not abilities for writing the life of an *ephemeron.*'

If this wasn't true it was, at any rate (apart from an underrating of Boswell's capabilities) splendid stuff though, perhaps, not of a sort to cause a smile to its victims.

✱   ✱   ✱   ✱   ✱

Soon after it had become apparent that the first volume of *Lyric Odes* was going to prove a financial failure Wolcot had another stroke of the good fortune that so often came to his aid. A Mr Penneck introduced him casually to John Taylor the one-time oculist who, in an admirably versatile way, had become the dramatic critic of the *Morning Post*. Taylor, nineteen years the doctor's junior, introduced into the paper—which he was later to edit, and finally to own—many of Wolcot's unpublished works, and brought the name of Peter Pindar into such prominence that the publisher Kearsley approached him. The result was a long and successful business association which began with a second volume of *Lyric Odes* attacking the Academy of 1783.

Wolcot compared it to Sodom—if there were ten paintings that deserved not to be damned he would burn his odes. The whole Exhibition, he maintained, was so flat and unprofitable that people would be better employed in going to see the conjuror Katterfelto and his Cat and, prone to encourage youthful talent though he was, he was forced to remark of the young painters exhibiting that year:

> There's many a painting puppy, take my word
> Who knocks his silly head against a board
> That might have helped the State—made a good jailor
> A nightman or a tolerable tailor. . . .

—a comment which is still valid in certain circles today.

Benjamin West was again attacked for his portraits of George III and of Oliver Cromwell, although Wolcot had to admit that these canvases would do as well as those by Caravaggio for stuffing holes and keeping the draughts out of the Royal stables as was being done by the king's servants in the North of England.

Even Gainsborough, whom he admired, he accused of stealing his picture of dogs from Snyders, and although he accorded him a certain amount of praise he told him that he had 'kicked Nature out of doors'. This volume proved a financial as well as a critical success and towards the end of the year—which must disprove any stories of a serious breach—he went on a tour of the West with his old friend John Opie and his young bride. In August Amy the survivor of the two aunts who were so responsible for his character had died and in December his mother, a figure even more shadowy than her sisters-in-law, also joined the other members of the Wolcot family in Fowey churchyard. It is not certain whether John saw his mother before she died or whether he extended his tour with Opie from Wales to Cornwall, after the event, to wind up the family estate—only one of the older generation (uncle William who had married into the family of Newcomen the engineer) survived—and put the old property at Dodbrooke on to the market.

Always he had loved the old house with its barn and walled garden and with its pleasant lawns sloping down to the estuary where the swans floated on the full tide and the chestnut trees cast a shade in which he had played in the happy carefree days before his father had died and he had been sent to live in Fowey. Often he had talked of returning there to live but now he was forced to try to sell it. Presumably the rewards of his writing had not yet sufficiently offset the debts that he is likely to have contracted in the dreadful winter of disillusion that he had just passed through. And there may well be a touch of autobiography in his advice to Landscape Painters to escape from London:

> Claude painted in the open air
> Therefore to Wales at once repair
> Where scenes of true magnificence you'll find
> Besides this great advantage—if in debt
> You'll have with creditors no tête-à-tête
> So leave the bull-dog bailiffs all behind
> Who, hunt you with what noise they may,
> Must hunt for needles in a stack of hay.

This state of probable indebtedness—though publication fees were at last beginning to trickle in and perhaps there were some legacies from Fowey as well—makes it all the more curious that Wolcot seems to have written no major work for publication this year. The only volume that appeared in 1784—and here was evidence of a speedy fame—was a pirated edition, published in

Dublin, of his *Collected Works*. Yet he was in London, at any rate from April onwards, in time to witness the tumultuous scenes of the General Election of that year.

The collapse in 1782 of Lord North's administration had led to two years of exceptional political instability which led, inevitably, to a lively election. The London mob had already shown something of its explosive potentialities, the year before Wolcot had come from Cornwall, in the Gordon Riots and the electioneering scenes in Covent Garden were of a nature that it would not be exaggerating to call robust.

Wolcot wrote to his old friend Thomas Giddy:

'We are in the midst of bustle and confusion—Hood, Wray and Fox battling it every day at Covent Garden—bribery, knavery and threats are the weapons made use of by Fox and his partizans who *bona-fide* are a set of highwaymen—a desperate banditti let loose on the Constitution. I am sorry to say Pitt is also connected with almost as complete scoundrels—your House of Commons is a House of Thieves—by them your liberties will be lost says old Montesquieu and it will prove so—however the State must undergo a pretty severe convulsion before that will happen—I abhor the thought of a Member of Parliament from the *known* abuse of so sacred a trust as is committed to their charge. The moment they enter the House they dream of nothing but robbery or Peerages but enough of them.

The Duchesses of Devonshire and Portland I met meanly canvassing in the street—they were hooted exceedingly by the Mob and deservedly but let me drop the subject for it makes me half mad to think that those men we choose for our defenders should be the fellows to *tomahawk* us. . . .'

It is a form of disillusion that many decent and by no means illiberal men sometimes come to feel about professional politicians.

*   *   *   *   *

But there were—as fortunately there often are—other distractions for a man of sensibility. For Wolcot music ranked high amongst them. Handel's Jubilee was to be held in Westminster Abbey and although, at first, he did not intend to go (he thought Handel 'a fine fellow to be sure but when I go to a feast I expect variety') he was at last persuaded, and at the Abbey 'was almost frightened' by the Dead March in Saul which 'surpassed almost everything in sublimity'. His admiration for Handel however stopped short of the enthusiasm of George III who at the queen's concert went up to Mrs Sheridan who was singing that night. 'Mrs Sheridan,' said the king, 'I have a favour to beg of you. The queen too has consented to my asking it, who by no means loves Mr Handel's compositions, will you sing me *Return O God of Hosts*?' At the conclusion His Majesty snapped his fingers with delight and exclaimed to the company at large: 'There's music for ye! One bar is worth all the music of the present day.'

'So much for the king's taste and manners,' commented Wolcot—for whom the king could do no right—a little unfairly.

His own musical taste was catholic. Haydn he found 'the Apollo of the day' and 'certainly very fine but at times he plays the devil with the ear with his chromatics'. There was a deal of good music making its appearance; young Stamitz he reported to be in high repute, Koswarra he found 'a charming composer but a damned rogue', Abel was still writing, Clementi had 'gone off in a pet because a performer (a stranger) was particularly noticed at Lord Abingdon's concert', Nicholai was 'much reputed and his lessons sweet things', Dibdin was in the King's Bench composing burlettas for Hughes' circus.

Armed with his musical appreciation Wolcot went both to public concerts and to the private houses of musicians. He visited Schroeter. He drank tea, during a most pleasant afternoon, with Miss Guest the celebrated harpsichord player. Rasuzzini was also there and Miss Guest showed him some of Wolcot's Ballads with which he expressed himself delighted and swore that he would set one or two of them to music. 'He is thought a very fine composer,' commented Wolcot with a certain complacency. 'Burney mentions him on his German tour.' He heard with amazement young Cramer on the pianoforte, he admired Fischer on the hautboy and Kampferr on the double bass. Above all he worshipped Madam Mara. 'Nothing was ever equal to her. She has so frightened the other songstresses that they tremble to open their mouths.' He attended her benefit at the Pantheon where during the concert she left her place in the orchestra and came down under it to hear Crosdell 'the first violoncello player in the world' play, inter alia, The Air in *Ariadne*. Wolcot kept his eyes glued upon her all the time. 'You cannot conceive her pleasure on the occasion—"Bravo! Bravo! Bravissimo!" she could not help exclaiming several times.'

The Exhibition at the Royal Academy was less than a fortnight away and there were scandalous things happening. Sir Joshua had told him that Gainsborough after sending in his pictures had sent for them back in a huff, because, it was presumed, he was displeased with the lighting arrangements. Reynolds himself had painted an inimitable picture of Mr Pott the surgeon. Yet Wolcot's Muse, lost in the giddy intoxicating round of all that London had to offer—art, concerts, theatres, his favourite resort *The Hummums* in Covent Garden—was silent. It is almost as if, freed for ever from the voices that had ordered, advised, directed and nagged, he had thrown off the shackles and in an ecstasy of moral independence produced nothing.

But by the end of 1784 the time had come to call a halt. On November 25th he wrote urgently from 37 Broad Street, Golden Square, to his solicitor George Prideaux at Kingsbridge:

> '*Hath* any Person or *is* any Person about taking my house at Dodbrooke. I wish to know before I visit it which will be in about three weeks or a month. My good Friend, do return me an Answer by Return of Post with as many other Particulars as you please. . . .'

The need for money and financial independence was again reasserting itself.

* * * * *

The Royal Academy again attracted his critical attention:

> The Academy is like a microscope
> For by the magnifying power are seen
> Objects that for attention ne'er could hope

In the preamble to the odes for 1785 he briefly mentioned some of the outstanding works of the previous unnoticed year. Benjamin West had exhibited *Moses on Mount Sinai receiving the Law*, *Jeremiah*, *Isiah* and the *Apotheosis* but, complained Wolcot, his Israelites had all possessed Christian faces and his angels were duck-winged; Rigaud's work had all been trash; Mrs Cosway's *Sampson* had been 'between two garden rollers staring'. He had only refrained from saying so the previous year for fear of the punishment that Lord Mansfield might deal out to him from the Bench.

> Although as sterling as the Holy Bible
> Truth makes it (MANSFIELD says) the more a libel!

It was only when he asked himself

> Where is the glorious freedom of our Isle
> If not permitted to call names

that he returned to the attack. This at any rate was his excuse and it is quite possible that it may contain an element of truth. For even though he had concluded his previous volume with the couplet

> What rage for fame attends both great and small
> Better be damn'd than mentioned not at all!

there must have been many artists who would readily have dispensed with the publicity he brought them and have stopped his pen by whatever means they could.

One contemporary satirist went so far as to state categorically:

> Peter thou know'st thou art a very coward
> And fear'st to meet the man thou hast lampooned
> Hast thou forgot when Cosway's visage soured
> How soon thy courage fail'd how soon thou swooned?

And he added a footnote to the effect that Wolcot, in fear, had apologized to Cosway for his attacks on Mrs Cosway's art.

But now, it seemed he had taken fresh courage and to those who might ask by what right he criticized the Academy he replied that through the taxes on candles and shoe-leather and butchers' shops he had helped to pay for it and he attacked West more devastatingly than ever: his landscape with a white sow and sucking litter he felt might fairly be called the 'dotage of the art'.

> Thou really dost not equal Derby Wright
>   The Man of Night
> O'er woolen hills where gold and silver moons
> Now mount like sixpences and now balloons.

Peter Pindar's own work was showing a new neatness of phrase. Writing of Ramsay, who had left 'nine rooms well stuff'd with Kings and Queens' which were bought by ambassadors and plenipotentiaries to show abroad the progress of British art, he commented:

> Whether they purchased by the pound or yard
> I cannot tell because I never heard.

Many of his similes showed a slickness that was refreshing: starlings he referred to:

> All talking gabbling but none listening
> Just like a group of gossips at a christening.

And young artists whom he attacked for their propensity for finding fault with each other rather than trying to excel he compared happily to dogs quarrelling over a bone given to one of them at the table.

But it was Nathaniel Hone, who had just died, who was the subject of the most telling ode:

> There's one RA more dead! Stiff is poor Hone!
> His works be with him under the same stone;
> I think the sacred art will not bemoan 'em.
> But Muse! *De mortuis nil nisi bonum*
> As to his host a traveller, with a sneer,
> Said of his dead small beer.

This jest might still earn a man the reputation of a wit in a pub in one of the older University towns.

★   ★   ★   ★   ★

Technically, too, Wolcot was advancing. To avoid dullness he was varying the pace of the various odes that made up a volume: suddenly he would drop an old-fashioned ballad into the pages, either in a spirit of parody of

> . . . those dismal times
> When naught my sighs avail'd and naught my rhymes
> When at the silent solemn close of day
> My pensive steps would court the darkling grove
> To hear in Philomela's lonely lay
> The fainting echoes of my luckless love,

or, perhaps, simply using up some old but revised fragment of his youthful amatory verse, *To Cynthia* or the like.

He widens the scope of his attack by engaging in diversions which have nothing to do with the main subject of the *Lyric Odes*; as an example of this technique he switches suddenly to Cornwall and talks of the pilchards which, in his day, made Fowey smell so disgusting:

> Pilchards! whose bodies yield the fragrant oil
> And make the London lamps at midnight smile
> Which lamps, wide-spreading salutary light
> Beam on the wandering Beauties of the night
> And shew each gentle youth their cheeks' red roses
> And tell him whether they have eyes and noses.

The response to this new and improved Wolcot was most gratifying. He had been forced to increase the price of his volume from 1s. and 1s. 6d. to half a crown:

> For things are desperately ris'n, good Lord!
> Fish, flesh, coals, candles, window-lights and board
> Why should not charming poetry then rise
> That comes so dev'lish far, too—from the skies!

107

The complaint has a familiar ring. But the higher price did not prevent the *Lyric Odes* for 1785 achieving a real success.

*   *   *   *   *

It was in this year 1785, too, that Wolcot branched out into what was an entirely new line of popular pamphleteering. In the twentieth century the idea that public figures in general and the members of the Royal Family in particular are not entitled to the personal privacy demanded by a nonentity has become so generally accepted that it is difficult to realize the momentous step that John Wolcot was taking when he decided to turn his attentions to the Crown. And to those who enjoy photographs taken of royal dukes in night-clubs at a carefully chosen moment when they look both drunk and moronic only the honest directness of Wolcot's approach is likely to cause a momentary comment. Wolcot was no hypocrite. He did not find it necessary to disguise his attacks behind the newspaper diarist's professed concern for the dignity of the throne or for the welfare of those faced with the choice between duty and inclination. He did not profess loyalty, yet, though it becomes sometimes hard to remember, he was in fact a Loyalist. And many a later journalist has perhaps made a more lucrative living as the indirect result of Wolcot's example. He was the first of a new generation of political satirists to attack the king. Wilkes and Junius, it is true, had addressed the throne with some acerbity, but generally speaking the monarch and his private life had been sacrosanct.

There have been many, including his contemporaries, who tried to find convincing reasons for this sudden iconoclasm. It was of course a time of revolution but this, though it made *lèse-majesté* acceptable, was not the reason. Some said it was because George III had slighted Opie, others that it was because he had insufficiently appreciated Reynolds, others still that his treatment of Wilson had aroused Wolcot's contempt. It was none of these things. Wolcot—who in any case was never loth to shock—was determined to make money and he was almost the first to realize that a quick way of making money was at the expense of the Royal Family. And in 1785 he started work on the first of five cantos dealing with the king's discovery of something moving upon his dinner plate.

108

'How, how? what, what?—what's that, what's that?' he cries
  With rapid accent and with staring eyes.
'Look there, look there—what's got into my house?
  A louse, God bless us! louse, louse, louse, louse, louse!'

But this publication, the *Lousiad*, will be dealt with in its
proper place; before it appeared the Academicians were to receive
another drubbing.

*   *   *   *   *

The *Farewell Odes for 1786*, as he called them, indicate perhaps
that Wolcot had his ear sufficiently well attuned to the public
taste to realize, as some writers less astute than he have failed to
do, that there are times when a writer must not stand still, that
there may be a limit to the number of times that it is possible to
sell variations on the same theme and that some popular vein of
material must be abandoned even before it is fully worked out if
the readers are to avoid satiety.

The *Farewell Odes* mark the end, for many years, of his art-
criticism in this form and the first of the odes gives a gay picture
of the artists all celebrating that fact that Peter Pindar intends in
future to spare them. There was an account, too, of the Academy
dinner at which the members

> . . . had no stomach over grace to nod
> Nor time enough to offer thanks to God
> *That* might be done they wisely knew
> When they had nothing else to *do*.

It was inevitable that Peter Pindar should notice that the Prince
of Wales arrived late at the dinner and found it difficult to get
anything decent to eat, and that Lord Bessborough also fared
badly and left early to seek a proper meal at Brookes.

As for the pictures in the exhibition they were much the same
as they always had been and always would be. Benjamin West,
who during the year had apparently said some rude things about
Wolcot's verse, was again the main object of attack:

The Holy Scriptures say 'All flesh is grass'
With Mr West all flesh is brick and brass
Except his horseflesh which I fairly own
Is chiefly of the finest Portland stone.

Moreover Wolcot expressed himself with sound common sense on a subject which in later years was responsible for a good deal of nonsense being written in angry letters to *The Times* and *Telegraph*:

On faults that modern works would tarnish
Time spreads a sacred coat of varnish.

And he again attacks the public who will praise any Old Master simply because it is an Old Master which like some poor raddled old duchess

Draws from the gaping mob the envious look
Because her husband chanc'd to be a Duke.

But really his spirit does not seem to have been quite so wholeheartedly in the attack this year. His rhyming is ingenious, his variety of subsidiary subjects greater than ever—the story of the Pilgrim and the Peas which Gillray illustrated and which Wolcot first heard from old Mrs Polwhele when she was complaining of breadcrumbs in her bed occurs in this volume—but there seems not quite the gusto, not quite the same number of memorable touches, as there had been the previous year. And although, once again, the work was well received and its financial success assured it was probably a wise decision to launch out into other branches of criticism.

* * * * *

The first cantos of the *Lousiad* in due course appeared. It is a work now interesting mostly for having been allegedly translated into German by no less a figure than Goethe and for the inside knowledge that Wolcot displayed of Buckingham House—a knowledge gained by dining several times, both in London and at Windsor, in the royal kitchens with the cooks who had been compulsorily shaved as a result of the Louse and whose reactions formed the main basis of the *Lousiad*.

The effect of the poem on the reading public was considerable: kings were still referred to, at any rate in public, as sacred. The Divine Right was still, theoretically, theirs. Even his closest friends and well-wishers were horrified and begged Wolcot to desist from attacking the 'best of kings'. This in itself he must have found a pleasing tribute to his skill in being shocking. And he received, too, some welcome and, indeed, symbolical publicity when Opie took an old portrait of Wolcot, painted some years earlier, and inserted it in an historical canvas to depict the doctor as a murderer of royalty in the *Assassination of James I*.

To those who had spread gossiping stories this was additional confirmation of a violent break between the two friends. Opie, it was said, had already included Wolcot's portrait in a study of Milton's *Fallen Angels*, but the doctor being at that time unknown the joke had not taken. Now 'irritated by the doctor's malevolence he painted a portrait of him in one of his most furious rages and substituted it for the head of the murderer'. And when, the following year, Wolcot appeared again in an Opie historical canvas this time as an assassin in *The Death of Rizzio* there could surely be no doubt that the artist was hitting his old friend hard.

But certain doubts may be permitted to intrude. In the first place Opie had also included as an assassin of James I his own self-portrait—and a much fiercer murderer he made than Wolcot, who, in the words of J. Jope Rogers, 'seems in no kind of rage and enters upon his duty in the most kindly manner and with the air of a light-hearted, well-bred gentleman'. And secondly there is strong contemporary evidence that Wolcot 'by a strange whim was actually introduced in this horrible character by his own particular request'. The *Gentleman's Magazine* had no doubts about it:

Thine, Peter, thine, the strong mark'd portrait there
'Twas thine own choice to wear the murderer's vest. . . .

And when, later on in the verse, the writer added:

III

> Well art thou mark'd amid the ruffian crew
> With eye of rancour and with treacherous mien
> The cruel mind the skillful artist drew
> And made thee hero of each deathful scene,

this was, of course, almost literally, exactly what the doctor ordered: it was all part of the scheme to build up the character he most wished to present to the public, the sort of character not unknown today whose fame and financial prosperity depend upon the continual outrageousness of his, or her, public pronouncements.

★   ★   ★   ★   ★

His output in 1786 was prodigious. In addition to the *Farewell Odes to the Academicians* there came from the publishers the first of his literary criticisms, the *Congratulatory Epistle to James Boswell on his Journal of a Tour to the Hebrides with the Celebrated Doctor Johnson.*

> Triumphant thou through TIME's vast gulph shalt sail
> The pilot of our literary whale

he prophesies, accurately enough, and he has a pleasant phrase to describe Boswell's preoccupation with minutiae:

> Thou charming haberdasher of small ware [he called him]
> Who like a watchful cat before a hole
> Full twenty years, (inflam'd with letter'd pride)
> Did'st mousing sit before Sam's mouth so wide
> To catch as many scraps as thou wert able—
> A very Laz'rus at the rich man's table.

The *Epistle* was vastly successful: it went through no less than ten editions in three years and it was followed also in 1786 by *Bozzy and Piozzi or the British Biographers*, a work which made great fun of the preoccupation of those suffering from the almost universal 'Johnso-mania' to deal in any matter, however small and inconsiderable, that had once fallen from the great man's lips.

Strong mids't the RAMBLER'S cronies was the rage
To fill with SAM'S *bon mots* and tales the page
Mere flies that buzz'd about his setting ray
And bore a splendour on their wings away:
Thus round his orb the pigmy planets run
And catch their little lustre from the sun.

Although *Bozzy and Piozzi* suffers from the fact that a satire on dullness may itself be dull, the work was an even greater success than the *Congratulatory Epistle*. Ten editions were published in two years. According to Cyrus Redding in what is possibly an exaggeration, at the height of this period of his fame between twenty and thirty thousand copies of his work were sold in a single day. He was, in any case, a force to be reckoned with. Boswell was not amused. John Taylor sitting next to him at a dinner at the Royal Academy proposed in a convivial moment to introduce him to Wolcot. Boswell answered vehemently and indignantly that he would never know that man for that he had abused the king: though it is very probable, adds Taylor, that

'his loyalty on this occasion was not unmixed with the resentment which he felt at the doctor's poetical epistle to James Boswell. Wolcot would have had no objection to take him by the hand and it was a settled point with him never in the slightest degree to attack those whom he had before satirized after he became at all acquainted with them.'

As an example of this Taylor quoted how after meeting 'the ingenious Mrs Cosway' Wolcot 'changed the tone of his lyre and wrote some elegant lyrics in praise of her talents and personal worth', but whether this was indeed the result of the meeting or of the threats by Mr Cosway reported elsewhere is a matter of conjecture.

Sir Alexander Boswell, on the other hand, asked Taylor to introduce him to Peter Pindar, and when the latter expressed surprise in view of the way that James had been attacked by Wolcot, 'Pooh,' said Sir Alexander, 'that was fun and not malice. He is a man of original genius and I should like to know him.' This was, however, an introduction that never took place, for the baronet, who also had a turn for satire, was involved through his pen in a quarrel which led to a duel in which he lost his life. It was evident that he had not had Wolcot's advantage before the duel of seeing from his bedroom window his opponent walking up and down with a brace of pistols on a cold morning.

*   *   *   *   *

There were others beside James Boswell who were not amused. The Privy Council took notice of the scandalous libels published against the king—quite apart from the *Lousiad* there was hardly a poem of Wolcot's that did not introduce some ridiculous story of the king's behaviour. Said Wolcot: 'It was agitated to attack me for my writings, particularly the *Lousiad*. But on its being discovered that the poem had its foundation in truth all idea of prosecution was extinguished. "Are you sure of a verdict?" said a Lord high in the law [the Chancellor Thurlow]; if not so, by God, we shall look like a parcel of fools." '

In *Ode Upon Ode*, his first work for 1787, he wrote:

> No! free as air the Muse shall spread her wing
> Of *whom* and *when* and *what* she pleases sing
> Though privy councils, jealous of her note
> Prescribed of late a halter for her throat. . . .

He adds a footnote which says simply, 'This is secret history.' And a Gillray caricature of Lord Lansdowne, published in 1787, shews his Lordship with, *inter alia*, a list of premiums that have been paid: they include £1,000 to P. Pinder [sic].

Whatever form it may have taken the attempt to silence Wolcot was singularly without effect for in *Ode Upon Ode, or a Peep at St James, or New Year's Day or What You Will*, a satire against the Poet Laureate Thomas Warton, Wolcot reached new heights.

The king was attacked at many points along a widely extended front; for his meanness to Madam Mara and Mrs Siddons, for his refusal to pay an outstanding bill to Capability Brown, for going to the theatre when in mourning for his aunt, for attempting to close Drury Lane, for yawning and quizzing strangers in church, and for anything and everything that could be made the subject of a rhyme. *Ode Upon Ode* was followed by an *Apologetic*

114

Postscript which contained the ludicrous account also illustrated by Gillray of the king's bewilderment at the manner in which an apple got inside a dumpling. This was followed, still in the same year of 1787, by *Instructions to a Famous Laureate* with the account of George's visit to Whitbread's Brewery:

> Full of the art of brewing beer
> The monarch heard of Mr Whitbread's fame:
> Quoth he unto the queen, 'My dear, my dear
> Whitbread hath got a marvellous great name
> Charly we must, must, must see Whitbread brew
> Rich as us, Charly, richer than a Jew;
> Shame, shame we have not yet his brewhouse seen!'
> Thus sweetly said the King unto the Queen.

Too long to be quoted here in full the ode contains a number of noteworthy passages. Whitbread of course was filled with a natural anxiety at the approach of the visit:

> Muse sing the stir that Mr Whitbread made,
> Poor gentleman! most terribly afraid
> He should not charm enough his guests divine
> He gave his maids new aprons gowns and smocks
> And lo! two hundred pounds were spent in frocks
> To make th' apprentices and draymen fine.

> Arriv'd, the King broad grinn'd and gave a nod
> To Mr Whitbread, who had God
> Come with his angels to behold his beer
> With more respect he never could have met
> Indeed the man was in a sweat
> So much the brewer did the King revere.

The scene at the brewery was animated. The place was filled with employees jabbering with excitement:

> Reader! my ode should have a simile
> Well! in Jamaica on a tam'rind tree
> Five hundred parrots gabbling just like Jews
> I've seen—such noise the feather'd imps did make
> As made my pericranium ache
> Asking and telling parrot news.

The King was full of his usual lively curiosity:

> And lo! no single thing came in his way
> That full of deep research, he did not say
> 'What's this? hae hae? What's that? What's this? What's
> that?'

His Majesty was interested, too, in statistics. The brewer told him that if all his barrels were placed side by side they would reach to Kew,

> On which the King with wonder swiftly cried
> 'What, if they reach to Kew then side by side
> What would they do, what what, placed end to end?'

Whitbread made a hasty calculation and replied, 'Almost to Windsor. . . .'

> Now did the King for other beers enquire
> For Calvert's, Jordan's, Thrale's Entire—
> And after talking of these diff'rent beers
> Ask'd Whitbread if his Porter equall'd theirs?
> This was a puzzling, disagreeing question
> Grating like arsenic on his host's digestion. . . .

George then took out a memorandum-book and made some notes:

> *Mem*
> Tis hops that give a bitterness to beer
> Hops grow in Kent, says Whitbread, and elsewhere.

> *Quaere*
> Is there no cheaper stuff? Where does it dwell?
> Would not horse-aloes bitter it as well?

> *Mem*
> To try it soon on our small beer
> Will save us several pounds a year.

At last the king put away his notebook and began asking more questions:

> To Whitbread now deign'd majesty to say
> 'Whitbread, are all your horses fond of hay?'
> 'Yes, please your majesty,' in humble notes
> The brewer answered, 'Also, sir, of oats:
> Another thing my horses too maintains
> And that, an't please your majesty, are grains?'
> 'Grains, grains,' said majesty, 'to fill their crops?
> Grains, grains—that comes from hops—yes, hops, hops, hops.'
> Here was the King like hounds sometimes at fault.
> 'Sire,' cried the humble brewer, 'give me leave
> Your sacred majesty to undeceive:
> Grains, sire, are never made from hops, but malt.'
> 'True,' said the cautious monarch with a smile
> 'From malt, malt, malt—I meant malt all the while.'
> 'Yes,' with the sweetest bow, rejoin'd the brewer,
> 'An't please your majesty, you did, I'm sure.'
> 'Yes,' answered majesty with quick reply
> 'I did, I did, I did, I, I, I, I.'

The grand tour of inspection continued. The bell used for summoning the draymen to lunch was inspected and demonstrated; the brewer's pigs were shown and Farmer George was graciously pleased to compare them favourably with his own before launching a new spate of questions:

> Whitbread, d'ye nick th'excisemen now and then?
> Hae, Whitbread, when d'ye think to leave off trade?
> Hae? What? Miss Whitbread's still a maid, a maid?
> What, what's the matter with the men?
> D'ye hunt?—hae, hunt? No no you are too *old*
> You'll be lord may'r—lord may'r one day—
> Yes, yes, I've heard so—yes, yes, so I'm told.

> Whitbread, d'ye keep a coach or job one, pray?
> Job, job, that's cheapest—yes, that's best, that's best—
> You put your liv'ries on the draymen—hae?
> Hae Whitbread? You have feather'd well your nest,
> What, what's the price now, hae, of all your stock?
> But Whitbread, what's o'clock, pray what's o'clock?'

The brewer was trying to decide which question to answer first but the king skipped off without waiting for any reply and Wolcot produced a splendid simile:

> Reader, dids't ever see a waterspout?
> 'Tis possible that thou wilt answer 'No'.
> Well, then, he makes a most infernal rout
> Sucks like an elephant the waves below
> With huge proboscis reaching from the sky
> As if he meant to drink the ocean dry.
> At length so full he can't drink one drop more
> He bursts—down drop the waters with a roar
> On some poor boat or brig or sloop or ship
> And almost sinks the wand'rer of the deep.
> Thus have I seen a monarch at reviews
> Suck from the tribe of officers the news
> Then bear in triumph off each wondrous matter
> And souse it on the queen with such a clatter. . . .

So the visit went on until it is time for the Royal Family to return to Buckingham House:

> Now through a thund'ring peal of kind huzzas
> Proceeding some from hir'd and unhir'd jaws
> The raree-show thought proper to retire
> Whilst Whitbread and his daughter fair
> Survey'd all Chiswell-street with lofty air
> For, lo! they felt themselves some six feet higher!

And, concluded Peter Pindar,

> Now God preserve all wonder-hunting kings
> Whether at Windsor, Buckingham or Kew-house
> And may they never do more foolish things
> Than visiting Sam Whitbread and his brewhouse.

In some respects he was reaching the height of his powers and was aware of the fact. Before publication he referred to the foregoing odes, which ran through seven editions in a single year, as being 'of a higher fantasy'. He was certainly, as the gusto of his writing indicates, enjoying himself vastly. He was living in Great Newport Street next door to Reynolds when he wrote to Giddy:

'Sir Joshua would astonish you with some of his latest portraits. Take him for all in all, he is the greatest painter that ever lived; and yet some of his pictures are execrable; but let it be remembered that he was *obliged* to paint them. I believe Sir Joshua very rarely makes a bad picture when his own enthusiasm is concerned. . . .'

He was still as fond as ever of the theatre. Colman he dined with, now and then, and found him a *bel esprit*: a fortnight before the odes quoted above appeared he could report that 'Colman was well pleased with them'. He went to see Mrs Siddons in *Macbeth* and considered her performance the *ne plus ultra* of fine acting. But, more intoxicating still, a production of his own was played on April 24th, 1787, at Covent Garden. It was a translation of *Nina: or The Love Distracted Maid*, an opera by N. Dalayrac to which had been added two airs by Haydn and Gossec.

Nina was performed as a Benefit either for Mrs. Martyr or, more probably, for Mrs Billington and is described as a '*petit piece* . . . well received', but there is no evidence that it remained for long in the Covent Garden repertoire. But it was another feather in John Wolcot's cap. His name, so recently unknown, was now everywhere to be seen—sometimes in the most unexpected places.

There was, for example, the portrait that in 1787 was offered for sale in London. An engraver named Benjamin Smith had published a portrait of John ('Horse') Pond the compiler of the Racing Calendar—a man whose sister rode 1,000 miles in 1,000 hours and ended up in Bedlam, but who was otherwise 'notorious for nothing but getting drunk'. The portrait failed utterly to sell and not wishing to lose money on the publication Smith simply erased the name of Pond and without making any alteration in the features or figure substituted that of Peter Pindar. The engraving was distributed and appeared in shop-windows all over the town and many a portrait collector 'enriched his book with it as the true and lively effigy of the man who cared not whose character he traduced'.

Wolcot had acquaintances in all sorts of society.

> 'My life [he wrote] is chiefly among the arts and sciences in order to lay up a little stock of knowledge for old age. Now and then I am invited to murder a day at the house of a Lord and like murderers ought to be hanged for the offence.'

Concerts still drew him to them. 'The Crescentini at the Opera was only so-so.' He heard the violinist Solli and reported to Giddy:

> 'his powers on the fingerboard are wonderful! But he abounds so much in Jack-puddingism by jumping from the bottom of the instrument up close to the bridge that I have no patience with the Puppy as nothing but vile squeaks are the result; he has a fine tone, a delicious one, but you very seldom have it. His music had no subject; it was no melody. A brilliant shake with about a thousand capers over the strings constituted his solo. . . .'

Haydn's work he still found too learned. 'Give me,' he said, 'Jomelli's overture, with the chaconne, in preference to everything.' Parke, the famous hautboy player who had adapted the choruses and the greater part of the airs of *Nina* to Pindar's words, together with Mahon the clarinettist and 'two or three capital hands besides', gave Wolcot a present one Sunday of a little concert at Parke's house.

Wolcot in fact knew many people of note and was known to an ever-widening circle. His pen, it is said, was so dreaded that he not only had the right of free admission to all places of public amusement himself but might take a friend with him. He enjoyed it all immensely.

'I never knew happier hours than at present,' he told Giddy. 'I *command* London and at the same time London does not *command* me.'

Since that day when John Wolcot had arrived in the city, an unknown doctor from the country starting out in middle age upon a new career, less than six years had passed.

9

THERE are glimpses—not all of them complimentary—of Wolcot, now fifty years old, enjoying hugely his belated fame around town. He was often at the house of Murray the Bookseller in Fleet Street where he sometimes met the Reverend Dr Thomas Somerville. Since neither man played cards on these occasions they were thrown together. Wolcot told Somerville that he had three hobbies—poetry, painting and metaphysics, in the last of which Somerville 'suspected his attainments to be superficial'. Wolcot claimed to be deeply indebted to David Hume and Adam Smith and the complimentary way in which he spoke of Scottish authors in particular and Scotsmen in general made the divine 'suspect that he was no stranger to the art of flattery'. But Somerville had made up his mind about Wolcot even before he met him. He found that there was 'in his conversation at table such a mixture of ribaldry, buffoonery and obscene allusions as coincided exactly with my preconceptions of this too much admired writer'. The prostitution of Peter Pindar's poetical talents in attacking the existing social order, he felt, called for 'the execration of every well-wisher of mankind'. They talked a little of Jamaica. 'Had I encouraged him,' complained Somerville, 'he seemed inclined to make the clerical duties a subject of profane jocularity.' Indeed, in view of the circumstances attached to Wolcot's ordination, he would have been a hypocrite had he done otherwise. He offered Somerville a season-ticket for the Opera at the Pantheon, which was refused. 'However fond of amusement, I disdained to be laid under an obligation to a person whom I so much despised.'

Clearly Somerville was just the sort of man in front of whom Wolcot, who when he wished could be the very model of propriety, took a fierce delight in misbehaving. He was certainly more at home in the company of those with whom there was never any need to keep up appearances. There were convivial little parties at the rooms of Mr Mitchel the Banker, in Beaufort Buildings in the Strand. 'Well do I remember,' recalled Henry Angelo in after years, 'sitting in this comfortable apartment listening to the stories of my old friend Peter Pindar whose wit seemed not to kindle until after midnight at the period of his fifth or sixth glass of brandy and water.' By this time in the evening Rowlandson would be at this twelfth glass of punch and, said Angelo, the two of them told stories 'that would make a modern Boccaccio'. A motherly lady, the wife of an actor at whose house Wolcot used sometimes to pass the evening, had once said, 'Dr Wolcot's wit seems to lie in the bowl of a tea-spoon,' and Angelo noticed at Mitchel's that 'each time Peter replenished his glass goblet with cognac and water, in breaking the sugar the corners of his lips were curved into a satisfactory smile and he began some quaint story as if, indeed, the new libation begot some new thought'. He decided to try a little experiment. He invited the doctor one evening to supper at his house in Bolton Row and arranged with a hoaxer named Wigstead—afterwards a magistrate—to have some fun of a joke-store kind with Wolcot. Wigstead arrived at the house armed with some small square pieces of alabaster and as the contents of Wolcot's glass got low, Wigstead slipped them into the sugar bowl. When the doctor reached the hot water and poured in brandy, Wigstead handed him the sugar tongs and advanced the basin of alabaster.

'Thank you, boy,' said Wolcot putting five or six pieces into the glass and beginning to stir.

'Well, sir—and so the old parish priest. What I tell you'—his spoon was at work—'happened when I was in that infernally hot place Jamaica'—he stirred the drink again—'Sir, he was the fattest man in the island'—he tried pressing the alabaster with his spoon —'yes, damme sir, and when the thermometer at ninety five was dissolving every other man, this old, slouching, drawling son of the church got fatter and fatter until, sir—curse the sugar, some devil black enchanter has bewitched it. By—sir this sugar is part and parcel of that old pot-bellied parson—it will never melt.'

And he threw the contents of the tumbler under the grate.

The company burst out laughing although their joke had cost them the conclusion of the story.

One evening Wolcot went with John Taylor to the house of Mr Pope the actor and was formally introduced as 'Peter Pindar' to the widowed Lady Hill who seemed to be an intelligent and well-bred character—at any rate she paid Wolcot many compliments on his work and even recited many passages from them. The doctor who, like a few other writers, was not averse to being flattered, was delighted by this reception. And as Taylor walked away from the house he asked Wolcot how he had liked Lady Hill. Still glowing with pleasure Wolcot answered that she was a very agreeable, elegant and intelligent woman. Taylor asked if he knew who she was.

'I suppose, the widow of some Irish Lord.'

'No,' said Taylor, 'she is the widow of that celebrated physician Sir John Hill.'

John Hill had been the subject of Garrick's well-known epigram:

> For physic and farces his equal there scarce is
> His farces are physic his physic a farce is

and Wolcot exploded with indignation.

'What! the widow of that old quack! Have I been praising her? Damn me I will go back and spit at her.'

But then reflecting on the nice things she had said about his work he added reflectively:

'But she is, however, really a very agreeable woman.'

Another agreeable woman on Wolcot's visiting list was Mrs Billington the singer, a pretty woman who lived at Brompton. One evening when he was dining there with John Taylor the famous Irish orator, Curran, was also in the party. Before dinner Mrs Billington, making polite conversation, said to Curran, 'I hear you are to be Lord Chancellor for Ireland and then I hope you will procure some appointment for me.' Instead of modestly expressing doubt whether he would ever be raised to such a situation, Curran merely replied that he should always be pleased to testify his respect for her. They went in to dinner. Wolcot was staring hungrily at one of the dishes and Mr Billington, waggishly observing this, winked at Taylor and entirely disregarded the doctor's plate while busily serving everyone else around him. At last Wolcot, slavering with appetite, could bear it no longer. He leaned over, exclaiming, 'Damn me, I will have this!' and thrust his fork into the dish 'to the surprise and amusement of all present'. After the meal was over Wolcot was cornered by Curran who seemed anxious to impress him with his powers of conversation. Unfortunately what the Irishman said has not survived beyond one apparently typical expression, noted by Taylor, 'a concatenated series of consecutive arguments'. After being talked at in this manner for some time Wolcot abruptly left the room and made for home, exclaiming in the hall on the way out, to the anxious Taylor who thought he might have been taken ill, 'Talk of Dr Numpskull he would cut into a dozen such fellows as Curran.' And on another occasion he remarked that 'he would not insult his magpie by offering her that fellow's brains for a dinner'.

Not all Mrs Billington's parties were on this scale for the financial uncertainties of a stage career existed then as now: one day when Wolcot arrived punctually for tea the sugar was brought to the table in a paper bag.

'What the devil is all this, Mother Billington?' said Wolcot. The actress was not in the least embarrassed.

'Everything is at the pawnbrokers and the silver sugar-dish is sent to get the tea.'

Enjoy himself he might in these and other ways—he who when Polwhele had first known him had hardly drunk spirits, could now, when the occasion demanded, spend a whole night drinking fairly heavily—but he did not let it interfere with his output of verse.

★   ★   ★   ★   ★

Brother Peter to Brother Tom, a satire against the Poet Laureate and, through him, against, of course, his royal master, provided the opening subject for 1788. It is noteworthy for one of the first explanations that he made about his attitude to the king:

> The world may call me liar, but sincerely
> I love him—for a partner, love him dearly
> While his great name is on the *ferme*, I'm sure
> My credit with the public is secure.
> Yes, beef shall grace my spit, and ale shall flow
> As long as it continues George and Co
> That is to say in plainer metre
> George and Peter.

And if it is possible to adduce a biographical detail from the internal evidence, Wolcot was thinking again of returning to the elysium of Kingsbridge:

> Yet, as some little money I have made
> I've thoughts of turning squire and quitting trade
> This in my mind I've frequently revolved
> And in six months or so
> For all I know
> The partnership may be dissolved.

In the meantime he continued to pour out ridicule upon his partner's head:

> My verse is somewhat like a game of whist
> Which game, though play'd by people e'er so keen
> Cannot with much success, alas! exist
> Except their hands possess a king and queen.
>
> I own my muse delights in royal folk
> Lead-mines producing many pretty pounds
> Joe Millars furnishing a fund of joke!
> Lo, with a fund of joke a court abounds.
>
> At royal follies, Lord! a lucky hit
> Saves our poor brain th'expense of wit
> At princes let but satire lift his gun
> The more their feathers fly the more the fun.
> E'en the whole world, blockheads and men of letters,
> Enjoy a cannonade upon their betters.

Certainly everybody seemed to enjoy Peter Pindar's cannonade against the throne which still seemed both novel and daring.

In fact so popular was his work and so many were the pirated editions that his publishers at this time were offering a reward of twenty guineas to anyone who could secure the conviction of a pirate publisher. John Taylor frequently begged him to drop the subject of the king, but while Wolcot was still chasing his will-of-the-wisp of financial independence all such appeals were ignored. However, he submitted much of his work while it was still in manuscript to Taylor who remarked in later years, 'I may confidently say that I induced him to make many alterations and suppressions which not only made his work less exceptionable but most probably saved him from legal consequences. . . .'

It seems almost certain that, since Wolcot was giving no chances of legal action, an attempt was made this year, possibly through the mediation of a Mr Yorke, to buy him off.

For one of his rival satirists wrote at this time:

> Three hundred yellowboys a year
> Would close thy silent lips and shut thine ear.

Wolcot himself produced, this year, a volume called *Peter's Pension*. In it he described:

> How the *exchange* and *coffee-houses* ring
> Nothing is heard but Peter and the King,

and the way in which the latter has 'given the gentle bard a pension':

> 'How are the mighty fall'n!' the people cry
> Meaning *me*—
> 'Another hog of Epicurus' stye
> 'This vile apostate bends to Baal the knee
> Lo, for a little meat and guzzle,
> This sneaking cur, too, takes the muzzle.'
>
> In vain I tell the world around
> That I have not a pension found
> Which speech of simple truth the mob enrages
> 'Peter this is an arrant lie
> The fact is clear, too clear,' they cry
> 'Thou hast already touched a quarter's wages.'

One of the difficulties in deciding exactly what happened on this occasion is due to the confusion which has arisen with a later and more carefully documented attempt to silence Wolcot politically.

It is possible that Wolcot, learning what was afoot, decided to 'beat the gun' and tell the story before he could be approached on a confidential basis:

> No sir! you never offered me a pension
> But then I guess it is your kind intention—
> Yes, sir, you mean a small *douceur* to proffer
> But give me leave, sir, to decline the offer.

The reason that he gave for the refusal was that the king could not possibly afford it. He had spent so much recently that

> the royal purse is poor
> Plagued with a dry consumptive cough.

For this reason alone:

> The pension was well meant, O glorious king
> And for the bard a very pretty thing;
> But let me, sir, refuse it, I implore
> I ought not to be rich while *you* are poor.

No doubt chuckling gleefully Peter Pindar, in the same volume, returned even more rumbustiously to the attack, with his disrespectful stories of The Royal Sheep and of The King and Parson Young in which latter tale the unfortunate parson who had been forced to go hunting with the king broke his neck.

> The monarch gaping with amaze look'd round
> Upon his dead companion on the ground.
> 'What, what?' he cried, 'Young dead! Young dead! Young
> dead!
> Humph!—take him up—and put him home to bed.'
> Thus having finish'd—with a cheerful face
> Nimrod the Second join'd the jovial chase.

It should have been quite clear by this time that Wolcot was incorrigible.

*   *   *   *   *

There were other distractions to come between himself and his work. The outside world, as it continually does on the man who working at home is considered not to be working at all, kept breaking in.

The Cornish baronet Sir John Seale, for example, used Wolcot as a go-between with Opie to get an altarpiece painted for a local church.

In June he wrote apologizing if his letter should 'break a chain of a well-designed Elegy . . . but if you are on the old Story I shall make no apology; you know I am a Loyalist, so are, in this clouted cream country, we all'. He had left at Wolcot's lodgings in Great Newport Street the dimensions of the picture required and asked what progress Opie was making with it.

Wolcot could get no satisfactory reply from the artist:

'he is so pestered by the Print Adventurers for Historical Matters [he wrote] that they hardly allow him a minute for other pursuits—Very soon however it shall be finished if I possess any interest with him—sufficiently have I badgered him on the subject and am determined to continue till I see a Painting that will do honour to the Church for which it is designed—Opie is exceeding willing to execute the commission and wishes to keep the drawing a little longer. . . .'

This certainly did not look as if there were any serious break between the two men. And when in 1791 he gave Opie a sketch of Edmund Burke by Sir Joshua the gift should have dispelled for ever any story of a violent breach between Wolcot and his former protégé. But then, as always, the public believed only what it chose to believe.

*   *   *   *   *

Not all Wolcot's attack, this year, was aimed at the king, for there appeared also *Peter's Prophecy* and *Sir Joseph Banks and the*

128

Emperor of Morocco, both addressed to the President of the Royal Society. The poet who had dared to advise princes

> Stoops from the zenith of his eagle flight
> To give instructions to a simple knight.

And it says a great deal for the general standard of education of his readers that a satire which dealt almost entirely with the individual intellectual quirks of various members of the Royal Society should have had any fairly general sale.

Yet Wolcot's success continued unabated. And he could afford at the Academy Exhibition, that year, to pay fifty guineas for Sir Joshua's second version of *The Sleeping Girl*.

The Academy was rich in historical paintings for which the connoisseurs' taste seemed insatiable and Wolcot stepped forward in his *Subjects for Painters* to suggest a few contemporary scenes that might well be used when the world of Shakespeare and Milton had been exhausted.

A Member of the House of Lords Eating His Own Words was one such subject; Charles Lennox, Duke of Richmond, Earl of March, Master General of the Ordnance, Lord Lieutenant and Custos Rotulorum of the County of Sussex, Duke of Lennox in Scotland and Aubigny in France, Knight of the most noble Order of the Garter etc etc refusing to pay an innkeeper one and sixpence for a roasted duck which had been ordered as part of a meal and returned to the kitchen untouched, was another.

But for the most part the work was a collection of assorted anecdotes on a wide range of subjects recounted in rhyme. They included the story of the Earl of Peterborough who, being mistaken by the mob for the close-fisted Duke of Marlborough, to prove that it could not be he, threw them sixpence, and, at the other end of the social scale, the old Jewess whose son having fallen from the gallery of the theatre and expired before the rise of the first-act curtain demanded her money back on the grounds that he had not seen the show. Only two of the verses were about the king and Sir Joseph Banks. And in fact one of the secrets of Wolcot's continuing popularity with his readers lay in the fact that he could still anticipate public sentiment. Before people could become utterly satiated with attacks upon one victim he switched his assault to another:

> Muse, having dropped Sir Joseph and the king,
> What sort of gentry shall we deign to sing?

The answer was Pitt and his government. In 1789 a *Poetical Epistle to a Falling Minister* opened the broadside against the race of politicians he had come so much to despise. It was followed by *Expostulatory Odes to a Great Duke and a Little Lord* [Osborne and Jenkinson] and from its contents it seems clear that yet another attempt was being made to hang some legal indictment on John Wolcot.

> Most noble peers there goes an odd report
> That you, prime fav'rites of an *honest* court
> Are hunting treason 'midst my publications . . .
>
> Yes! Yes! I hear that you have watch'd my note
> And wish'd to squeeze my tuneful throat
> When Thurlow your designs most wisely scouted
> Swearing the poet should not yet be knouted.

Those in authority are always ready to tack an ugly label on to adverse criticism. In time of war comments on the conduct of affairs, however constructive and from whatever motives made, are condemned as disaffection. Wolcot's criticism of George III must therefore be treason. Unfortunately for the bureaucrats (and fortunately for the man in the street) the lawyers have stricter standards of interpretation. John Wolcot had made many enemies who would have welcomed his destruction but treason was not one of his faults. Kindly John Taylor, though he did not wish to palliate attacks upon the king, could in his old age

'venture solemnly to say that the Doctor entertained the highest notion of the kingly character and it was therefore because our revered monarch did not reach to his *beau ideal* of what a monarch should be that he continued his satirical hostility. Indeed it must be admitted that pecuniary advantage

130

was not without its influence on his mind for though he possessed landed property it was but small. . . .'

Wolcot himself told Taylor that he reverenced the Constitution and held its political head in due veneration but that he felt justified in sporting with the peculiarities of the private character of the monarch.

> Right honest watchdogs of the State
> I like to smile at kings, but Treason hate.

Taylor in vain 'opposed these opinions and referred him to Blackstone to show the punishment annexed to works that were calculated to bring the character of the monarch into contempt. In short he found the topic too profitable to be abandoned.' And, indeed, when one day an old acquaintance hesitated to shake hands with him because of his abuse of the king Wolcot replied good-humouredly, 'Pooh pooh! I bear no ill-will to His Majesty—God bless him! I believe him to be a very good man but I must write upon characters that the world are interested in reading about. I would abuse you but I would get nothing for it!'

Once, too, in another moment of candour, he remarked, 'The king has been a good subject to me but I have been a bad subject to His Majesty.'

His attitude to the Prince of Wales was very different, and at the time of the *Expostulatory Odes* verged on the nauseating. The Prince of Wales was, in fact, one of Peter Pindar's most constant readers and advance copies of the works as they appeared, particularly those attacking his royal father, were sent to Carlton House for his amusement. But it was surely erring on the side of flattery to answer the hypothetical accusation:

> Poor rogue thou hast not got the trifling spirit
> To own thy king e'er did one act of merit

as did Peter Pindar.

> My lords with great submission to your sense
> Giving the lie, yet hoping no offense;

An act is his my heart with rapture hails—
George gave the world the Prince of Wales
A prince, who when he fills Old England's throne
The virtues and fair science shall surround it
And when he quits the sceptre all shall own
He left it as unsullied as he found it.

It might almost be represented that this was in itself satirical, but it is clear from the context that it was not so intended and although, later, disillusionment was to come from 'the youth who dares at times unbend', at that moment Prinny could do no wrong.

In view of the way that Peter Pindar's satires on the king were received at Carlton House there is something rather hypocritical about the prince's attitude on meeting Wolcot.

Taylor was in a private room at the old Opera House when the heir to the throne

'condescended to permit Dr Wolcot to be introduced to him. The prince received him in the most gracious manner and in a short conversation observed with dignified affability that he admired his genius but sometimes thought it ill-directed. The doctor seemed to sink with humility and self-reproach and made a mumbling inaudible apology. The prince maintained the same dignified ease and affability and Wolcot recovered his spirits enough to express his hopes that his royal highness would have less reason hereafter to find fault with his humble muse. Nothing could be more graceful than the manner in which his royal highness took leave of the doctor. . . .'

Another time Taylor was going up the stairs at the Opera House with the doctor when they met the Duke of Cumberland 'who with perfect good-humour said, "How do you do, Pindaricus?" Wolcot felt abashed, but not to the same degree as before the Prince.'

This account contrasts strangely with Wolcot's own version of a meeting with the Duke of Cumberland behind the scenes at a play for which Wolcot had written the prologue. Here, if his story is to be believed, he had treated the duke with less than respect and had actually made a rather unkind jest which was aimed at Cumberland's reputed lack of even the most elementary education. But in this the doctor was doing no more than does any man who thinks up a crushing retort half a minute after it is too late to use it—except in recounting the incident. Wolcot was nothing if not intensely human and the man who had spent both youth and early middle age in trying to escape from female domination, greatly though he might wish to appear in the guise of a bold bad devil-may-care man about town, the scourge of the ignoble, however great they might appear, could bring himself to be offensive only upon paper.

Taylor was, in fact, often surprised at the freedoms he took 'not only with the royal character but with many of the upper ranks . . . as he was really a timid man'.

★   ★   ★   ★   ★

For a timid man who has made a vast number of enemies—in the *Expostulatory Odes* he refers constantly to this not improbable fact—it must have been a relief, every now and again, to get away from it all. In fact he may have felt, about this time, that a temporary absence from London would be strategically advisable.

> I've been disgraced, too—felt a monarch's frown—
> And consequently quitted town

he wrote the following year. But in any case he must have enjoyed leaving the jungle and going down once again to the happy estuary of Kingsbridge and the cathedral calm of Exeter where Jackson the organist—one of the few men whose intellect Wolcot respected—had set his romantic lyrics to music.

From his own account he was hoping to get married, to whom is not known. One of his reasons, so he maintained in the *Expostulatory Odes*, for not wishing to be convicted of treason was that he wanted to go on living firstly to see George the Fourth upon the throne and also

> My lords I fain would live a little longer
> For lo! desire as to a bosom wife
> Undoubtedly the greatest bliss of life
> Hath taken deeper root and stronger.

Whether this refers to one of his old flames or not—certainly nothing came of the desire—he made for the West bringing with him to the simple pursuits of the country a breath from the great literary world of London, for a prologue by Peter Pindar was, that year, spoken by Sir Francis Bassett at his Little Theatre at Tehiddy Park in Cornwall.

Wolcot went to Fowey to see his sisters. Amy had married Robert Stephens, a surgeon; Ann was still unmarried. 1790 was a year of elections: he joined the local fray with gusto, taking the side of the Tories. Moreover he openly proclaimed his political faith in the name of the 12½-ton sloop (perhaps used as a pleasure boat) the *True Blue* which he owned jointly with Mrs Austen and a Scottish naval surgeon called Thomas Mein. He renewed his contacts with his old friends. From Plymouth he wrote, in June, to Polwhele, who had propounded some sort of literary project that Wolcot could not fully understand. He promised to visit Polwhele in Exeter to hear more of the matter. Polwhele, who was engaged on writing a history, lived at Kenton some ten miles away from the city and while he and Wolcot were awaiting the guests who had been invited to meet the great Peter Pindar a ragged boy passed the window on a donkey. The boy, pale and emaciated, was, said Wolcot, rotten from the marsh miasma they were all breathing. In less than ten minutes he produced 'an admirable sketch' of the ass and its rider. In due course Polwhele's other guests arrived and Wolcot was introduced to the members of the 'Alps Club'. There was Mr Prebendary Swete and his lady, Mr Archdeacon Andrew and his lady, Mr and Mrs Lee and Dr and Mrs Downman. What Wolcot, who was staying the night at Kenton, thought of the company is not recorded though it may be inferred. For Polwhele, who had planned an outing on the estuary for the following morning, had invited another and no doubt similar party of his friends from Starcross to meet the great man, 'and we were willing to anticipate a pleasant morning on the Exe enlivened by the wit of P. Pindar'.

As soon, however, as he got up in the morning he found, he said, a note on the breakfast table to the effect:

'Your pestilential air has almost been the death of me! Adieu!'

The servant said that Dr Wolcot had left the house some hours previously. The sailing party was abandoned and Polwhele followed Wolcot to Exeter where apparently without rancour he dined and supped with him at Dr Downman's. Polwhele and Downman explained to Wolcot the scheme mentioned in their earlier correspondence which seems to have been for some kind of Poet's Co-operative. Wolcot's reply was not encouraging: 'a coalition of poets was only a competition invidious at best and terminating often in unpleasant consequences. . . .' He therefore begged leave to decline the honour of becoming a member of what Polwhele called 'our Heliconian fraternity'.

In spite of the abstention of the man who would have provided the great attraction of such a venture the Exeter poets went ahead.

In due course they published combined volumes of verse—the one for 1792 contained, in addition to contributions from Downman, Swete and Polwhele, verses by a number of other clergymen and gentry including the Revd Thomas Warwick—as the brother of Wolcot's old Truro antagonist Warrick called himself. What Peter Pindar in fact thought of them all emerges in a letter written from London to Downman on St Valentine's Day 1793 by a Mr A.B.

Sir,
    As I was reading the paper a few evenings since at the Turks Head Coffee-house my attention was taken up by the conversation of two gentlemen in the adjoining box, upon the subject of literary publications. After mentioning the works of several authors one of them said 'I see the Monthly Review gives a great character to some plays of Downman's of Exeter.' 'Does it?' said the other 'have you met with them yourself?' 'No.' 'If you do, kick them out of your way or ******** with them; for **** me, if ever the man wrote a line of poetry in his life. There are a parcel of mud-headed fellows down in that country who write the **** things ever were read, which they have the impudence to call poems. There is a little spitting toad of a parson and a blustering son of Mars who write and review their own nonsense. Downman and several of them have got hold of Williams and they are likewise intimate with that old Scotch son of a **** in Fleet-street; but their career is almost over. A new society of Reviewers will soon make their appearance and will lay all their impositions

before the publick. I intend giving them a lash or two on reviewing their own works. There is one devilish clever fellow amongst them who has more genius and understanding than all the rest of them put together—I mean Kendal. He is the son of an architect at Exeter. Take him out and Polwhele and the others are only fit to ***** upon.'

Without punctuation it is difficult to tell in which category Polwhele was included, but since it is quoted in his own works it is at any rate clear in which sense Polwhele understood it.

A.B. was, at this point, called out of the room on business and heard no more of the conversation. He had a look at the speakers and reported:

'I do not recollect having ever seen either of these gentlemen before. One of them was a thin man of a pale complexion about forty. The other who seemed to condemn everything without mercy was a set fat man of a dark complexion who appeared to be five or six and fifty, or more. He swore most abominably. . . .'

This was not a bad estimate. Wolcot was at that time nearly fifty-seven so it is evident that the disreputable life his enemies declared that he led—taking money from whores and begetting bastards in the Borough were two of the milder offences—does not seem to have had any undue effect on his appearance.

★   ★   ★   ★   ★

In the meantime in 1790 the Exeter poets as an organization were still only in the process of being founded and no shadow of criticism had arisen to cloud the friendship with Doctor Downman. At supper, perhaps the same evening, in the middle, Polwhele says, of an animated conversation Wolcot started up in great perturbation:

' "Zounds!" he cried out, "I've dropped a letter in the post without directing it!" and he hurried off to the music of the glasses that danced at his exit most merrily. By good luck he recovered the letter. It was addressed to a young woman in London, a poor orphan whose charms he said (but we did not believe him) he had had the fortitude to resist from a regard for her welfare and to whom he had given much good advice (religious I suppose!) accompanied with a considerable sum of money to set her up as a milliner.'

Polwhele seems to have been in an unwontedly frivolous mood. As for the milliner she may well be the pretty one to whom some eighteen months later Wolcot published an ode.

'Oh nymph with bandbox tripping on so sweet' he opened an amatory verse that certainly has a far greater carnality about it than is usual in Peter Pindar's work and is a far cry from the formal passion which he usually declared for such incorporeal ideals as Delia, Cynthia and Chloe. Towards the end of the ode it becomes apparent that the pretty milliner is incorruptly chaste, and that Wolcot's lust, which brings a wholesome blush to her cheek, surely includes an interesting element of eighteenth-century fetishism.

> Oh nymph, so sweet, forgive my wild desires,
> That knave, thy bandbox, wak'd my lawless fires.

But if the ode is, in fact, autobiographical Wolcot did, *pace* Polwhele, respect her virtue.

> Go guard that honour which I deem'd departed
> O yield thy beauties to some swain kind-hearted
> Whose soul congenial shall with thine unite.

His own soul, he clearly realized, was not in the same class as the pretty milliner's.

* * * * *

Even on his visits to the West work had to go on. While at Exeter he employed a printer named Trewman to prepare some of his verses for the public. One of the proof sheets he shewed to Polwhele who damned it so thoroughly that Wolcot left the proof behind, saying that his old friend could keep it and, said

Polwhele, it was never printed.[1] The first work that did appear in 1790 was a *Benevolent Epistle to Sylvanus Urban*, alias Master John Nichols, Printer, attacking the *Gentleman's Magazine*.

> A magazine! A peddlar's, huckster's shop,
> That harbours brush and cabbage-net and mop
> Pan, gridiron, button, buckle, bodkin, bead
> Tape, turnip, malkins, nightcaps green and red,
> Pins, pipkins, garters, oatmeal, jorden, dish
> Stale loaves and rusty nails and stinking fish.

Literary squabbles are, even when fresh in the mind, duller than most. It seems likely that had this volume contained nothing but his dispute with John Nichols the sale would have been strictly limited. But Wolcot, without any great attempt at continuity, attached every other kind of poem to the title work, from verses to his barn at Kingsbridge (where with his love of the theatre he had sheltered a band of dispossessed actors) to verses in defence of keeping mistresses and, even, a *Consolatory Stanza to Lady Mountedgcumbe on the Death of her Pig Cupid*.

> O dry that tear so round and big
> Nor waste in sighs your precious wind
> Death only takes a single pig—
> Your lord and son are still behind.

The pig was buried beneath a monument with a superscription written by Lady Mountedgcumbe's son and, in a later footnote, Wolcot tells of the occasion when George III stood pondering near the grave. The queen from a distance asked him what he was looking at and the king with ready humour replied, 'The family vault, Charly, family vault, family vault.'

Advice to a Future Laureate was the next of the year's productions and it was followed by a *Complimentary Epistle to James Bruce Esqre, the Abyssinian Traveller*.

But it is noteworthy that amidst all this variety of subject matter Wolcot's attacks on the throne are, that year, almost altogether abandoned.

[1] In this Polwhele flattered himself for it was certainly printed in the *Collected Works* of 1794 and 1816.

10

THE whole subject of the monarchy was an extremely delicate one. At the end of 1789 Farmer George had become certifiably mad and there had been great heart-searchings by the Government over the problem of the Regency. For if the Prince of Wales became Regent it would mean the fall of the existing Tory Government, and what party of professional politicians was tamely going to put up with that? At the time when Pitt was seeking some way out of the unpleasing situation John Taylor was editing the *Morning Post* and Wolcot was a constant visitor to his office and a contributor of what Taylor described as whimsical articles.

> 'I endeavoured all I could [said Taylor] to procure a regular salary for Dr Wolcot having a high opinion of his inventive powers and humour but the surly proprietor was taught to be afraid of the freedom of his muse. I even offered the doctor half of my weekly salary but neither his pride nor his delicacy would permit him to assent and he still supplied his gratuitous effusions chiefly of the poetical kind. We were plentifully supplied with punch, the doctor's favourite beverage, and as far as our limited party admitted the meeting might be considered as Comus's Court. . . .'

During one such party the 'confidential agent of a high personage' came into the *Morning Post* office to tell Taylor about a 'lady supposed to be in great favour with the high personage and not merely connected by the ties of mutual affection'. It seemed that she had 'determined to assert claims not sanctioned by law, but which if openly developed or rather promulgated could perhaps have been attended by national agitation'. In short, said the mysterious agent, the lady was demanding £6,000 per annum and a peerage to stay an action that 'would have put an effectual stop to all further proceedings on the subject of the intended Regency'.

Wolcot's instant reaction that the matter could easily be settled—Mrs Fitzherbert could be quietly done away with by the Government (by poison, he suggested)—was not regarded as being entirely serious. But Taylor none the less drew the moral from it that such was the impression that history had made upon the doctor's mind and that such was his opinion of foreign courts that he could impute the possibility of such a desperate expedient being used in England.

The king's temporary recovery, however, put for the time an end to the Regency, and there arose the far greater problems brought about by the start of the French Revolution. There was a spirit of revolt in the very air. Said Peter Pindar:

> A spark will now set Kingdoms in a blaze
> That would not fire a Barn in former days.

Just at first moderate, liberal-minded opinion in England was in favour of the revolutionaries: it was optimistically thought that some kind of free institutions based on a British democratic parliamentary system might be established across the Channel. For as Wolcot expressed it:

> To this great truth a universe agrees
> He who lies down with dogs will rise with fleas.

Surely something of her neighbour's democratic principles would infect France. The situation there was hopefully compared to that in England a century earlier. Political clubs were founded in support of the Revolution: the Constitutional Society, the Revolutionary Society, the Club of the 14th July and, most violent of all, the Corresponding Society were some of those formed to give moral support to those struggling, as it was thought, for liberty in France. But as time went on second thoughts began to creep into the English mind. There was a gradual falling off in sympathy with the ideals of the Revolution, the Whigs were divided amongst themselves, clubs in opposition to the revolutionary ones were organized, the excuse was eagerly seized to postpone all measures of Reform, and the Tories again were swept into power in the election of 1790.

Where stood Peter Pindar in all this? In spite of his detestation of Pitt, in spite of his admiration for the Prince of Wales, Wolcot, as has been shewn, had in Fowey supported the cause of the Tories. Disconcertingly to those who thought that because he had brought ridicule upon the throne he must himself be a revolutionary, he put Tom Paine firmly in his place both publicly and privately. In 1791 his *Song by Mr Paine* so exactly struck the right note that it is valid today:

> Come, good fellows all—Confusion's the toast
> And success to our excellent cause—
> As we've nothing to lose, lo, naught can be lost;
> So perdition to monarchs and laws.
>
> As we all are poor rogues, 'tis most certainly right
> At the doors of the rich ones to thunder
> Like the thieves who set fire to a dwelling by night
> And come in for a share of the plunder.
>
> Whoever for mischief invents the best plan
> Best murders, sets fire, and knocks down
> The thanks of that club shall be giv'n that man
> And hemlock shall form him a crown.

And though Wolcot had been a visitor to Lord George Gordon's cell in Newgate (and there is a caricature by R. Newton of him in this situation) he let it be known in the same song that his presence could not be held to imply approval of that madman's projects:

> Our Empire has tower'd with a lustre too long;
> Then blot out this wonderful sun;
> Let us arm then at once, and in confidence strong
> Complete what dark Gordon begun.

In private he was equally antipathetic to Paine. On a flyleaf of

The Age of Reason belonging to Royall Tyler he wrote an epigram which ended

> Though Beelzebub's absence from Hell I'll maintain
> Yet we all must allow that the Devil's in Paine.

Wolcot met the revolutionary once at the lodgings of a mutual friend where the meeting was described by Tyler. Paine was dressed for the occasion in a snuff-coloured coat, olive velvet vest, drab breeches, and coarse hose with shoe buckles the size of half a dollar. He asserted that 'the minority in all deliberative bodies ought in all cases to govern the majority'. Wolcot simply sat and smiled. 'You must grant me,' said Paine, 'that the proportion of men of sense to the ignorant among mankind is at least as twenty, thirty or even forty-nine to an hundred. The majority of mankind are consequently most prone to errour and if we atchieve the right the minority ought in all cases to govern.' Wolcot continued to smile. The discussion continued. In the end Paine's theory was put to the vote of the company present and all arose to vote with Paine. All, that is, except Wolcot. He continued to sit and smile. 'I am,' he said, 'the wise minority who ought in all cases to govern your ignorant majority.'

★   ★   ★   ★   ★

In 1791, with a sideways dig at both Paine and the monarch, he also published *The Rights of Kings or Loyal Odes to the Disloyal Academicians* who had refused to comply with the king's expressed desire that Lawrence should be elected to the Academy and had chosen Wheatley in his place by sixteen votes to three. But the old rumbustiousness of the attack against the king is missing. Wolcot's nineteenth-century biographer Theodore Reitterer considered that the high-point of Peter Pindar's satire had been reached this year. But compared with some of his earlier effusions the spirit had gone from his verse. Perhaps something of the deadly lack of humour of the revolutionary had at last infected Peter Pindar so that political satire became almost as dull as the object attacked. It is hardly to be wondered at that he found escape again in music.

'You know what a luxury music is to me,' he wrote in November 1791 to Giddy:

'nor am I yet satiated. I dined with Mara a few days since who is on the wing for Italy-Venice for two years. I fear she will lose much of her voice before the expiration of her engagement. There will be no serious opera for the season. Could you hear Jarnowich; what a treat! I have been lately pretty much with Giardini who has not lost an atom of his fire I am told. He is a most extraordinary creature. But the most wonderful fellow is Crosdell on the violoncello; he beggars everything. The difference between him and the son of old Nosy Cervetti is that Crosdell is superior to the instrument, but the instrument is rather superior to Cervetti. . . .'

It was while dining with Crosdell and the ubiquitous John Taylor at Madame Mara's house in Foley Place, Marylebone, that Wolcot, earlier in the same year, had made an exciting new acquaintance. Before the wine was removed from the table Salomon the great violinist arrived bringing with him a stranger, speaking no word of English but greeting Madame Mara in German as an old friend. It was the great Franz Josef Haydn, on his first visit to England, and as soon as they were introduced the high-spirited Crosdell—'an enthusiast for musical talent of all kinds'—gave three cheers for their distinguished visitor. Haydn heard his name mentioned but, apparently, did not understand that kind of welcome, and, still seated, gazed around at the standing, cheering company with amazement. When they were finished Salomon explained to him what it was all about. He was so modestly confused with the unexpected novelty of his greeting that he put his hands before his face and, says Taylor, 'was quite disconcerted for some minutes'.
However

'finding that he was in company with so celebrated a musical performer as Crosdell and so popular a poet as Peter Pindar whose fame had reached him in Germany he felt himself comfortable and we did not separate till a late hour to the perfect satisfaction of Madame Mara who was delighted to see so great a genius as Haydn enjoying the animated character of Crosdell, the sarcastic shrewdness of Salomon and the whimsical sallies of Peter Pindar.'

A few months later, when Haydn had acquired some knowledge of English, Salomon invited John Taylor and Wolcot to dinner with the great man, now a Doctor of Music of Oxford University, in a private room at the coffee house in Vere Street. Salomon was in great form and entertained them with anecdotes of distinguished characters in Germany. He amplified for their benefit some of the observations that Haydn made in his halting English on the works of Handel, Mozart and other musicians. At last, inevitably, the name of Pleyel was mentioned and Wolcot, who was inclined to say the first thing that came into his mind, burst out into an enraptured eulogy of that now neglected master, dwelling at length on his taste and genius as a musician. So far, in fact, did he go that Haydn at last, while readily admitting the merits of Pleyel, could not help adding a little warmly:

'But I hope it will be remembered that he was my pupil!'

Wolcot felt this to be a rebuke and attempted a confused apology. However it is certain that Haydn did not allow the matter to rankle.

In November, a week after Wolcot had written to Giddy, Haydn attended one of the four farewell performances that Madame Mara gave at the King's Theatre in the rôle of Mandane in Arne's *Artaxerxes*. The star also sang to a harp accompaniment, and, presumably as an extra number, an aria from *Idalide* for which Wolcot had written new words: it was an immense success and Madame Mara had not only to give an encore but to repeat the song a third time. It is not known whether this suggested to Haydn that Wolcot might perhaps write the libretto for his first composition with an English text but on February 24th, 1792, a great concert took place. The programme included a symphony by Clementi and a new quartet by Gyrowetz which was played by Salomon, Damen, Hindmarsh and Menel. There was also the first performance of *The Storm* by Haydn, a work for a Quartet of Soloists, Chorus and Orchestra with the libretto by Wolcot. Miss Corri and Miss Poole, Mr Nield and Mr Bellamy were the soloists and the performance was an immense success.

The *Morning Chronicle* talked of the 'matchless Haydn' and although the work is not now greatly discussed by musical enthusiasts it achieved a quick and widespread success, soon becoming well known in Vienna and being published in Leipzig by Breitkopf and Härtel.

'From the opening measures [said a later critic] the spectator is cast in the midst of a storm in which time, syncopation, accidentals, discords, abrupt dynamic oppositions, all the colours spread on the palette of an 18th century musician, are brought into play. The choir expresses its fear of the roaring of the winds by imitating their chromatic moaning. . . .'

It certainly gave Wolcot an opportunity to exercise his dormant taste for the Gothick:

Hark the wild uproar of the winds and hark
Hell's genius roams the regions of the dark
And thund'ring swells the horrors of the main.
From cloud to cloud the moon affrighted flies
Now darkened and now flashing through her skies.
Alas! Bless'd calm return, return again.

But, in any case, this venture, exciting and stimulating though it must undoubtedly have been, was outside the normal run of his work.[1]

'Thank God [he wrote to Giddy] there is an asiatic famine in Poetry. Now is a fair time to write verses. I daily compose some nonsense and am lucky to meet with folks to buy it. Anacreon is on the stocks and as we have no translation but Fawkes's which is very so-so I think I may adventure upon him. I must, as Queen Elizabeth said of her Latin, rub up my old Greek and considering the many editions of the old Toper I shall not have much difficulty. . . .'

[1] There exists a somewhat confusing and undated *Collection of Original Songs with an Accompanyment for Pianoforte or Harp composed by W. A. Mozart, etc., etc., the Poetry by Peter Pindar*. Only one song—'The Fair Thief'—is in fact by Mozart and this does not appear to be in Köchel. On the other hand it is noted that the words of 'The Violet' (K. 476) are supposedly by Wolcot.

Nothing came of this excursion into the Classics, but 1791 saw the publication of a work that was to involve Wolcot in legal trouble.

A Commiserating Epistle to Lord Lonsdale was a satire of the most blistering kind, not less effective for the fact that it pretended to sympathize with the Earl.

It was prefaced by an Argument which gives the flavour of Pindar's attack:

'The noble Earl, as naturally in Pursuit of his Coal as a Sportsman of his Hare or Fox, happening in a Coal-chase to undermine a parcel of Houses belonging to the Lord-knows-who, of Whitehaven (no Votes, perhaps, for a Borough or a County) but particularly of a Mr Littledale—what does this insolent Littledale but *Complain*! Nay, not contented with Complaint he insists upon it that his Lordship has no Right to pull down his House about his Ears—nay, what is still worse, the Fellow brings an Action, absolutely brings an Action against his Lordship—nay, what is still more horrible, the Knave gets a Verdict in his favour—and, what is more atrocious still, the Villains of the Town and Neighbourhood illuminate their Houses, as if for the Birth-nights of our *beloved* King and Queen, and exhibit equal Symptoms of Joy. Notwithstanding this saucy Opposition to their great Superior; notwithstanding the wicked Action; notwithstanding the vile and unnatural Verdict; notwithstanding the triumphant Illumination and brazen-faced Delight on the occasion; how sublimely his Lordship behaves! Though he most spiritedly suspends his Coal-works for a Time to shew the Power of his Vengeance; lo, he promiseth to open them again on Condition he has full Liberty to undermine any Houses that may impudently stand in the way of his Coal for the future—What an Act of Humanity! partly for the Benefit of *himself*, a *poor* Individual; but principally for the Advantage of the Town of Whitehaven! Who, besides his Lordship, would have done this? It is too humane—it is too great—for as it has been observed by some celebrated Divines, that a Man may be *over*-righteous, so verily a great Peer may be over-*forgiving*. Such is the ground of my Epistle to Lord Lonsdale. . . .'

'Shades of the Lowthers, [cried Wolcot], armed with vengeance rise,
And shake this Lonsdale who his birth belies.'

In the course of five hundred years, he claimed, no Lonsdale had ever shewn a trace of virtue or generosity; when had there been one Lowther trunk that was not rotten at the root?

> Ah do not so unfashionably dote
> And stitch one spangle on an old black coat

exclaimed Peter Pindar still in the roistering satirical spirit of his preface as he proceeded to urge his Lordship at some length to grind the faces of the poor of Cumberland in a way that would really do credit to his illustrious forbears:

> Humanity's a pigeon-hearted fool,
> Soft, puling, as the girl at boarding school.

The activities of spiders, hawks, and alligators he described in bloodthirsty detail:

> These be thy great examples—careful mind 'em
> And do not in a tittle lag behind 'em.
> Be *thou* the spider that devours the flies
> Be thou the tyrant kite that scours the skies
> Be thou the hard mouth'd subtle alligator. . . .

The poem ended with the couplet:

> Thus at thy feet shall dumb Obedience fall
> And Hell, in lustre, yield to Lowther Hall.

The *Commiserating Epistle* sounded a new note of savagery. Nothing that Wolcot had written had been quite so fierce and, in a comparatively short space, so devastatingly libellous. It was more than his Lordship could be expected to suffer. In February 1792 he brought an action in the Privy Council against John Wolcot.

But although the case was eventually allowed to drop, the subsequent ode which he addressed to Lord Lonsdale on the subject was by comparison so mild that it seems almost as if Wolcot had at last realized that it was possible sometimes to go too far.

II

AT THE age of fifty-four Wolcot had reached the stage of being that familiar phenomenon the ubiquitous Man of Letters; the man contributing to a variety of newspapers and magazines, the man with a new book continually at the booksellers, the man seen about Town at all the literary haunts and taverns, the man asked to review and compile anthologies and write pieces for the theatre. In addition to *The Storm* the year had seen his usual spate of ephemeral or occasional poetry. Like all such verse it was of unequal merit. There were *The Tears of St Margaret*, *Odes to Kien Long*, *Epistles to Lord Macartney and his Ship*, *Odes of Importance* (which included the mild reply to Lord Lonsdale) and *More Money*. In the latter work he resumed his attacks upon the king and in them, as seems always to have been the way, he was at his happiest and most inventive: the account of the royal visit to Wilton House supplies an example of his sunnier manner:

> . . . 'My lord, you've got fine statues,' said the King.
> 'A few, beneath your royal notice, sir,'
> Replied Lord Pembroke—'Stir, my lord, stir, stir,
> Let's see them all, all, all, all, *ev'ry* thing.
> Who's this? Who's this?—Who's this fine fellow here?'
> 'Sesostris,' bowing low replied the peer.
> 'Sir Sostris, hey?—Sir Sostris?—'pon my word
> Knight or baronet, my lord?
> One of my making? What, my lord, *my making*?'
> This, with a vengeance, was mistaking!
>
> '*Se*-sostris, sire,' *so soft*, the peer reply'd
> 'A famous king of Egypt, sir, of old.'
> 'Poh, poh!' th'instructed monarch snappish cry'd
> 'I need not *that*—I need not *that* be told.

'Pray, pray, my lord, who's that big fellow there?'
'Tis Hercules,' replies the shrinking peer.
'Strong fellow, hey, my lord? Strong fellow, hey?
Cleaned stables! Crack'd a lion like a flea;
Kill'd snakes, great snakes, that in a cradle found him——
The queen, queen's coming! Wrap an apron round him.'

All this literary activity was not without its rewards. His publications sold in thousands at prices ranging from 1s. 6d. to half a crown and even more. In the early part of the year he had been able, so it was said, to place a considerable sum in the Funds which, at that time, were regarded as a safe investment. Yet Reitterer noticed that, with an inconsistency more common to-day, socialist tendencies were creeping into his work. He quotes Wolcot's *Ode to the Shoemakers* counselling resignation in the face of a rejection of their wage claims as a masterpiece of bitter irony, the earliest example of the poetry of the Social revolution and comparable both in tone and subject to Shelley's *Masque of Anarchy*:

> Lo to the great we breathe the sigh in vain
> A zephyr murm'ring through the hollow walls
> Our tear, that tries to melt their souls, the rain
> That printless on the rock of ages falls. . . .

It is a fair sample of Wolcot in his more responsible mood, the mood that might be expected from a middle-aged *enfant terrible* who was growing up. Perhaps it was this sense of social conscience that endeared him to Burns who remarked, 'Peter is a delightful fellow and a first favourite of mine.' In any case it was with Robert Burns that Wolcot was now joined in an improbable collaboration.

*　　*　　*　　*　　*

Some musical amateurs in Edinburgh, led by George Thomson, had formed a project for *A Select Collection of Original Scottish Airs*. The work was to be more 'elegant' than James Johnson's *Museum*, there was to be no 'indelicacy' and English

149

words were, with a rare lack of Nationalist feeling, to be preferred to Scots. Pleyel was to re-set the music and Wolcot was
approached to undertake the English side of the task. It was
clearly one that caused him considerable difficulty for on January
24th, 1793, Thomson wrote from Edinburgh to Burns:

> 'That eccentric bard Peter Pindar has started I know not
> how many difficulties about writing for the airs I sent to him
> because of the peculiarity of their measure and the trammels
> they impose on his flying Pegasus. I subjoin for your approval
> the only one I have yet got from him, being for the fine Air
> *Lord Gregory*. . . .'

Burns read Wolcot's verses with a real pleasure. On January 26th
he replied to Thomson:

> 'The very name of Peter Pindar is an acquisition to your
> work—His *Gregory* is beautiful.—I have tried to give you a
> set of Stanzas in Scots on the same subject which are at your
> service.—Not that I intend to enter the lists with Peter; that
> would be presumption indeed.—My song though much in-
> ferior in poetic merit has I think more of the ballad simplicity
> in it.'

This verdict, from such a poet as Burns, was praise—and
modesty—indeed. It was also lacking, a little, in critical judgment
for it can hardly be disputed even by those to whom dialect in
general and the Scottish idiom in particular induces tedium, that
Wolcot's lines which began

Ah ope, Lord Gregory, thy door

were in fact greatly inferior to Burns's variation which began

Oh mirk mirk, is this midnight hour

There seems in fact always something a little spurious and un-
convincing about Peter Pindar in sentimental vein. That seriousness clearly did not agree with his temperament is confirmed by

John Taylor's comment that 'Dr Wolcot used to read his own compositions and the comic productions of others with admirable ease, humour and spirit, but he read all grave poems with a kind of ludicrous quaintness. . . .'

It seems likely that the fitting of serious English words to Scots airs was one that gave Wolcot a disproportionate amount of work. His satirical output for 1793 amounted to little more than the short volume containing his *Epistle to the Pope*. Nor was this apparently in any way offset by a great production of ballads for the Edinburgh poetry lovers. In August 1793 Burns wrote to Thomson, evidently urging him to get more contributions from John Wolcot:

'. . . one thing I must hint to you, the very name of Peter Pindar is of great service to your publication; so get a verse from him now and then. . . .'

Thomson reassured him: 'I shall be glad to see you give Robin Adair a Scotish dress. Peter is furnishing him with an English suit for a change and you are well matched together.'

And on September 1st, sending twenty-three songs to Burns for setting, he wrote:

'I have burdened the pleasant Peter with as many as it is probable he will attend to; most of the remaining airs would puzzle the English poet not a little; they are of that peculiar measure and rhythm that they must be familiar to him that writes for them.'

Pleyel was in difficulties, too. When the second set of songs was published the editor deemed it necessary 'to inform the Public that he used every effort in his power to obtain from Mr Pleyel at Paris the Symphonies and Accompanyments promised by him but in vain'. Eventually Thomson applied to the 'equally celebrated Mr Kozebuch'.

The joint work was still in progress a year later. On October 14th, 1794, Thomson told Burns, 'Peter Pindar has at length sent me the songs I expected from him which are in general elegant and beautiful. . . .'

It is not altogether easy to estimate how many songs Wolcot in fact produced. In the whole collection there are no more than six

that are definitely credited to Peter Pindar: *Here Awa' There Awa',
Will ye go to the Ewebughts, Marion, O, Mirk Mirk is this Midnight
Hour, Oh, I hae lost my Silken Snood* (Wolcot's version read 'Gone
is my heart for ever gone'), *Blythe ha'e I been on yon Hill* (Wolcot's
'Dear Colin quit thy Love-sick Tale' called for 'an additional
quaver for the first word or syllable of every line') and *Now in her
Green Mantle blythe Nature arrays.*

But in addition to poems by many other writers such as
Otway, Falconer, Whitehead, Smollett, Collins and Allan
Ramsay—to name only a few—there are many unattributed
which may be by Wolcot's hand or, perhaps, by his adaptation
from traditional lyrics.

His connection with the work was not universally approved,
for as Thomson added to his letter of October 14th an English-
man called Ritson had also just published a book of Scots Airs:

> 'He snarls at my publication on the score of Pindar being
> engaged to write songs for it; uncandidly and unjustly leaving
> it to be inferred that the songs of Scottish writers have been
> sent a-packing to make room for Peter's.'

Burns commented on Wolcot's final contribution:

> 'If you insert both Peter's song and mine to *The Bonnie
> Brucket Lassie* it will cost you engraving the first verses of both
> songs as the rhythm of the two is considerably different. As
> *Fair Eliza* is already published I am totally indifferent whether
> you give it a place or not; but to my taste the rhythm of my
> song to that air would have a much more original effect.'

And in December, 1794, he again wrote to Thomson:

> 'It is, I assure you the pride of my heart to do anything to
> forward or add to the value of your book; and as I agree with
> you that the Jacobite song in the *Museum* to *There'll never be
> peace till Jamie comes home* would not so well consort with
> Peter Pindar's excellent love-song to that air I have just framed
> for you the following
> *My Nanie's awa*—Tune: There'll never be peace. . . .'

But eventually the two long years of work neared their end, for on December 20th, 1794, Burns wrote to Mrs Dunlop to tell her of 'a superb Publication of Scottish songs which is making its appearance in your Great Metropolis and where I have the honour to preside over the Scotch verse as no less a personage than Peter Pindar does over the English. . . .'

In January, 1795, perhaps to celebrate the end of the task, George Thomson presented the poet with a set of Wolcot's *Collected Works*:[1] Burns thanked him for the 'elegant present. . . . The typography is admirable and worthy of the truly original bard.'

Robert Chambers, the biographer and editor of Burns's works, commented with characteristic Victorian disapproval on this fondness of his hero for Peter Pindar and added: 'It must ever be a humiliating consideration that this modern Aretin was richly pensioned by the Booksellers while Burns, the true sweet singer, lived in comparative poverty.'

But what John Wolcot thought of his collaborator and whether George Thomson presented him with the Works of Robert Burns is not recorded.

* * * * *

The reference to a rich pension from the booksellers relates to an impressive incident that occurred possibly in the winter of 1793–4 and which set the final seal of success upon Wolcot. About the exact details of the arrangement and of the subsequent legal actions that took place there is a certain conflict of evidence. But what seems to be the most probable account reports that three booksellers, Messrs Robinson, Goulding and Walker, got together and decided to offer the great man either an annuity or a lump sum—whichever should be acceptable to Wolcot—for his copyrights. Wolcot, then aged fifty-seven, chose an annuity. Walker was deputed to be the spokesman and it so happened that when he called one evening to arrange the matter the doctor

---

[1] According to Professor John Nichol, Burns to his indignation received for 100 songs in the collection no more than 'a shawl for his wife, a picture by David Allan representing the *Cotter's Saturday Night* and £5'. If John Wolcot was rewarded on a similar scale his comments must have been worth hearing.

was in the throes of a severe attack of the asthma from which he still suffered. Walker went home in a state of some alarm and told his wife that it seemed unlikely that Peter Pindar would live to sign the agreement. This remark somehow got back to Wolcot and when the bookseller arrived on the next occasion he was met with a fit of coughing of such violence that he hastened the business without arguing too much about the details.

Henceforth the booksellers were to pay the doctor £250 a year for the copyright in his works. Wolcot was assured of a reasonable income for life. The independence he had always sought was now in fact his. And in his immense satisfaction he took a gleeful pleasure in exaggerating the way the agreement had come to be signed so quickly, making it appear that he had craftily overreached the booksellers, that he had forced their hands with a variety of amusing deceits. His genuine infirmity was turned to advantage for the purposes of a good story: he had received Walker in a nightcap, he had purposely abstained from shaving for four days, he had assumed a hollow cough. Between coughs he had gasped out that it made little difference what the annuity might be as all would soon be over with him. With each fit of coughing the price of the annuity was raised. The story grew with the telling. He had taken walks in the November fogs to increase his cough. When the bookseller called, Wolcot had been incapable of speech until he had gulped down a full glass of brandy. 'But after I mixed water with my brandy the Spring came on and I lost my cough.'

Eventually the story was told that Peter Pindar had powdered his cadaverous unshaven face with chalk to increase the effect of having one foot in the grave, 'but no sooner than the document was signed he wiped the chalk away and went dancing for glee out of the room'.

How much of all this was of Wolcot's own imagining and how much grew from his spiteful but envious critics is not known. Cyrus Redding who was a close friend for fourteen years indignantly denied any such stories—no amount of chalk would have whitened that mahogany countenance. Nor was it the sort of trick that Wolcot, 'one of the most open, candid men that ever lived', would play. But Redding had to admit that his friend was fond of a joke and often made one out of little.

But documents signed in haste are often a rich source of income for the lawyers. The agreement with the booksellers was loosely worded. Both parties thought they knew what it meant to convey. Messrs Robinson, Goulding and Walker were convinced they had bought the right to all works both past and future without further payment. But Wolcot argued, 'It was *not* a part of the agreement that they were to have my *future* works included in the annuity; these they were to purchase if I chose to sell them. . . .'

A long-drawn-out law-suit was to follow. But in the meantime Wolcot's income was assured.

* * * * *

Another aspect of Wolcot's ubiquitousness in the literary world of the seventeen-nineties was his appearance as a book critic. This appointment arose, no doubt, from his membership of the *Packhorse Club* which met at the Inn on Turnham Green. This coterie included Edward Jerningham, John Taylor and Jesse Foot amongst its members as well as Dr Griffiths the editor of the *Monthly Review* to which, from June 1793 to February 1796, Wolcot now contributed. In common with the rest of the reviewers his criticisms were published anonymously. And it is significant of Wolcot's character that behind the veil of anonymity his reviews were notable for their mildness of tone and the kindly way in which he strained to find something pleasant to say about productions of a worthy but indifferent kind. Thus of Lady Sophia Burrell's *Poems* he reported that he found them

'possessed of perspicacity ease and vivacity. We confess that we have perused some of them several times and are pleased to *recollect* them; a circumstance which confers fame if the assertion of Mr Malherbe be true "*que la pierre de touche des beaux vers etoit quand on les apprenoit par coeur*".'

Malherbe or Horace—Wolcot could bring many a classical quotation to the aid of the aspiring author and to the production, at the same time, of an urbane critique. Of George Cumberland's

155

Some Anecdotes of Julio Bonasoni the worst he could find to say after a review by no means wholly unfavourable was that 'the anecdotes are dry and uninteresting'.

Of the *Poems* of William Kendall he remarked:

> 'the Muse of Mr Kendall is a lady of no mean appearance. Far from disgracing the celebrated old Mount her *tout-ensemble* does credit to Parnassus.' But . . . 'we must confess that though we have been pleased with a number of Mr K's stanzas many require correction.'

The *Life of Hubert* by The Revd Thomas Cole, D.D., called forth more quotations from Horace and the comment that Cole's works 'cannot boast much of Parnassus; they possess too little of the *aura divina* to excite envy. Yet they have merit sufficient to secure them from creating disgust.' And in his review of *Imitations on the Epigrams of Martial* he noted with approval that the 'many indecencies' of the original had been 'laudibly softened' although even more might have been achieved in that direction: expressing disgust at such obscenities as survived, he added: 'right sorry should we be to find the library of a gentleman disgraced by the licentious labours of an Aretine'—All the same he allowed that the imitations, not without fault though they might be, had also considerable merits. All this was soft-pedalling indeed. Literary schizophrenia could scarcely go further. But relieved by his anonymity from being the dread character he had so carefully fashioned for himself he could relax into the essentially kindly being that, in private and amongst his friends, he was. And in the pages of the *Monthly Review* he could encourage, as he had encourage Polwhele and Opie, the aspiring poets whose sensitive feelings on the publication of their precious books he himself knew only too well:

> Child of my love, go forth, and try thy fate
> Few are thy friends and manifold thy foes!
> Whether or long or short will be thy date
> Futurity's dark volume only knows.

*   *   *   *   *

In public, however, he must continue to shock. 1793, filled as it was both with Scottish ballads and also the setting of one or more songs by Haydn, had been a comparatively unproductive year. But it had not been without its moments of exuberance.

Poor Richard Cosway, who had already suffered at Peter Pindar's hands, moved from Pall Mall to No. 1 Stratford Place, a fine house with a lion on the top of it. Someone—and it was generally believed to be John Wolcot—fixed to the door a verse which read:

> When a man to a fair, for a show, brings a lion
> Tis usual a monkey the sign post to tie on
> But here the old custom revers'd is seen
> For the lion's without and the monkey's within.

This caused, so it was said (but mistakenly), the sensitive Cosway to move house again.

Now in 1794 the scourge of Throne and Government lashed out once again.

Celebration or The Academic Procession to St James's recounted how the king had refused, on the ground of the institution's poverty, permission for the Royal Academy to subscribe to a memorial to Doctor Johnson; how the king had vetoed, also on the grounds of poverty, the proposal that the Academy should print an elegant edition of Sir Joshua Reynolds' discourses; but how on the other hand His Majesty had welcomed with acclamation the proposal that the Academicians should give a vast banquet to the Royal Family and present to the king and queen, to the Prince of Wales and the Princess Royal memorial medals of solid gold.

Pathetic Odes carried the expression of Wolcot's social conscience even further. *The Ode to the Poor Soldier of Tilbury Fort* who was reduced to gathering driftwood on the shore for a living

> Glean'd with the very hand that grasp'd the sword
> To guard the throne of Britain's sacred lord

dwelt on a problem that still was not satisfactorily solved 150 years later.

Britain was again at war with a France that had announced a crusade against all monarchies and the war was made—as war always is—the eagerly seized excuse for further whittling away, purely as a temporary measure by the Government, of individual liberty. Cried Wolcot:

> Now God bless our good King and this good war
> And damn that wicked word we call Reform
> Breeding in Britain so much jar
> So witch-like conj'ring up a dangerous storm!
>
> Yet in the mouths of Pitt and Richmond's lord
> *Once* what a sweet and inoffensive word!
> Thus proving the delightful proverb true
> What's meat to *me* may poison be to *you*.

When a man of Wolcot's influence, a man who commanded such a circulation, and whose works were so eagerly read and discussed, wrote in this vein it is small wonder that the eye of authority began to be turned bleakly towards his activities.

*   *   *   *   *

The remaining publication for 1794 proved however to be of a nature less exceptionable to the politician. *Pindariana or Peter's Portfolio* provided his public with what is really the hall-mark of the successful writer—an *olla podrida* of every kind of scrap and fragment of verse from the files—some 130 altogether—of such a diversity as could not conveniently be included in any other volume.

He was now a law unto himself. As befitted a character publicly accepted as disgraceful he could afford a certain carelessness about his personal appearance. In fact if the Reverend Richard Warner, writing from memory thirty-five years later, is to be believed he now presented a figure almost too Bohemian:

> 'Dr Wolcot . . . had often pressed me to visit him when I went to London. I called on him in company with a friend at his chambers in (I believe) New Inn. As we entered the

room a dirty drab rose from the table (for the poet was break-fasting at one o'clock) and glided into an inner apartment. Pindar himself wore a greasy night-cap on his head and was involved in a flannel mantle marvellously discoloured; on his foul table cloth were spread plates of sausages and ham, eggs and muffins; tea in a pot without a spout; and a bottle sending out the odour of British spirits. Around on the dusty and dingy carpet lay a mingled mass of pamphlets and manu-scripts, muddy shoes, a hat with a hole in it and two old wigs! We talked for an hour. Peter said some *strong* but coarse and offensive things. He was very indignant at the execution of Coigly for sedition which had just taken place. "Sir," said he, "it was murder and nothing else. It was the devil bringing his action and trying it in hell." '

The picture is neither attractive nor, it must be admitted, isolated and it shews Wolcot in a light which ill accords with the opinion held of him by the fastidious John Taylor. Eighteenth-century standards of personal cleanliness were not altogether exacting and from his youth he had never been noted for paying undue attention to his appearance, but John Wolcot was welcome at a number of houses where such sluttishness would not have gone unremarked. The suspicion must occur that in the presence of certain visitors—always male and often Anglican divines—he was on his worst behaviour.

$$\star \qquad \star \qquad \star \qquad \star \qquad \star$$

Freed, so it appeared, from financial cares and literary lion that he had become, he now lived, says Reitterer 'a life full of the pleasures of the table and of love'.

At houses where he had been invited for the evening he was apt to stay overlong and this was particularly the case with a family living in a house identified only as being in —— Place.

One of the daughters of the house eventually in a friendly manner pointed out to him this failing. The next time he pro-posed a visit he wrote to them a note:

Tell me sweet girls of —— Place
If at the Opera or the play
You mean this night to add a grace
And steal a heart or two away
If not, I sip my tea with you at seven
Dead or alive I'll leave you at eleven.

As a result of that evening an agreement was reached that the maid would always come into the parlour with Wolcot's cane on the stroke of eleven o'clock. One night, however, the clock struck the hour at a moment when he was in the middle of one of his best tales and the summons was temporarily omitted, 'which the doctor no sooner observed than he triumphantly declared the treaty broken and himself absolved from the engagement'. Just to point the moral he 'nearly sat out the night'.

To his pleasure the great Haydn was back in England. They met again in Brompton at the house of Mrs Billington. There was a large party including Shield the composer and John Taylor. Also among the guests was a journalist named Williams who wrote under the name of Anthony Pasquin. He was a man not without a certain amount of talent and in humour not very greatly different from Wolcot. According to Taylor, however, he was also 'vain, vulgar, insolent and overbearing' and his works were marked by a 'low malignity'. As if this was not bad enough he appears to have existed largely on a species of blackmail. 'He was the terror of the middling and lower order of actors and artists and would call on them in a morning, ask them if they dined at home and finding that they did would impudently order them to get a particular dish and sometimes bring an acquaintance with him at the appointed hour. This practice he carried on for many years almost subsisting on timid painters and performers, musical and theatrical, who were afraid of his attacks in the newspapers or in his abusive verses.'

All in all he was not the sort of companion that Wolcot and his particular friends would have chosen on this or any other occasion. At dinner Williams was seated opposite Haydn and suddenly addressed him.

'Mr Haydn, you are the greatest genius I ever saw.' Apart from the sudden brusqueness there would have been no harm in this if he had not qualified the remark by concluding 'with a very

160

Dr. John Wolcot
Formerly attributed to John Opie

Good morning sweet BARD!!!

Dr. Wolcot at Bath
By Cruikshank

coarse and violent asseveration'. Haydn showed signs of confusion and the whole company were shocked not only by the vulgarity of Williams' salutation but by the general coarseness and obtrusiveness of his manners.

The matter was passed off and at last the evening neared its end. From the general conversation Williams had learned that Taylor, Shield and Wolcot had ordered a coach to take them back to Covent Garden and made up his mind to cadge a lift. He kept a careful watch on the three friends and as they were getting into their coach he forced his company upon them, insisting that of course he would pay his proportion of the fare. Kindly William Shield instantly consented but Wolcot could hardly conceal his disgust. They all piled into the coach. Shield and Taylor sat on one side, Wolcot and Williams, facing them, on the other. The coach swayed off over the uneven roads towards Knightsbridge. Taylor nudged Shield and remarked how gratifying it was to find oneself a passenger with two men of great genius who had both distinguished themselves under assumed names. Shield, who enjoyed a joke as much as the next man, agreed. How gratifying it would be to everybody, continued Taylor, of only they were to collaborate. He even proposed that the two writers should there and then shake hands to seal an agreement. Williams at once stretched out his arm and declaring that he should feel great pride to take part in such a literary alliance attempted to seize Wolcot's hand. The latter however was greatly unwilling and held Williams' hand 'as if he feared contagion in the touch'. Taylor was delighted with his little jest and was quite unable to leave well alone. He returned to his subject and began to predict a wonderful success for their joint production. Wolcot could bear it no longer and with great warmth accused Taylor of trying to make trouble. Taylor protested. He appealed to Shield; had he not done everything to promote harmony between two eminent writers? But there was something in Shield's manner that gave the game away. Wolcot fell silent, but nothing would induce him for the rest of the journey to turn towards Williams.

At last the coach pulled up outside St Paul's, Covent Garden, and now that the moment for paying the fare had arrived Williams, as soon as the driver dismounted and opened the door, leaped out and bolted away in the direction of the Strand. Wolcot, seeing him run off, immediately imitated him and tore away as fast as he could in the opposite direction. Taylor chased him but there was really no need to do so: John Wolcot seized hold of the church rails as though claiming sanctuary and burst out laughing.

'As soon as I saw Gibbet run I resolved to follow his example,' he panted and he came back readily enough to hand over a share of the coach which Shield, feeling rather guilty for having admitted Williams to their company, wanted to pay for on his own.

'We then concluded,' adds Taylor, 'a pleasant night together.'

★   ★   ★   ★   ★

There had been, some time earlier in the year, a meeting between Wolcot and another man with whom he had little in common. The Duke of Leeds had been one of those in authority who, Wolcot believed, had been trying to silence his Muse:

> When Majesty was in a monstrous passion
> And grimly Thurlow thunder'd out damnation
> And Leeds and Hawkesbury joined their jowls together
> Brewing like witches of Macbeth foul weather
> I cannot truly say my heart was light. . . .

But it had not been so heavy that he had not at once subjected the duke to a few verses of a satirical nature in which, *inter alia*, he described not too savagely his Grace's personal appearance:

> With lath-like form, whey face and cheeks so thin
> With some old gentlewoman's nose and chin

Now suddenly they came face to face in the Green Room of Covent Garden. The duke was probably the less embarrassed of the two.

'Ah, Ποιητης!' he exclaimed with an apparent geniality that really did him credit. Peter Pindar, whose nervous attitude, so inconsistent with his writings, on being confronted with the great has already been noted, gave some kind of nervous salute.

'When were you in Cornwall last?' asked the duke, clearly intent on being gracious.

'About two years ago! Pray when was your Grace in that province?'

The duke had been there, with the duchess, during the previous year.

'Godolphin is wildly situated,' said Wolcot and as he began to feel more at ease he began to shew off a little. 'If I mistake not, Cornwall was made the scene of the diableries of the old Spanish and Italian writers of romance.'

'Hem, hem!' agreed the duke with a smile and a nod. If he did not know what Wolcot was talking about he was not disclosing the fact and he steered the conversation on to more general topics of literature. Himself an amateur poet he spoke easily and with knowledge on the subject of Shakespeare, Dryden and Pope: he had moreover what Wolcot describes as the poet's 'desultory disposition, leaping from earth to heaven in his phrensy' for he suddenly broke off in the middle of a quotation from Shakespeare to say abruptly:

'How came you, sir, in your ode to attack my nose?'

This was certainly an awkward question.

'My Lord Duke, when your Grace, Lord Hawkesbury, Lord Thurlow, Lord Sidney and others, your colleagues in administration, took it into your heads to attack me, I thought a poor poet had a right to the laws of retaliation.'

'But why attack my *nose*, sir; why attack my nose?'

Before Wolcot could reply the duke was back again on the subject of the poets from whom he took many quotations and spoke them well but then, suddenly, in the middle of a passage from the classics he burst out again:

'But why attack my *nose*? Is there anything *uncommon* in my nose?'

Wolcot was forced to admit that he had known nothing of his Lordship's nose other than what he had heard in reports of it, but that he knew that the duke had power and meant to use it against him. The duke stood silent for a moment or two. Then he said:

'I will introduce you to the duchess.'

The two men left the Green Room arm in arm and made their

way to a stage box where Wolcot was introduced to the duchess and to her sister Miss Anguish.

'My love,' said the duke, 'I have been asking the doctor what provoked him to attack my *nose*.' He turned to Wolcot. 'Pray, Doctor, what provoked you to attack my nose?'

The embarrassed Wolcot was forced to produce a rather feeble compliment, muttering something to the effect that if he had seen his Grace's nose before he wrote the ode he would have written a panegyric instead of a satire as the nose was really a very good nose indeed.

The duke seemed pleased with this. His ladies smiled and Wolcot leaned over the edge of the box to shew the audience what splendid company he was keeping. The conversation, freed from the weight of the nose, became quite cheerful, and after one or two pleasantries Wolcot bowed and left the box, thinking that the hatchet had by this time been decently buried. But at the very next public dinner that the duke gave he recounted the interview in a way which caused a considerable amount of amusement to his guests.

He made much, no doubt, of the contrast between the poet's daring on paper and his deferential manner when faced with his victim: Peter Pindar was made to look as ridiculous as possible. The ducal nose was, in some small degree, avenged.

12

IF THE Duke of Leeds spoke truly when he told Taylor that he
had never advised a prosecution against Wolcot and that, in
fact, he revered the freedom of the Press, then he was one exception in governmental circles. Faced, after a succession of disasters
in the war with France, with invasion, desperately unpopular as
the result of the level of taxation, unwilling to curb in any way
governmental extravagance and resentful of criticism, the
Administration sank to pitiable depths of witch-hunting. Criticism of the rulers was a risky business. In Edinburgh, where the
ministerial influence was strong, prosecutions had been instituted
against loyal citizens who had done no more than associate to
discuss Parliamentary reform. Two men who had read the works
of Tom Paine and had expressed a partial and qualified approval
were sentenced to fourteen and seven years' transportation res-
pectively. In the South in general and in London in particular
the prosecutions were less successful: a bookseller, arrested for
publishing pamphlets of a democratic tendency, was acquitted
by a jury. But every such trial and its verdict brought more riot-
ing and unrest, for each side, both prosecutor and prosecuted, had
a mob ready to cause trouble if they did not agree with the result
of the case. In the summer of 1794 members first of the Corresponding Society and then of the Society for Constitutional
Information had been arrested, and in November a great series of
State Trials was planned. Erskine was in his usual rôle of defending
counsel and after the first batch of acquittals had made it clear
that English juries were to be neither intimidated nor panicked
by the State's false cries of Treason and Disaffection the remainder
of the accused were released without trial. But the persecution
continued. Satire was a dangerous trade and it is greatly to be
counted in favour of Wolcot's moral courage that 1795 saw a

greater outpouring of his attacks against the Government than ever before.

★   ★   ★   ★   ★

It is clear that John Wolcot was in the unhappy position of many a liberal-minded man who has become disillusioned with all politicians. He cannot hope for any form of totalitarian régime, yet his own leaders have through expediency betrayed their principles. The fact that he attacked Pitt—and his attack was the more savage because of the admiration he had felt for Chatham— put him automatically by the simple black and white reckoning of English politics among the enemies of the Government and therefore, by an easy stretch of casuistry, among the enemies of his king and country. He has in fact been described as one of the 'leading *sans culottes* in the country'.

Yet his attitude was never in doubt to those who knew him. Towards the end of 1793 he had called in the company of Opie and John Taylor on Joseph Farington, and the Diarist recorded:

> 'In a conversation on Political Constitution the Doctor steadily maintained that a King and Lords were essential parts in a good Government and less liable to corruption than the third estate, the Commons. That the political distinction be-tween the Lords and the Commons placed the former at a distance which causes them to be more neutral judges than it is likely they would be, or than has ever been found, where equality or rather the name of it has been boasted.'

But to attack the Commons was almost worse than to attack Holy Writ. It was un-English behaviour. No amount of loyalty or patriotism could excuse it.

★   ★   ★   ★   ★

> Mercy to England yield, the poor lean cow!
> Thy busy fingers have forc'd milk enow
> Through frequent rushing the lank teats to tease
> How patiently the beast has borne thy squeeze!

166

Just shak'd her head and wincing whisk'd her tail
When oft thou fill'dst a *puncheon* for a *pail*:
But now she bushing roars and makes a pudder
Afraid thy harden'd hands may steal her udder. . . .

Hidden among the more amusing images in *Hair-powder*—an attack upon the new taxation—there lay serious passages urging the Government not to regard too lightly the swelling discontent of the nation and warning the Prime Minister not to become over-ambitious:

Believe me, Pitt, not yet is *thine* the realm
Not *thine* the ship because thou hold'st the helm.

In attacking Pitt in this manner John Wolcot was in no doubt about the way his verse would be received:

Such is the song and do not thou, severe,
With *treason, treason* fill a royal ear.
A gentle joke, at times, on queens and kings
Are pleasant, taking, nay *instructive* things:
Yet *some* there are, who relish not the sport,
That flutter in the sunshine of a court;
Who, fearful *song* might mar their high ambition
Loose the gaunt dogs of state and bawl 'Sedition'.

The title page of the bitterly sarcastic *Convention Bill: an Ode* carried the quotation

Odi profanum vulgus et arceo
Favete linguis
Horace

and beneath it

I hate the mob—avaunt the vulgar throng
Be padlocks plac'd on ev'ry Briton's tongue!
Pitt's translation.

This was hard-hitting and fairly justifiable pamphleteering. Yet with his acute sense of what his readers wanted he was careful—and no doubt relieved—to lighten the gloomy picture that 1795 presented with *The Cap*, a book dedicated to Sheridan and

167

containing a highly critical survey of the dramatists of the day and with two volumes devoted to nothing more serious than the eccentricities of the monarch. And, as always, in these he was at his gayest and least inhibited. *The Royal Visit to Exeter* is handicapped for the general public by being written throughout in Devonshire dialect but *The Royal Tour and Weymouth Amusements* bubbles and sparkles with the poet's enjoyment of his own lines. He compares the drive to the coast with the flight of the chariot of the sun, the wind of the royal passage is like the mighty blast of Aeolus:

> Straws from the lanes, dispers'd and whirl'd in air,
> The blustering wonders of his mouth declare
> Heav'd from their deep foundations with dread sound
> Barns and old houses thunder to the ground
> And bowing oaks, in ages rooted strong
> Roar through their branches as he sweeps along.

But then comes a delicious change of key:

> George breakfasts on the route, gulps tea, bolts toast,
> Jokes with the waiter, witty with the host;
> Runs to the garden with his morning dues;
> Makes mouths at Cloacina's; reads the news;
> Now mad for fruit he scours the garden round;
> Knocks ev'ry apple that he spies to ground;
> Loads ev'ry royal pocket, seeks his chaise
> Plumps in and fills the village with amaze
> He's off again—he smokes along the road. . . .

Safely in Weymouth his holiday is interrupted, as royal holidays are prone to be, by the Prime Minister:

> Lo! Pitt arrives! Alas, with lantern face!
> 'What, hae, Pitt, hae—what, Pitt, hae *more* disgrace?'
> 'Ah, sire, bad news! a second dire defeat!
> Vendée undone and all the Chouans beat!'
> 'Hae, hae, what, what?—beat, beat?—what beat agen?
> Well, well, more money—raise more men, more men.
> But mind, Pitt, hae—mind, huddle up the news
> *Coin* something and the growling land amuse.'

But there are other things to attract the attention of a king. The proprietor of the Royal Hotel passes on his way to the shops:

> 'See see! see! Stacie—here, here, Stacie, here—
> Going to market, Stacie?—dear, dear, dear!
> I get all my provision by the mail.'

According to Wolcot, still tilting even in his relaxed mood at governmental extravagance, the coach cost the public at least fifty pounds every day of the week during the royal stay at Weymouth. Every day, more sutler's cart than mail-coach, it rolled heavily into the town:

> The mail arrives! hark! hark! the cheerful horn
> To majesty announcing oil and corn
> Turnips and cabbages and soap and candles
> And, lo, each article great Caesar handles
> Bread, cheese, salt, catchup, vinegar and mustard
> Small-beer and bacon, apple-pie and custard;
> All, all from Windsor greets his frugal grace
> For Weymouth is a damned expensive place.

The simple pleasures of the king are, as usual, ruthlessly vivisected. His bargaining for bullocks and pigs, his enjoyment of the Dancing Dogs, his rushing down to the water's edge to see the fishermen hauling in their nets, his investigation of the book Lady Cathcart is reading (it turns out, to his disgust, to be *War with America*), all is breathless and gay and very much in the happy strain of the *Visit to Whitbread's Brewery*. But since that day Wolcot's social conscience had developed, and in the *Visit to Weymouth* a serious note was allowed to be sounded. The king and queen are suddenly confronted with an unwelcome sight:

> A sailor pops upon the royal pair
> On crutches borne—an object of despair
> His squalid beard, pale cheek and haggard eye
> Though silent, pour for help a piercing cry.
>
> 'Who, who are *you*? what, what? hae, what are you?'
> 'A *man*, my liege, whom kindness never knew.'

'A sailor, sailor, hae; you've lost a leg.'
'I know it, sir, which forces me to beg.
I've nine poor children, sir, besides a wife—
God bless them! the sole comforts of my life.'

'Wife and nine children, hae—all, all alive
No, no, no wonder that you cannot thrive.
Shame, shame to fill your hut with such a train!
Shame to get brats for others to maintain.
Get, get a wooden leg, or one of cork:
Wood's *cheapest*—yes, get wood and go to work. . . .'

'Oh! had I money, sir, to buy a leg!'
'No money hae? nor I—go beg, go beg. . . .'

Later, a thought strikes the king:

'How, sailor did you lose your leg, hae, hae?'
'I lost it, please your majesty, at sea
Hard fighting for my country and my king.'

'Hae what—that's common, very common thing
Hae, lucky fellow that you were not *drilled*.
Some lose their heads and many men are killed.
Your parish? where's your parish? hae—where, where?'

'I served my 'prenticeship in Manchester.'

'Fine town, fine town—full, full of trade and riches
Hae, sailor, hae, can you make leather breeches?
These come from Manchester—there, there I got 'em!'
On which great Caesar smacks his buckskin bottom.

'Must not encourage vagrants—no, no, no—
Must not make laws, my lad, and break 'em too.
Where, where's your parish, hae? and where's your pass?
Well make haste home—I've got, I've got no brass.'

The king's sudden descent into the vernacular seems a particularly
happy touch.

✱   ✱   ✱   ✱   ✱

The last of his political productions for that sour, spy-ridden year of 1795 was *Liberty's Last Squeak*, a volume which included, in addition to the title elegy, three *Odes to an Informer* and an *Ode to the Jurymen* before whom Peter Pindar thought it probably he might soon appear.

The times for liberal-minded men were dangerous and their flavour is given by a sinister incident that now took place. Many of the malcontents of London were in the habit of flocking to Copenhagen Fields in St Pancras and there listening to inflammatory speeches against the Government. Occasionally, as happened at the end of October, after a meeting of the London Corresponding Society, scenes of mob violence ensued—the king on his way to open Parliament was surrounded by a vast crowd from which he could get away only with difficulty and not before a shot from an air-gun had shattered a window of the State Coach. Meetings at Copenhagen Fields were naturally closely watched by Government informers and the participation of notable characters marked for future reference.

One day, out of curiosity, Wolcot attended a gathering organized by the Friends of the People. It was nearly dark by the time he got back to his rooms in Tavistock Row and hardly had he settled down for the evening when his old friend Opie burst panting into the room. Wolcot, he gasped out, was in imminent danger of arrest. Pitt's men were after him. Even now . . . he peered out of the window and, drawing back with an exclamation of alarm, motioned to Wolcot to join him: the two men then peered cautiously out from behind the curtains. There in the gathering dusk stood a man, in a slouched hat and coat with the collar turned up, watching the house. Clearly there was no time to be lost. Opie darted to a back window, flung it wide and helped Wolcot to scramble out. He watched his old patron stumble away into the night in full flight for Windsor—the last place that any governmental agent might think of searching for him. Then, roaring with laughter, Opie and Ozias Humphry— the sinister watcher in the twilight—went off together to celebrate the success of their practical joke, a success so complete that it was a fortnight before Wolcot thought it safe to return.

*   *   *   *   *

171

All in all 1795 could not be called a happy year and for John Wolcot it must always have been held the most unwelcome and shaming of memories: it was the year when, in the heat of the battle, he capitulated to the enemy. The degree of surrender is a matter for argument; the stories that were told conflict on vital points and the protagonists themselves were certainly speaking with bias.

The reasons were, almost certainly, financial. Either, as his enemies always averred, he cared for nothing but money and would do anything to get more of it—an accusation that his own declared reason for attacking the king had done nothing to discount—or, in spite of his vast success, he had been living up to the limit of his income and now, with the additional weight of penal taxation, he was actually in urgent need of hard cash from whatever source it might come.

The frame of mind that this worry might induce coupled with the gloomy outlook for any British satirist—for even if he were to continue fearlessly to attack authority might not the booksellers soon become alarmed and refuse for the sake of their skins to publish what he wrote?—must have made the time propitious for the Devil to whisper in Wolcot's ear with some chance of being heard.

Of all the tales that were told of Wolcot's fall it seems probable that Taylor (although writing in after years he was apt to be muddle-headed) came nearest to the truth, came nearer even than Wolcot himself, though his story and Peter Pindar's story of the dreadful thing in many respects agree.

The two friends had been invited to dinner by Heriot of the Tory *True Briton*, a journalist in the closest contact with a member of the administration. During the course of the evening Wolcot began to comment with great vehemence against the French Revolution and against the principles upon which it was founded. His reputation as a *sans-culotte* was such that Heriot must have shewn symptoms of surprise at this diatribe and Taylor who, as has been seen, enjoyed taking a rise out of his friends, said jocularly:

'The doctor seems to shew signs of *bribability*!'

Herot took up the joke.

'Come, Doctor,' he said, 'with these opinions you can have

no objection to support the Government—shall I open a negotiation?'

Wolcot passed the matter off, but the seeds of temptation were planted. What arguments he used to himself in the darkness of the night in his lodgings in Tavistock Street, though they may be guessed at, are unlikely ever to be known. In the morning he called on Heriot and asked him if he had been serious. Heriot managed to control the surprise he felt that the fish had, so many hours later, risen to the improbable lure. But he was a keen supporter of the Government and well aware of what a powerful weapon ridicule, particularly in the hands of Peter Pindar, could be to any political party. He told Wolcot that, quite seriously, if he really felt inclined in future to support the Government with his pen then almost certainly it would be possible to procure for him some form of patronage. Wolcot wriggled a little upon the hook. He was engaged on a number of works attacking various ministers individually and would be prepared, if that was sufficient, to suppress them: really he did not think he could be actively employed on behalf of the Government. But Heriot was too old a hand at negotiating to allow such a misunderstanding to arise. He smoothed the way with a compliment to the doctor's talents but said suavely that really there could be no basis of discussion on such lines. If such attacks were to be published they would make the author liable to prosecution; it was therefore clearly unthinkable that he should be actually paid not to publish them. Wolcot's emotions must have been all too transparent for it was at this moment that Heriot remarked that, after all, in supporting the Government he would only be acting in accordance with his own declared principles which were so hostile to the system by which the French monarchy had been overthrown. This was a statement that had the merits of paving the way for further discussion. No doubt Wolcot dearly wished to be convinced. In the end he was convinced; he gave Heriot permission to approach the Government on his behalf. In due course he was given an introduction to Charles Long, Secretary to the Treasury, who was in the closest confidence of the Prime Minister. He confirmed rather pompously that the patronage of the administration might, under certain conditions, be extended to Peter Pindar.

'There are certain sums, Dr Wolcot, floating in His Majesty's Treasury for those who defend the cause of Government.'

A considerable discussion arose as how much might be expected to float in Peter Pindar's direction: Wolcot demanded five hundred pounds per annum but eventually had to be content with three hundred. An advance was made—or he borrowed the sum—of ten pounds to seal the bargain. The sudden change from Wolcot the all-powerful to Wolcot the corrupt politicians' hireling sent contemptuously on his way with ten pounds in his pocket on account of services to be rendered is painful to contemplate. Nothing can be said in his defence other than that he was human; the fact that he was human must, too, have made him who had been the bright star suffer the more as he contemplated himself in the rôle of Faustus.

The exact extent of the bargain is not disclosed: if it was indeed to set to and write panegyrics of Pitt and his colleagues then Wolcot showed a fearful and natural repugnance for the task. According to Taylor he wrote nothing but a few epigrams which he sent to the editor of *The Sun*. This, if true, was in itself a dreadful degradation for he had long been active in attacking George Rose and his two newspapers *The True Briton* and *The Sun*. Of the last 'never emitting a single ray' was about the mildest criticism he had made. Support for the administration on such a limited scale was not considered adequate.

Taylor used frequently to rebuke him and advise him to be more active, 'but a sort of shame hung about him for having engaged in support of a Government which he had so often abused, or rather its members, and I could never rouse him into action'.

It is possible—although sensibility towards political corruption was less acute than it is in England today—that 'a sort of shame' was something of an understatement: Wolcot's embarrassment was, in any case, increased by the difficulties that arose over the manner in which he might be paid. The urbane Mr Heriot refused point-blank to have anything more to do with the affair and Wolcot it seems 'was prohibited from going himself to the quarter where it was to be received'. Taylor, himself a Tory and thinking highly of the advantages that the Party might gain if Peter Pindar were really to do his best, offered to act as go-between. Wolcot eagerly accepted the offer but, so long as he was really doing nothing to earn the money, Taylor was reluctant to ask for it on his behalf. Wolcot however continually urged his old friend to 'bring the bag', as he put it, and eventually Taylor delayed so long in his application that Wolcot, evidently desperately in need of the money, asked if he might go himself to the treasury agent.

He was tired, anxious and had been overworking. He was fifty-seven—elderly in the eighteenth century—and he had produced in addition to his reviews six new books in the year. He may well have been heading for a nervous breakdown: in any case his lack of proportion had by this time grown so great that he apparently believed that the Government had really agreed secretly to pay him £500 a year, but that Taylor and Heriot were dividing the other £200, and since Taylor was aware of and hurt by this suspicion he replied coldly that he thought it would indeed be best for Wolcot to manage his own business in future. Angrily Wolcot went in person to the fountain-head and found that the proposed pension was, indeed, only £300 and that Taylor had spoken in the highest terms of the return the Government might expect to get for this sum. There was an implied query about when they might expect to see something tangible from the great Peter Pindar. At this the doctor flew into a rage and declining to have anything more to do with the business returned the £10 he had borrowed and went growling away. Taylor, quite disgusted with the unworthy suspicions Wolcot had held of him, reproached him bitterly and the two friends parted angrily. It was many years before they were to come together again.

*　　*　　*　　*　　*

Wolcot's own account of the affair differs essentially only in the degree of his culpability. In the first place the opening move had not come from him:

> 'As for the imputed pension, the fact is this; application was made to me by the friends of government that if I would employ my pen in their favour, they would remunerate me with a pension. My reply was, in a jocular way, that as for varnishing knaves, I would never consent to it; I had no

whitewash for devils; but if they would give me three or four hundred pounds per annum to be *mute* I might accede. This I said without the most distant idea of the proposal being accepted; however they *did* accept it; a half year elapsed when it was intimated to me that *something* was expected from me in favour of the administration. My reply was that they had infamously violated the agreement and that sooner than write for a set of men I despised, it should be void from that moment; and I pronounced it void; adding with some acrimony that rascality might think itself happy in passing without notice. As I had taken up ten pounds of the annuity I sent it back to them and gave the pitiful scoundrels their half-year's due. This is a fair picture of the matter which they may have impudence enough to deny but not powers to refute. I called on and complained to Mr Long but his answers were ministerial—that is to say replete with equivocation.'

But there is little comfort to be drawn from this story. The champion of Free Speech, the tilter at the windmills of political corruption, the man so essentially sound, the man who sneered at those who made money their God, had, on his own admission, allowed his silence to be bought. It had all started as a joke and but for the urgent desire for money it could all have ended as a joke. Not the least distressing aspect of the whole sad business was that it really need never have happened at all.

Tired and depressed Wolcot had gone down to Kingsbridge to see his old house. For a long time it had gone unsold and there had been occasions when he had intended to abandon London altogether and there in the Arcadia of the South Hams build himself on his property a neat little house of nine rooms—a plan that drew from an observant friend the comment that there would be just one room for each of the Muses. Now, after all these years on the market, the old house was suddenly bought by the Reverend Nathaniel Wells who proceeded to demolish the greater part. Wolcot found himself with capital in hand, clearly enough for any present needs. He had sold himself uselessly and in vain. Perhaps this was as hard as any of the other burdens that having acted in expediency he was forced to bear.

*   *   *   *   *

William Gifford, Editor of the Quarterly Review
Replica by John Hoppner

Richard Wilson
After A. F. Mengs

> Farewell, O my pen and my tongue
> To part with such friends I am loth
> But Pitt, in majorities strong,
> Voweth horrible vengeance on both.

he had written in *Liberty's Last Squeak*.

> The meanness no more of high folk
> In the rope of your satire shall swing
> For behold there is death in the joke
> That squinteth at queen or at king. . . .
>
> . . . No more must ye laugh at an ass
> No more run on topers a rig
> Since Pitt gets as drunk as Dundas
> And Dundas gets as drunk as a pig.

The once great Pitt—whose money John Wolcot had been prepared to take—was drinking himself to death. With Dundas he
would appear staggering at Westminster and be helped to the
place where he sprawled on the Front Bench. The Leader of the
Opposition had declared a boycott on Parliament and never came
near the House. It was not even possible any more to respect one's
political enemies. They were bitter days for any man who had
believed in Parliamentary government. They were more bitter
still for a man who could no longer even respect himself.

When Wolcot had forecast in 1795 that he would be silenced
there can have been few, including himself, who believed that it
would ever happen. Yet 1796 saw without warning the torrent of
his satire against the Government dry up. To account, in part, for
this drought, there was of course the interval of six months in
1795 when nothing had been written that could appear in the
booksellers' in the New Year, but this was not enough to account
for the whole year that went by without a single word from Peter
Pindar.

Wieland's *Neuen teutschen Mercur* for April 29th, 1797, suggested satirically that he was 'an einem Halsübel erkrankt'—that he
was suffering from a disease of the throat brought on by a gift of
money. But Wolcot had, eventually, taken no money. The disease of the throat, if the simile may be continued, was a lump too

choking to be smiled away. He had estranged his closest friend, he had lost his self-respect. It was difficult, if not impossible, to recapture the fine notes of righteous contempt for a party whose sins were scarcely greater than his own. In the misery that was all of his own making he could not find it in his heart to make merry with the caricaturists at such natural targets for 1796 as the additional tax on wine and the new tax upon dogs.

That he was bitterly ashamed of his action may be assumed from the fact that he, who was so ready to make fun in his early days of the pension that might be offered to him, made no mention whatsoever of the pension that was his for the earning. His quarrel, too, with Taylor was significant. It was with Taylor and his love of solemn jesting that the whole trouble had started. Taylor of all his friends was the only man who knew the whole beastly business from beginning to end. In his corruption he had vented his spite on Taylor with an accusation of equal corruption that he must have known, in his inmost heart, to be untrue. In shame he quarrelled and in shame, his criticisms for the *Monthly Review* ended in February, he fled from London and his reputation before the fall. He made for the West Country. In August Dr Downman reported him in Exeter and making for Cornwall. And there in the calm of the Duchy, John Wolcot found something of himself again. The tensions eased; the strain relaxed. There came, even, one small piping note of verse: *The First Book of Chings* addressed to his friend the chymist and apothecary John Ching of New Bond Street. It consisted of a mere twenty-eight verses cast in Scriptural phraseology and referring to the miraculous effect of Ching's medicine 'on the king and his courtiers, on his captains over fifties and his captains over hundreds'. The fact that Ching had invented 'a medicine for the destroying of worms without prejudice to the constitution of the patient' and had presented a free supply to George III struck Wolcot, even in his misery, as being irresistibly comic. Since the poem does not appear in the *Collected Works* it was presumably regarded as substandard and perhaps, even, was never printed at all.

It shewed that Wolcot had turned the corner and was directing his footsteps once again along the old road. But it was a road that would never again be such a joy to tread.

13

THE way back proved by no means easy. After so great a crisis nothing could ever again be quite the same. Never again were there to be the joyous ebullient outbursts at Farmer George's follies. They belonged to the past. The old gaiety had gone into a decline and, in print at least, even though his satirical volumes began once again to appear at the booksellers', it never revived. His critic P. M. Zall writing from Cornell University in 1952 has noted that 'his popularity of the eighties and early nineties was never regained. In his engrossing programme of saving England from the Hanoverian, Peter had neglected the humorous little tales, the odd techniques of caricature and language-mangling that had been his trademark. Matter had become more important than manner.' It seems likely that this was because the manner of his own existence had altered; he was, in a sense, like one who having apparently completely recovered from the effects of a stroke is gradually seen by his friends to be only a walking shadow of the man he once was.

The first work that he published after his return was *One Thousand Seven Hundred and Ninety-Six*—an attack on Pitt, certainly, but an attack both listless and resigned: in the mock dialogue between Peter and Tom (the latter being a rising young satirist straight from the university and eager for reforms) it is almost as though in young Tom with his burning enthusiasm for attack and in Peter with his quiet elder-statesman air of disillusioned caution Wolcot is contrasting his old and his new self:

Cried Tom:

> Full of my mighty *self* from college down
> I rush to blaze a comet on the town!

To tear from Slavery's neck the galling chain
And raise a nabob fortune by my *brain*
On skins of hungry wolves, the courtiers, thrive
A Nimrod! leaving not a beast alive! . . . .

. . . Arm'd with the light'ning's pointed fire, my pen
Brand thou, my arm, black Guilt to open day!
Such are my projects!—how d'ye like 'em, pray?

Peter replied:

Nobly resolv'd! A pious resolution
Would Fortune kindly crown the execution.
But . . .

And there followed a long list of objections to the hopeless task of
ever uprooting Pitt from his position:

'I'll pour a broadside into courts . . .' [boasted Tom].
. . . 'Forbear,' [answered Peter].
'Court folly charms of all the eye and ear:
Sink it and Satire mourns his useless dart
While Ridicule, a bankrupt, breaks his heart. . . .'

So the cautionary dialogue continued, with the young man
growing wilder and Peter ever more restraining until:

PETER: Heav'ns! Tom, be cooler; take advice—
TOM: I won't—
Wilful will do't—my soul is fix'd upon't.
Ah, Peter, you're a *courtier.*
PETER: No such thing
I never drank at Adulation's spring.
TOM: No! Peter never dealt in praise!
PETER: I *have.*
There is a time ere *any* man's a knave—
Some start in youth, some sin at bald fourscore;
But known—the voice of Fame is heard no more. . . .

This sad, sick statement was the nearest he ever got to an apologia
and the volume ended on the same note of tired resignation:

Tom:	So then, you laugh at hopes of *reformation*?
Peter:	Pitt finds a tame old hack in our good nation
	Safe, through the dirt and ev'ry dangerous road
	The beast *consents* to bear his galling load
	And, spite of all that we can sing and say,
	Fools will be fools and ministers—betray.

The writing was clearly upon the wall for Peter Pindar's audience to read.

*　　　*　　　*　　　*　　　*

There were threads of his old social life to be picked up too. And while he was doing so there must have been many occasions for embarrassment—even though the news of Peter's Pension does not seem, at any rate at first, to have been very widely talked about—at meeting old colleagues in the struggle against the Government. And John Wolcot must have felt a terrible irony when the famous Polish patriot, General Kosciusko, came to England. For the great fighter sent a note from Sabloniere's Hotel in Leicester Fields to Peter Pindar, apologizing for not calling in person and asking the poet to visit him. And when Wolcot went, at once, he found Kosciusko lying on a sofa suffering from wounds which prevented him from rising. The reason, he said, for his summons was that while he had been imprisoned by the Czar in St Petersburg his gaoler had lent him a volume of Wolcot's works and he had been so impressed by the freedom with which the Great were treated in England and by the spirit of fearless Liberty that Peter Pindar represented that he determined that the doctor should be one of the first people he met when he came to England: now, at last, they were met. It is not difficult to imagine Wolcot's particular and private circle of Hell. Yet he constantly visited the general during his short stay in England and, on finally parting, presented him with a couple of his crayon landscapes. In return Kosciusko gave Wolcot 'a bottle of real Falernian, or what was said to be so, of which he had but a couple left'. Wolcot was to take wine with him in order that they might pledge each other in the wine of Horace.

Wolcot afterwards observed that the only notables who called on Kosciusko were Charles Fox and Mr Grey, 'so little sympathy did the fate of Poland excite in England'.

There were other, older friends to be sought out. In January 1797, when Farington called on Opie, Wolcot was there. In March his friend William Godwin married Mary Wollstonecraft and in September he called on Wolcot—who had just returned from Exeter—with the happy but illusory news that Mary had sufficiently recovered from the birth of their child for him to be able to leave the house and take a walk across the fields to Kensington. But these contacts apart there are, during the years 1797 and 1798, comparatively few references to social activities, although he seems to have struck up a fairly close acquaintanceship with the Duke of Hamilton.

Gradually, of course, the pain began to lessen and the memories mercifully to recede. And quite unchanged was his willingness to help and foster aspiring genius. In December he called on Sir Christopher Hawkins and was shewn some verses by a miller's daughter. 'I do not use the word "miller's" as an opprobrious epithet,' said Wolcot a little snobbishly, 'as I understand the father is a very respectable man. . . .' The verses seemed to shew more than an ordinary talent; moreover the girl had gone to the trouble of learning Latin, French and Italian. The poem that Sir Christopher shewed to Wolcot was a rather lengthy *Ode to Philosophy*; Wolcot noted that

'she seems to prefer things to words, substance to shadow, simplicity to affectation, in short a shirt without ruffles to ruffles without a shirt. I should like to see more of her poetical attempts and, if she wishes, make her known and put money in her pocket. There is on her a head of truly classic taste and if some lines of the Ode belong not to other Authors Miss Dennis will cut no mean figure on Parnassus—one line is particularly happy, viz.: "And make the mental desert bloom." '

However, when he repeated this line on Christmas Eve, at the Duke of Hamilton's, 'a Lady of much reading and great literary acquirements' agreed with Wolcot that it was beautiful, but believed that it was not original.

Wolcot wrote to Giddy asking for further specimens of her work; a correspondence arose on the subject and Wolcot went to considerable trouble to proffer her, through his old friend, sound advice:

'As for heroic measure I would not wish her to cultivate it, it is so difficult to manage in order to keep attention awake. . . . Bid her hunt nature for interesting objects (for nature abounds) and she can never be at a loss for a subject for her muse to work on—an Ode to Winter—to Summer, etc—to the sea—to the mountain—to the moon—to the sun—to Hesperus—to the bee—to the spider &c &c &c. . . .'

But he still had one eye on his pocket:

'If she wishes me to see more of her compositions—let them be directed to me (under a cover) addressed to his Grace the Duke of Hamilton &c Half-moon Street, Piccadilly, London, by which means I shall escape a good deal of postage.'

Of his own life he told Giddy:

'I go on in the usual tracks of rhyming, crowding and painting, steal out now and again among the little Great to enjoy a laugh and return much better pleased with my own humble station. To be what is termed a great man is, in my opinion, to be damned before one is dead.'

Some of his painting, in fact, received about this time the accolade of being published when Samuel Alken produced a set of six Aquatints of Wolcot's Landscapes of Bristol, Penzance, Plymouth and Fowey, with Poetical Inscriptions.

Not many of Wolcot's original drawings survive. There is a crayon drawing of 'Perdita' Robinson in Bristol which has been described by a competent modern critic as 'a work shewing sensibility but slight in character'. From a mid-Victorian writer it might be supposed that he anticipated the Impressionists:

'When seen near the eye [the drawings] seem to be composed only of random scratches and masses of black chalk of different densities and depths of that colour; with here and there a streak and blot of white and others of red. There did not appear to be any defined objects such as a tree, house, figure, etc but when viewed as a whole . . . each of them appeared to be a landscape representing morning or evening in which the dark and light of the sky and the foreground, hills, trees, towers etc could be made out by the fancy in the smallest space of time allowed for the imagination to come into play; and then the effect was certainly very good and a surprise to the beholder. . . .'

As far as rhyming was concerned his second production for 1797 was an *Ode to the Livery of London on their Petition to His Majesty for kicking out his worthy Ministers*—a gently sardonic work the first part of which ended:

> Thus is Politeness turn'd clown—
> Wisdom in gothic gloom benighted
> The world turn'd fairly upside down,
> I fear me, never to be righted.
> When such things are 'mongst cobblers, tinkers, tanners
> The Lord have mercy on the people's manners.
> Then, sirs, no more your wanton venom spit
> At kings and queens and worthy Master Pitt.
> Should the ship founder in this blowing weather
> Like friends and neighbours let us sink together.

The volume however is greatly lightened by the most human tale of the married couple who after a desperate quarrel over nothing at all angrily placed in the middle of their double bed a board between them:

> . . . Two, three, four nights the sulky pair
> Like two still mice, devoid of care,
> In philosophic silence sought repose;
> On the fifth morn it chanc'd to please
> John's nose to sneeze—
> 'God bless you, dear!' quoth Joan at John's loud nose.

184

At this John gave a sudden start
And, popping o'er the hedge his head,—
'Joan, did you say it from your *heart*?'
'Yes, John, I *did*, indeed, indeed!'
'You *did*?'—'Yes, John, upon my word'—
'Zounds, Joan, then take away the board!'

'Thus it will be with you and Pitt agen . . .' he told the Liverymen. He was, it appears, recovering his spirit, but the increased spate of prosecutions for sedition must have made it difficult to persuade the booksellers to take the risk of publishing the old sort of lampoons on those in authority which had made him famous. Peter Pindar must now tilt at smaller fry such as Sir Joseph Banks whose appointment to the Privy Council gave a splendid opportunity for letting imagination run riot on the subject of the President of the Royal Society in attendance at a meeting of the Council:

While Pitt harangues on Spain and France
Sir Joseph's on a beetle's brain
A fly, a toad, a tadpole's tail:
While Pitt is on the emperor's loan
For Britain's jaws so hard a bone
Sir Joseph's on a weed and snail!

And when a moth flies into the Council Chamber, Sir Joseph of course is away leaping after it, upsetting benches and statesmen in the chase.

There were signs however that readers felt that, quantitatively at least, they were not getting their money's worth. His bookseller had assured him 'with a most solemn countenance', said Wolcot, 'that the public expect more for their half-crown than was provided'. So, for better measure, he threw in a *Jeremiad* to George Rose, to whose papers he had so recently been a modest contributor. Since the Government had declared

That Peter shall not laugh at queens and kings
Permit me, gentle George, to laugh at thee.

Permissible—and saleable—subjects became increasingly hard to

find, and in fact 1798, a year of greatly increased political persecution, saw no essentially political publications by Wolcot.
Instead there was *Tales of the Hoy*, an entertainment in a form, as
he admitted, 'borrowed from Chaucer who borrowed his hint
from the Decameron of Boccaccio who borrowed *his* hint from
the *Cento Novelle Antiche*'. It consisted of a gallimaufry of songs,
parodies, anecdotes and epigrams strung together by dialogue and
presided over by the captain of a hoy carrying passengers from
Margate to London. Many of the songs were of an impeccably
patriotic nature, and one at least Wolcot himself set to music.
This song—*Tom Halliard*—was of a frankly sentimental character
and much to the popular taste of the time:

> From the main deck to the quarter
> Strew'd with limbs and wet with blood
> Poor Tom Halliard, pale and wounded
> Crawl'd where his brave captain stood.
>
> 'O, my noble captain! tell me
> Ere I'm borne a corpse away
> Have I done a seaman's duty
> On this great and glorious day?
>
> Tell a dying sailor truly
> For my life is fleeting fast
> Have I done a seaman's duty?
> Can there aught my mem'ry blast? . . .'

The continued political repression and the many attacks upon
the liberty of the Press were no doubt responsible for Wolcot
busying himself with the production of an edition of Mathew
Pilkington's *Dictionary of Painters* which, his enemies alleged, he
'spoiled with his coarse comments'. But his graceful appreciation
of Richard Wilson of whose major paintings he owned at least
five examples is certainly a model of eighteenth-century art
criticism[1]—urbane and informed and, at the same time, quite
contrary to the then fashionable opinion of the painter.

---

[1] *See* Appendix A.

John Wolcot was enjoying himself again. And after Elizabeth Fry had been to see him she was able to write:

'I had a pleasant, merry day with Peter Pindar.'

$$\star \quad \star \quad \star \quad \star \quad \star$$

All the same the sky of his new life was not entirely free from clouds. Already there had been, inevitably, a dispute with the booksellers over the interpretation of the hastily drawn terms of his annuity. Equity, in the opinion of at least one of his contemporaries, was clearly upon his side in the contention that the booksellers had merely bought the existing copyrights and an option on future works. After all, ten years' purchase at the age of sixty was only £2500 at the rate of Wolcot's pension. And it was pointed out that 'in our own time £3000 have been given for a single poem'.

An action at Common Law was begun and followed soon after by a suit in Chancery. The legal details are not available— the case dragged on in the customary eighteenth-century manner until 1801—but Wolcot's interpretation of the agreement was eventually upheld, and for the rest of his life the annuity was paid with a satisfying regularity, first by the Robinsons and after their deaths by Walker. But according to one of Wolcot's obituarists,

'much *skirmishing* constantly took place on these occasions; and when the receipt was presented at the end of every six months, many angry words passed so that Peter was at last obliged to employ the good offices of a third person to transact the business. On these occasions he was particularly bitter, being accustomed to send most offensive messages which the good sense of his friends of course either softened or suppressed.'

> Much like St Paul (who solemnly protests
> He battled hard at Ephesus with *beasts*)
> I've fought with lion's monkeys, bulls and bears
> And got half Noah's Ark about my ears:
> Nay worse (which all the courts of justice know)
> Fought with the *brutes* of Paternoster Row.

187

Like many a successful writer he had always professed a humorous enmity for his publishers, and now this affectation was heightened by his legal quarrel. He was reported to have attended a dinner 'along with a number of literary men at the house of a very spirited publisher'. It happened that 'our host was suddenly called out on some particular business, immediately after the cloth was removed. A long and awful pause ensued at the close of which it was proposed to drink the health of the bookseller at whose table we were then seated.

' "No!" exclaimed honest Peter, rising and at the same time brandishing a bottle of red Port in his hand. "No! let us drink a bumper to our own, for this is author's blood."

'The effect was electric and his advice was instantly followed amidst shouts of applause.'

On another occasion when John Wolcot called on a book-seller in Paternoster Row to enquire about his sales he was asked to take wine with the publisher and consented to 'a little negus as an innocent morning beverage'. The drink was served to him in a coconut goblet carved with a man's face.

'Eh! Eh! What have we here?' exclaimed Wolcot.

'A man's skull—a poet's for what I know!'

'Nothing more likely for it is universally known that all booksellers drink their wine from our skulls.' This seems to have been the beginning of a joke that Wolcot often repeated. Even Samuel Smiles of all people writes, 'I remember Peter Pindar saying one of the few times I ever met him that the booksellers drank their wine in the manner of the heroes in the halls of Odin out of authors' skulls.'[1]

* * * * *

But booksellers were necessary evils and in 1799 they published for Wolcot *Nil Admirari*, an attack upon Bishop Porteous and Miss Hannah More. The celebrated Blue-stocking had aroused Peter Pindar's derision by her *Strictures on Female Education*, a tract which referred to the harm done to youthful minds by un-expurgated editions of the poets. Wolcot might very well have

[1] But it is just possible that his memory was at fault for at the time of Wolcot's death Smiles was only seven years old.

let such a work pass quietly by among the other outpourings of the presses if it had not been that the work was praised by Bishop Porteous in terms that seemed to the poet to be somewhat extravagant.

The fact that he did not let it pass was to give rise to a really classic scandal in the London literary world at the turn of the century.

> 'Extraordinary and versatile talents [intoned Porteous] . . . such a fund of good sense, of wholesome counsel, of sagacious observation, of a knowledge of the world and of the female heart, of high toned morality and genuine Christian piety; and all this enlivened with such richness of imagery such variety and felicity of allusion, such neatness and elegance of diction, as are not I conceive, easily to be found combined and blended together in any other work in the English language.'

Total sales of her tracts had amounted in the first year to the respectable figure of two millions which, the bishop thought, helped 'very considerably to counteract the poison of those impious and immoral pamphlets . . . dispersed over the kingdom in such numbers by infidels and republicans'.

Wolcot, in fact, was inclined to blame Miss More less than the bishop:

> Hads't thou not fondly dragg'd Miss Hannah forth
> Plac'd her on high, and cried, 'Behold a wonder!'
> No soul had scrutinized the woman's worth
> Safe from the world her weakness and thy blunder.

> . . . I censure not Miss Hannah for sad prose—
> I censure not Miss Hannah for sad rhymes.
> God sees my heart! I only censure those
> Whose flatteries damn the judgment of the times. . . .

And he even suggested that Porteous had an interest in this flattery, that he was in fact largely the author of the *Strictures*. The bishop reacted strongly. The attack was 'a piece of gross and coarse ribaldry, rancour and profaneness', qualities which today it is not easy to read into *Nil Admirari* 'My crime,' wrote Porteous indignantly to Hannah, 'is too much complacency: yours is too great asperity.'

But quite apart from the storm of which the book sounded the first distant rumble it is interesting for its postscript. How long it has been the amiable habit of publishers to prevail upon their authors to provide their own 'blurbs' is not clear. It is possible that John Wolcot was starting something when he wrote:

> 'As I am destitute of friends among the Periodical Reviewers of Literature, I confess my fears of foul treatment, and tremble for this my youngest offspring; which in a moment of spleen or ignorance may be put to death by the tomahawk of criticism.
>
> Now as charity begins at home, and as every man is entitled to as much justice from himself as from his neighbour I have *sans cérémonie* given a free and impartial account of my own pamphlet. . . .'

The account was in the best style of author's modest self-praise. 'Executed in the poet's happiest manner . . . told with neatness precision and humour . . . tempered with a pleasantry that tickles even while it seems to wound . . .' These are phrases that would hardly be out of place on a modern publisher's book-jacket.

But the reviewers were not to be mollified and the reception of *Nil Admirari* was by no means entirely favourable. Wrote the critic of the *Monthly Mirror* for November 1799, '. . . we think the bulk so futile and nugatory, pointless and barren of amusement as to deserve no notice at all'.

Had Wolcot merely contented himself with making fun of the bishop and Miss More it is likely that the matter would have rested there and that the effects of *Nil Admirari* would have been short-lived. But in it Wolcot had also started the first of a series of satires against his fellow writers and the preliminary skirmishes were joined, and the jockeying for positions took place, for an epic struggle that was soon to explode upon the town.

14

THE first of his fellow writers to feel the lash was Thomas James Mathias, referred to in a footnote to *Nil Admirari* as

'This poor little wretch whose pamphlet misnomered Pursuits of Literature but whose true appellation should have been Pursuits of Rancour dared not acknowledge his own work. The enormity of its falsehood and impudence was quite a novelty and in spite of its contemptible imbecility gained the attention of the public. This Mathias mistook for fame; still he denied any connexion with the pamphlet—every paltry subterfuge was made use of to escape detection. At length a few literary hounds seriously pursued him, hunted him fairly to his hole and put the vermin to death.'

Nor was the verse to which this footnote appended any less violent for it began:

> Behold this human snake or human toad
> Sly, 'mid the windings of his murky hole.

Really, Wolcot cannot have been surprised when Mathias retaliated in kind. In Peter Pindar's own words in a postscript to his next work, *Lord Auckland's Triumph or the Death of Crim. Con.*

'Little Mister Mathias, the son of a cobbler (says Fame) nevertheless a rhime-monger and critic united in hostility against me with little squinting Master Aesop Gifford . . . and fearful of their own abilities . . . united themselves with a young gentleman cleped Master Canning. . . . Still to strengthen the phalanx the aforesaid three young gentlemen made a further union with a young gentleman who received the *best* part of his education at that long-established seminary celebrated for turning out as well as turning off genius of every description, called Newgate. Further still to augment their force, the aforesaid young gentlemen united with a fifth, the *élève* of little Aesop (Lord Belgrave). . . . This formidable association with the motto *Vis unita fortior* on their banners, having completed a battery called the *Anti-Jacobin Magazine and Review* for the purpose of confounding the enemies of their country, supporting the cause of literature and getting into lucrative employments, opened their fire on my poor pamphlet. . . .'

But, in this, as will be seen, John Wolcot was making a very vital, though understandable, mistake.

Certainly the *Review* for November 1799 trounced *Nil Admirari* severely. Though it started off in a sufficiently dignified manner:

'The maxim of ancient Satyrists was *dicere de vitiis, parcere personis*' . . . the reviewer soon came down from this level to talk about Wolcot's 'prostituted muse whose language and sentiments are those of the lowest street-walker in the purlieus of Parnassus'. Vicious Peter had dared to attack 'the two most spotless characters in the Kingdom'. He was, the writer declared contemptuously, one of those authors whose

'wretched productions of perverted genius or incorrigible dullness, particularly if seasoned with a tolerable sprinkling of abuse of virtuous and elevated characters, first attract the applause of some fool of fashion whose ideas are kindly adopted by his associates, then become the topic of conversation in the circle of roundheads[1] at Ridgeways or Debretts and from those *pure* authorities receive the stamp of general currency. . . .'

The review also talked about Wolcot as 'the profligate priest whose conversation exhibits a disgusting mixture of obscenity

[1] Cf. 'egghead' as a twentieth-century right-wing term of abuse.

and blasphemy'. He was moreover a 'monster in human shape' who wished to take a 500-year lease on life the better to indulge his sensual appetites, and who in this connection had blasphemously exclaimed 'God blast death! I could spit in God's face for inventing death!' And so on through six closely printed pages. For good measure the last page of the issue of the *Anti-Jacobin Magazine and Review* published 'Stanzas Addressed to the Muse of the falsely and self-named Peter Pindar' which began :

> Twas in a dark and treacherous hour
> Curst, inauspicious, crabbed, sour
> Thy mother brought thee forth
> At sight of thee the midwife squall'd
> And terrified the attendants call'd
> To view the horrid birth

and ended:

> Each true-born Briton views thy fall
> With eye prophetic; aye and all
> The loyal sing Te Deum
> Thy vulgar thoughts and low-bred wit
> For *Cloacina's* temple fit
> There find their *Mausoleum*.

According to a later correspondent in the same magazine the effect of the November issue was gratifying:

> 'That animated philippic stung him to the quick. It drove him almost to madness and drew from him such horrible execrations as terrified all who heard him. He had never before met with so powerful an adversary and he sunk under his correcting hand.'

It is possible that there is an element of wishful thinking in this. Wolcot was certainly angry with William Gifford, but he was far from sunk.

In his postscript to *Lord Auckland's Triumph*, during the recitation of the manner in which Mathias, Canning and Gifford had come together, Wolcot expatiated in return on William

Gifford's character. Formerly a cobbler of Ashburton in Devonshire—it will be remembered that at Truro many years earlier Cookesley had traded, with Giddy, Gifford's work for Wolcot's —he had become, so Wolcot asserted, tutor to Lord Grosvenor's son, lampoonist and betrayer of his friends and benefactors, swindler and pimp to his Lordship. His verse was so flatulent, Wolcot added, that his Muse must have eaten a dish of peas before getting down to work. 'Truth and Candour are the deities at whose shrine I sacrifice,' declared Peter Pindar, a trifle pompously, 'or may I resemble

> A poor, mean, sneaking, literary shrimp!
> Lie like M—s and like G—d p——!'

Whether this was true or not it was, as it happens, entirely beside the point. For the fact is that William Gifford and Mathias and Canning and the rest of them had nothing whatsoever to do with the *Anti-Jacobin Magazine and Review*. They had founded in 1797, some two years before the appearance of *Nil Admirari*, a journal called the *Anti-Jacobin or Weekly Examiner*. It had survived for about eight months and had then ceased publication. Contemporaneously with its disappearance John Richard Green had launched the *Anti-Jacobin Magazine and Review*. Though its policy was the same as that of Gifford's defunct *Examiner* there was no connection between the two similarly titled journals. And to add to the literary confusion into which others besides Wolcot fell[1] John Richard Green assumed the name of John Gifford.

★   ★   ★   ★   ★

Quite unconscious of the monumental misunderstanding that was piling up Wolcot went about his normal life. On Boxing Day, 1799, his old friend 'Perdita' Robinson died. Wolcot had visited her during her last illness and had spoken to her some words of rather doubtful consolation. Now she was buried at Old Windsor: 'the funeral was attended only by

---

[1] The *Encyclopaedia Britannica* (14th edn.?) in its article on William Gifford perpetuates the error.

two literary friends greatly valued by the deceased, whose friendship and benevolence had cheered her when living and followed her to the grave'. Gifford had accused Mrs Robinson of relying upon Peter as her 'flash-man' and warning her that she would find him a broken reed. Yet by going to Old Windsor with William Godwin, John Wolcot shewed himself faithful to the end. And for the living he was active, too. January and February 1800 found him enthusiastically lobbying, writing to Farington to urge his support, pressing Opie to use his influence, in the cause of a man named Spilsberry of Snow Hill who wished to become printer to the Royal Academy.

He was active, too, in his club life. There is a glimpse of him reported by a guest at a Jacobinical political society known as an Oyster Club, of which Wolcot was one of the leading spirits.

There were about twenty people present who after supper gathered round the fire. Punch was served in large rummer glasses and there was a good deal of telling of jokes and stories, many of them political and often a little vulgar into the bargain. One of the members who was called upon for a song told the company that a few days earlier Dr Wolcot had called at his chambers, and after he had left a manuscript had been found on the floor—it was inferred that it had been written and dropped by the doctor. The finder had set the song to music and would sing it.

It began:

> 'God bless all good kings and queens
> If such there be
> But if it should please Him to damn them all
> 'Twere all the same to me.'

There followed a jocular narrative in verse about George III selling rotten mutton to a butcher in Windsor and about the meanness of the queen in washing her own lace. Each stanza had the verse quoted above as a chorus in which everybody joined with gusto. The visitor came away with 'the lowest possible estimation of the social and moral character of the party'. But he had to admit that 'Dr Wolcot and a few others were rather more staid and well-behaved than the rest'.

The pace was quickening. In April the apocryphal account by 'Anti-Sordes' of the infant Wolcot's fall from his nurse's arms (to which reference has already been made) appeared in John Gifford's *Anti-Jacobin Magazine and Review*, and another, anonymous versifier anticipated his ultimate fate:

> O'er Peter's lone, deserted tomb
> Shall withered hags and wizards strew
> Each poisonous herb of deadliest bloom
> And rifle all the stores of woe.
>
> There kindred ghosts shall oft appear
> To fill with shrieks the ghastly grove
> And fiends of death assemble there
> To hail the Rhymer whom they love.
>
> Gaunt Blasphemy shall there be seen . . .

The rest of the poem was in similar strain. And in May the same magazine, reviewing a book on *The Infidel Societies of the Metropolis*, cried:

> 'Let that miscreant Peter Pindar contemplate, in these pages, with the malignant exultation of a fiend, a sight congenial to his heart; let him here behold a determined band of followers fully prepared to reduce principles to practice. Not that his name appears in the list of authors encouraged by these societies, but because his works intended to hold up to public derision the sacred characters of our Sovereign and our Prelates are eminently calculated to serve their cause and to aid the circulation of their tenets.'

If Wolcot noticed this at all he, no doubt, chalked it up, again mistakenly, against the score of William Gifford. The Pursuit of Literature, too, he thought to be partly Gifford's work. Nor was the confusion entirely one-sided: in the Critical Review an attack appeared on William Gifford which he thought mistakenly to be by Wolcot.

In June *Lord Auckland's Triumph* was published with Peter

Pindar prophesying an end to adultery if the Postmaster-General'
Bill became law:

> Auckland will give a deathful blow
> To some sad purlieus of Soho
> No longer there shall lofty beds of down
> Expect the muffled married dame
> And blushless youth of lawless flame
> Secure from husbands and the prying town.

He gave the names of a number of society pimps and salacious
publishers who would be put out of business but, as it happened,
Lord Auckland's Bill, like two other similar and earlier attempts,
by the Duke of Athol and the Bishop of Durham, failed to
convince Parliament that a private sin should be made subject to
the criminal law.

And of course it contained his violent postscript against
Gifford. Coming after months of a slowly developing hatred it
was altogether too much. Furiously Gifford sat down to write an
Epistle to Peter Pindar. Quite unaware of the approaching storm,
John Wolcot wrote happily to Giddy, in June:

> 'I still proceed in the rhyme and painting line which
> affords me all my amusement. I am attached to the great city
> and shall never leave it except for Bath the common re-
> ceptacle of Bachelors and Old Maids. My chief difficulty
> now is to select my pleasures for the day which has really
> been the case for a dozen years past. Providence has given me
> a very easy berth in life; how long this happy organization
> will continue I know not; I could wish to carry it in its present
> condition into the two thousand century; for I am as rapacious
> of life as Dr Johnson.
> The academic exhibition is a hungry one. No historical
> exertions. The landscape painters I think carry it. Opie has a
> good picture or two but finding it necessary to colour high
> like the rest of his rivals in order to be seen the modesty of
> Nature is greatly outstepped. It is a misfortune that will not
> be remedied so that the Institution will really undo the art.
> The death of Sir Joshua Reynolds made a great chasm in the

annual exhibition. He came like an amazing flash of lightning and in disappearing rendered the darkness more visible. He was of the highest order of genius. We have nothing like him now—*quod petis est nusquam.*'

Wolcot was sixty-two. One by one his old friends were disappearing. This was the last letter he was to write to his old roistering fellow-student Thomas Giddy. His enemies were growing in number and gaining in strength. In a note to correspondents at the end of the June volume of the *Anti-Jacobin Magazine and Review* John Richard Green sounded the warning:

'We have received a note respecting that miscreant Peter Pindar and it is with great reluctance we have been compelled to postpone for a month the chastisement we have prepared for him, on account of his new compilation of impudent falsehoods which is without exception the most atrocious libel we ever perused. We think, indeed, that it cannot fail to subject him to the lash of the law; our Correspondent may rest assured that we shall not relax in our efforts to exhibit this wretched Poetaster to the world in his true colours.'

And in July 1800 the *Anti-Jacobin* reviewed *Lord Auckland's Triumph.*

*   *   *   *   *

Although it would have been too much to expect from the *Anti-Jacobin* a reasoned review of any of Wolcot's work, its notice of *Lord Auckland's Triumph* really went almost as far as eighteenth-century literary criticism might be expected to go. The irony of the work was, in a manner not uncommon to the reading public, overlooked. The book was described as 'a hideous lump of ribaldry, obscenity and falsehood'. But the writer was not greatly concerned with the work itself; he was more anxious to score points in a personal attack upon its author. In particular he seized on Peter Pindar's claim to be a reformed character:

> Yes, I was once a sinner, I confess
> But now my morals wear a *sober* dress.

198

Had this been the case, exclaimed the *Anti-Jacobin*, the man would have been spared even though his writing was attacked. But this claim to sobriety was simply untrue:

'We will just recall to his memory his late visit to a favourite bookseller where his reception was such as to have disgusted any man who had one atom of feeling about him though it did not prevent Peter from *begging* a dinner from him; the scene which ensued we shall not minutely describe; suffice it to say the bard got beastly drunk with his favourite beverage, brandy, which he blasphemously denominated *the liquid Messiah* and when a prostitute with whom he had made an appointment for the purpose called to take him to the play he was unable to accompany her and was left to sleep off the fumes of the spirit in the corner of the warehouse where he lay lifeless as a bale of damaged goods. Such is the sober dress which the morals of Peter Pindar are still accustomed to wear. . . .'

Wolcot, still under the spell of his original mistake, naturally attributed this story, which may or may not have had an element of truth in it, to William Gifford. And it was William Gifford who, angered by the Postscript to *Lord Auckland's Revenge*, had, in fact, published in July the abusive and libellous *Epistle to Peter Pindar*:

> Come then, all filth, all venom as thou art
> Rage in thy eye and rancour in thy heart
> Come with thy boasted arms, spite, malice, lies
> Smut, scandal, execrations, blasphemies;
> I brave 'em all. Lo, here I fix my stand,
> And dare the utmost of thy tongue and hand,
> Prepared each threat to baffle, or to spurn,
> Each blow with ten-fold vigour to return.

The poem, from which extracts have earlier been quoted, dealt only with Wolcot's life until he arrived in London and as such would have been, even if true, which it was demonstrably not, rather *vieux jeu*. It consisted of a continual stream of abuse and vilification, utterly devoid of humour, failing even, in its desire for revenge, to make its subject appear ridiculous:

> But what is he that with a Mohawk's air
> 'Cries havoc and lets slip the dogs of war'?
> A bloated mass, a gross, unkneaded clod
> A foe to man, a renegade from God,
> From noxious childhood to pernicious age
> Sacred to infamy through every stage. . . .

One couplet was thought, even by reviewers friendly to Gifford, to be so unprintably indecent that it was omitted in later editions. The notes were hardly less vindictive than the text and threatened that if William Gifford were further provoked he would bring the disgusting story up to date. For, he held in his hand, so he said, a letter from an officer who had assisted in kicking Wolcot out of Maker Camp because of his scandalous indecencies there.

It is fairly clear from his introduction that William Gifford was aware that this was not the stuff of which first-class satire was compounded, for he admitted that there could be two objections made to the *Epistle*, 'its severity and its unvarying tone of reprobation', but these were justified by the fact that Wolcot had to be 'cut to the bone' before he would wince and that his life presented 'a horrid monotony' of evil-doing and depravity.

'Pause from thy pains and take my closing word;' William Gifford ended angrily:

> *Thou* canst not think nor have I power to tell
> How much I SCORN and HATE thee—so farewell.

The *Anti-Jacobin* welcomed this *Epistle* with pleasure:

> '. . . one of the most able and animated productions which we have perused for a long time . . . displays all the *nerve* and *spirit* which so strongly characterize the prose-writings of this distinguished author . . . the thanks of every virtuous man is due to the writer of this spirited *Epistle*. . . .'

But it is fair to point out that not all the reviews were as favourable. For Wolcot there was no alternative; he must retaliate to this appalling attack. But even while he was contemplating what action he should take William Gifford began to advertise for some back numbers of *The Times* in which, twelve years earlier, Wolcot had been rather obscurely accused of indecency. The first charge had appeared on March 19th, 1788:

> 'There is no palace into which foul things sometimes intrude not; witness the *Pages*. And there is actually a *Kitchen Rat* at Buckingham-House that was caught about twelve months since, in a trap with *Peter Pindar* in the *Bird-Cage Walk*, but let loose again on condition of amendment. If this same rat and Peter Pindar continue their disloyal and ******** intercourse let them beware.'

Then, on March 26th, followed:

> 'We advise *Peter Pindar*, alias the Cornish Apothecary, alias the Plantation Parson, alias the low *doer* of a fallen print, to restrain his goose's quill against the loyalty of other prints, and recollect that though his doggerel is too contemptible for notice—plain prose, his itch for treason, and the *Bird-Cage Walk* may endanger his ears.'

And again on March 28th:

> 'The impudence of the *Bird-Cage Walk* hero in the fallen print the *damnation* of which his stupidity has completed is very much in the style of this motley renegade—half apothecary, half parson.'

Such were the paragraphs that William Gifford was trying to find, but while he was waiting for a reply to his advertisement he received a letter from Wolcot which besides calling him an 'infamous rascal' threatened him with personal injury. Gifford at once published a second edition of his *Epistle* to which he appended a copy of Wolcot's letter. There was nothing left for

Wolcot, as a man of honour, to do, but, now that his threat was made public, to carry words into action.

And on August 18th, 1800, there took place what was subsequently described as the *Battle of the Bards*.

*   *   *   *   *

William Gifford was known to be in the habit of going every morning to the Piccadilly shop of his publisher Mr Wright, the leading political bookseller of the day. And it was there that John Wolcot sought him out. Gifford, according to Sir Walter Scott, was 'a little man dumpled up altogether and so ill-made as to seem almost deformed'. At least two other of his contemporaries have described this deformity which made him almost a hunch-back; as Wolcot himself put it, he was 'a fellow in the shape of a letter Z'. Wolcot on the other hand was big and burly and clearly all the odds (except that of age for Gifford was then forty-eight years old) in the struggle must have been on Peter Pindar. Wright was away from London at the time, but his two assistants—one was Peltier, a French journalist, and the other probably William Upcott—were there when Wolcot came striding into the shop. William Gifford was sitting reading a newspaper when the doctor accosted him.

'Sir, is your name Gifford?'

On being answered 'Yes!' Peter said, 'You are the fellow I have been looking for,' raised his cane and struck Gifford over the head.

But then something went wrong. The incredible happened. Sickly and deformed as Gifford was he managed to wrench the stick from Wolcot's hands and gave the doctor two terrible blows across the head. He was about to deliver a third when the bookseller's assistants intervened and hustled Wolcot out into the street. In the ignominious struggle his hat and wig had been lost and before the door was locked upon him they were flung contemptuously out into the mud of the gutter. The cane Gifford retained as a trophy of his victory.

Utterly humiliated, John Wolcot stood gasping there in Piccadilly; the blood streaming from his head attracted a mob of hackney coachmen, watermen and paviours. To anyone who would listen he blurted out his version of the case and then with a troop of boys jeering at his heels he made his way shamefacedly to a surgeon in St James's Street to have his wounds treated. After which, so it was said, 'he slunk home with his crack'd pate beplastered and bepatched like an old paper lantern'.

John Taylor, passing by the shop soon after the fracas, saw blood still wet upon the window, and on enquiring learned with sorrow that it was that of his old friend.

★　　★　　★　　★　　★

It is hardly possible, at this moment of complete ignominy, not to be sorry for John Wolcot. Ageing and surrounded by enemies, with the knowledge that there would be great numbers of those lesser men who had envied his fame and power and success who would be gloating at the toppling of the dreaded Peter Pindar from his pedestal, no very vivid imagination is needed to imagine the depths of shame and misery he must have reached that night alone in his lodgings off Portland Place. It was essential to do something to restore a little of his pride. The reasons for his defeat must be put before the public. There would be those who believed them. Perhaps, in time, he even came to believe them himself. He at once wrote a letter to the *Morning Chronicle* and delivered it so that it was in the issue of the following day. He had attacked Gifford and then had been disarmed by those in the shop, receiving in the struggle and while he was being hampered a blow from his adversary. Breaking loose from those who sought to restrain him he had weighed in with his fists *à la Mendoza* to such effect that he had driven Gifford to the other end of the shop. But then his hands had been seized and by superior force he was hustled out into the street where the door was locked against him. In vain he had sought to get into the shop again, but he had succeeded only in throwing in a letter which had been written before the encounter and the delivery of which, after the débâcle, seems singularly inappropriate:

'As there are certain expressions that require only a little of the severity of satire by way of a corrective, so there are others of so malignant a nature as to demand a horsewhip instead of words. Had you possessed something more of the human form I should have treated you as a man; but as things are you must be contented to be whipped as a malicious monkey.'

According to Wolcot he had then retired to the house of a friend—possibly this may have been the surgeon in St James's Street—and after about an hour had returned to Wright's shop to finish the affair; but the door was still locked, and Gifford, as he believed, still inside. He asked the shop assistant, who refused to admit him, to inform Mr Gifford that he could depend on every castigation due to his calumny and that in spite of his *noble* supporters he, Wolcot, would try to accomplish it.

'Gifford has given out, [wrote Wolcot], as a matter of triumph, that he possesses my cane and he means to preserve it as a trophy. Let me recommend an inscription for it. "The Cane of Justice with which I, William Gifford, late Cobbler of Ashburton, have been soundly drubbed for my infamy".'

That at any rate was John Wolcot's story, and it was one that he maintained among his friends as well as in the press. Some at least of his friends rallied to him. Mr Phillips, the bookseller in St Paul's Churchyard and editor of the *Monthly Magazine*, evidently sent round a note of condolence immediately for only two days after the fiasco Wolcot wrote to him:

'Dear sir,
    I am much obliged by your friendly intentions. It was but a fair piece of justice due to my character as a man to attack at any disadvantages such a calumniating ruffian as Gyfford [*sic*] the instant he came within the reach of my vengeance. Had not Wright and his customers and his Frenchman and his shopmen hustled me and wrestled the cane from my hand and then confined my arms I should have done complete justice to my cause. As it was he had a smart

204

taste of what he will experience in future whenever I find him. Such a pest of society ought to be driven from its bosom. . . .'

That this letter was written with one eye on posterity may be inferred from the fact that it is endorsed:
'Should you think this of importance enough to publish you have my free leave.'

John Taylor seems also to have rallied round, but the fact that he pointed out to Wolcot the mistake that he had made between the two Giffords and the two Anti-Jacobin journals does not seem to have led to any immediate resumption of their friendship.

In after years when the smart had gone out of the memory of that disastrous day, Wolcot 'often confessed he mistook his man. . . . He used however pleasantly to say that they both deserved it and therefore "it was all one".'

★   ★   ★   ★   ★

The reverberations of the Battle of the Bards were long in dying away. Not unnaturally several satires were produced at the expense of the satirists. The Irish poet, Thomas Dermody, wrote under the pseudonym of Mauritius Moonshine a mock heroic epic on the subject which contained the memorable couplet referring to Wolcot's first stroke on Gifford's head:

> His sconce impenetrable scorn'd a wound
> But hollow rang and gave a mournful sound.

In the literary world opinions were fairly equally divided. William Cobbett at the time approved the *Epistle* with the words: 'Pindar is politically and poetically defunct. Never did any writing produce so good and sudden an effect. . . .' But looking back on it sixteen years later he decried the attack and thought it had affected the sales of at least one of Wright's publications to those who did not wish to be associated with Gifford. To some the *Epistle* was couched too much in the language of Billingsgate, to others Gifford's strictures were well justified. Polwhele, on the other hand, writing in 1831, was sure that Wolcot was not the aggressor for 'in Satire Gifford was a Juvenal, Wolcot a Horace'.

And in sections of the public other than the purely literary the reactions were lively and lasting as Wolcot found one evening when strolling along Titchfield Street he saw the diminutive figure of Nollekens the sculptor leaning over his gate.

'Why, Nollekens,' said Wolcot, 'you never speak to me now; pray what is the reason?'

'Why, you have published such lies of the king and had the impertinence to send them to me, but Mrs Nollekens burnt them and I desire you'll send no more; the Royal Family are very good to me and are great friends to all the artists, and I don't like to hear anybody say anything against them.'

Wolcot placed his cane gently on the sculptor's shoulder. 'Well said, little Nolly! I like the man who sticks to his friend; you shall make a bust of me for that.'

'I'll see you damned first,' replied Nollekens, 'and I can tell you this besides, no man in the Royal Academy but Opie would have painted your picture; and you richly deserved the broken head you got in Wright's shop. Mr Cook of Bedford Square shewed me his handkerchief dipped in your blood, and so now you know my mind.' He called to his dog, 'Come in, my Cerberus, come in.' The dog followed him in and he left the doctor at the gate which he then barred up for the night.

The extent that the Battle of the Bards had taken hold on the popular imagination must have been considerable. A handkerchief dipped in Wolcot's blood as a memento of the occasion indicates partisanship on a considerable scale.

15

PHYSICAL violence was ended, but for some further time the wordy battle continued. John Taylor, a genial and friendly man himself and wishing all his friends to agree together, wrote in later years:

'When the matter was understood by both parties all enmity was at an end. I succeeded in making them send amicable enquiries as to the health of each other.' But this was clearly wishful thinking. Enmity was by no means at an end. William Gifford produced a third edition of his *Epistle to Peter Pindar* and included the scabrous advertisements from *The Times*. This was, of course, warmly welcomed by John Gifford in the *Anti-Jacobin*. Though he admitted that it was unusual to review a subsequent edition of a work already noticed, yet Peter Pindar's fall

'ought to be regarded as a matter of national importance. When a petty culprit expiates his crimes a simple record of the fact may suffice; but when a *Cartouche* feels the sword of justice, when after a long series of unheard of atrocities the hoary miscreant is dragged backwards from his den and stretched upon the rack, his sufferings should receive an ample detail; every torture that he endures should be described, every groan that he utters should echo; as in his life he has been the terror of the good, so in his death he should be the terror of the wicked.'

But there were others who were disinclined to take the advertisements in *The Times* at their face value. Thomas Dutton, the editor of the *Dramatic Censor*, was one who took Gifford severely to task for accusing John Wolcot of 'a crime at which human nature shuddered. . . . He brings no proof and knows it to be false.' Gifford well knew, also, said Dutton, that the newspaper on which he had based his charges had recently been prosecuted for dealing in exactly the same sort of libel and that the 'fabricator of the report' was the late Mr Finey, 'a name notorious for profligacy and an apt coadjutor of *The Times* in the habit of making this charge an engine of distortion'.

Wolcot's publishers had advertised on August 7th, a fortnight before the Battle of the Bards, that he would soon reply to the *Epistle*, that there was 'in the Press and speedily to be published . . . *The Horrors*—an Elegy written in a Bookseller's Shop, by Peter Pindar Esquire. Also *A Little Lash at a Little Liar* or *A Cut at a Cobbler.*'

According to a friendly obituarist of William Gifford this reply was actually written, but it was 'so lacking in wit and poetry and so filled with passion that it merely turned the people against him'. There is no such production in the *Collected Works*, and if Wolcot's own words are to be believed he changed his mind and never wrote the reply, 'thinking Gifford beneath the dignity of such an exhibition

> For should the Muse's satire bid him die
> The Goddess really guillotines a fly.'

But it was Wolcot, in fact, who had the last word in a footnote to *Out at Last* which was published the following year after the resignation of William Pitt. In it he repeated his charges against Gifford and added to them a considerable amount of circumstantial detail—Gifford had recommended one of Lord Grosvenor's cast-off strumpets to a teaching post in the school run by Cookesley's widow; she had wrecked the school with her Cyprian propensities; Gifford had gone through a form of marriage with an Ashburton girl called Mary Weeks; subsequently abandoned, she had died of a broken heart; Gifford continued 'in his favourite occupation of ministering as jackal to the constantly watering chops of the toothless old lion', Lord Grosvenor. As for Gifford's verse—and here Wolcot was on critically sound ground—it would appeal only

'to such readers (and they are not a few) as prefer bombast to sublimity . . . the vulgar eye is sooner fascinated by the stiff staring cabbage-rose brocade of the harlot than the modest and snowy robe of innocence. . . . So much inequality invades his verse that the Faculty would pronounce his Muse afflicted with the rickets. . . .'

This, as R. B. Clark, Gifford's biographer, has noted, was a fairly accurate estimate of the satirical style of this Tory pamphleteer.

★   ★   ★   ★   ★

Among all the shots fired in the battle there is one more curious than the others.

Richard Polwhele, Wolcot's old friend and pupil, had published in 1798 a work called *The Unsex'd Females*.

Always somewhat inclined towards solemnity he could see all too clearly the terrible dangers of the mixed botany classes that had, apparently, been advocated by Mary Wollstonecraft.

'How the study of the sexual system of plants can accord with female modesty I am not able to comprehend,' he confessed as he launched out into an anathema against women who

> More eager for illicit knowledge pant,
> With lustful boys anatomise a plant,
> The virtues of a dust prolific speak,
> Or point its pistill with unblushing cheek.

But there was something about the verse as it stood that did not satisfy the artistic conscience that Wolcot had, no doubt, instilled into him. He tried again:

> With bliss botanic as their bosoms heave
> Still pluck forbidden fruit with mother Eve
> For puberty in sighing florets pant
> Or point the prostitution of a plant
> Dissect its organ of unhallowed lust
> And fondly gaze the titillating dust.

An obvious improvement, this was the version that eventually appeared in *The Unsex'd Females*, a work which is mentioned here not so much for its merits as for the fact that in 1800 a new edition was produced in New York to which was appended quite gratuitously and utterly unconnected with the subject matter an extremely hostile account of John Wolcot, an account, moreover, which appears to have been taken almost verbatim from the pages of the *Anti-Jacobin*. It might well be inferred that Polwhele was the author of at least one of the offending articles in that paper, to which he was already a contributor. Yet the sentiments are quite contradictory to those he expressed about his old mentor at any other time, and it can only be assumed that the publisher used the volume for launching an attack by a different author and from a totally unexpected quarter upon Peter Pindar—a practice which if generally adopted by modern publishers might stimulate some interesting literary feuds.

*　　*　　*　　*　　*

But, as Wolcot himself had noticed, any publicity is better than no publicity at all. His name was still very much before the public. In New York a collected version of his works was published, thereby consolidating a fame which had already been established by the time of the Duke of Kent's visit to America. His Royal Highness while strolling in the country had, so it was said, entered a wayside cottage to find a pretty girl with a book in her hand.

'What books do you read, my dear?' said the duke.

And the girl had replied 'with the most artless innocence', 'Sir, the Bible and Peter Pindar.'

This at any rate was Wolcot's claim, and it was not disputed. It was fortunate that his fame rested securely on what he had already written for his new productions for the year 1801 were, by comparison, sorry stuff. The first of them, a miscellaneous collection of poems called *Tears and Smiles*—even the softness of the title has an uncharacteristic ring—is perhaps the best. It contains, in addition to a series of solemn elegies about a certain Julia, 'The Victim of Love', a lively and spirited ballad (though perhaps 265 verses and three interpolated songs makes it a little overlong) of Orson and Ellen. This not only tells the simple love

210

story of the country barmaid and the young farmer who was rich and fond of women,

> But he his neck to wedlock's yoke
> Would not consent to bow;
> Quoth he 'The man who milk can buy
> Should never keep a cow'

but also manages to interpolate into the ballad form a number of gibes at some of his old targets such as Bishop Porteous, Hannah More and Gifford.

But the remainder of the volume, which was a long one, consisted for the most part of a collection of New-Old Ballads, written in a presumed Elizabethan orthography and bristling with Meseems and Withals, but otherwise conveying no atmosphere whatsoever of an earlier age. As a verse form it seems now about as satisfactory as a pyrograph upon a Tudor teashop wall, but it may then have had something more of the charm of novelty. Certainly nothing like it had ever before come from Peter Pindar.

The next volume, *Out at Last*, an ode celebrating the resignation from the Government of his old enemy, William Pitt, contained scarcely one couplet that is worth quoting. Well might the reviewer of the *Monthly Magazine* exclaim:

> 'This publication has disappointed us . . . his ammunition appears to have been totally exhausted and the fallen minister must be kept in countenance by the expiring poet. . . . There is neither wit nor drollery in any stanza of this poem. . . .'

Nor were *Odes to the Ins and Outs* any better: there is an utterly pedestrian strain which makes them tedious reading.

The Epistle to Count Rumford who, as an associate of Sir Joseph Banks in the foundation of the Royal Institution, was a natural target for Wolcot, shewed little improvement. It has been suggested that with Pitt the enemy suddenly removed from the seat of authority Wolcot had lost his target, but in the old days Wolcot had never lacked for fresh targets. The fact seems to be that he was rapidly becoming the example, common to any age, of the literary lion who gradually loses touch with contemporary life and thought. His prejudices and his entire way of thinking remain stationary, embalmed upon some peak of his career. But the world goes remorselessly on; the values and idioms are changing, the public taste veers as new winds blow. The great man does not, at first, realize what is happening. He knows only that, inexplicably, his sales are dropping, his reviews becoming, book by book, increasingly contemptuous. At first the reviewers are gently chiding, recalling the lost days of brilliance, then they become without qualification unfavourable; finally they print no reviews at all.

John Wolcot, it seemed, was just entering this sad stage. But fortunately the public reputation of a literary lion does not die overnight. Amongst his friends and among his own generation who speak the same language and whose ideas have been formulated and crystallized at the same period, his conversation still seems to sparkle. He still meets interesting people. Young men are still brought to see him—if only for the purpose of pointing a cautionary tale. Though John Wolcot's literary star might seem to be scudding behind the gathering clouds the years of fame still paid dividends which were not solely financial.

In March 1801 he was invited by Beckford to Fonthill as one of a large house-party (which included Wyatt and Benjamin West) to meet Nelson and Sir William and Lady Hamilton. What Peter Pindar thought of West has already been mentioned. Sir William Hamilton and Emma had been no less harshly treated.

In a footnote to an *Epistle to Sir William Hamilton*, written in 1792 when the Ambassador in Naples was excavating around Mount Vesuvius, he had been sufficiently forthright to say:

'Sir William keeps an old antiquarian to hunt for him who when he stumbles upon a tolerable statue bathes him in urine, buries him and, when ripe for digging up, they proclaim a great discovery to be made and out comes an *antique* for universal admiration.'

He had accused Sir William, too, not only of passing off as his own the volcanic observations kept by an old Neapolitan monk but also of being responsible for the disappearance of a number of valuable antiques from the Royal Museum in Naples—a circumstance which Wolcot used in the *Epistle* to point a warning, in two final and scabrous verses (with appropriate footnotes), about Emma:

> O Knight of Naples, is it come to pass
> That thou has left the gods of stone and brass
> To wed a deity of *flesh* and *blood*?[1]
> O lock the temple with thy strongest key
> For fear thy deity a *comely* She
> Should one day ramble in a frolic mood.
>
> For since the idols of a *youthful* King
> So very volatile indeed, take wing
> If *his* to wicked wand'rings can incline
> Lord! who would answer, poor old Knight, for *thine*
> Yet should thy Grecian Goddess fly the fane
> I think that we may catch her in Hedge-Lane.[2]

It might have been anticipated that Wolcot's inclusion in the house-party at Fonthill would lead to a certain amount of natural embarrassment:

> 'The military formed a line on the lawn in front of the house, fired a *feu de joie,* and the band then played God Save The King. Just as this salute and parade were going on, the whole well executed under the command of Captain Williams, commandant of the day, the weather very thick and even foggy before, cleared up and displayed the whole scene to as great an advantage as the author of *Vathek* himself could have desired. He received Nelson and his friend Sir William Hamilton . . . on the marble steps in front of Old Fonthill House.
> Among the arrivals just then was the celebrated Peter Pindar. . . .'

[1] It is really true—the Knight is *married* to a beautiful *virgin*, whom he styles his *Grecian*. Her attitudes are the most *desirable* models for *young* artists.

[2] The resort of the Cyprian corps, an avenue that opens into Cockspur Street.

But, almost incredibly, there appears to have been no ill-feeling of any kind. The party retired

> 'to prepare for dinner which was to take place at six o'clock . . . the repast abounded in the usual fare of a good table. When coffee had been introduced a variety of vocal pieces were executed by Banti who had been procured from town on purpose. . . .'[1]

There were other eminent performers too, including Lady Hamilton who performed and 'displayed her vocal abilities which were of no common order. . . . Conversation and music filled the interval until the hour of twelve when supper was commenced. . . .'

And, in this conversation, the old literary lion, fading though his fame might be, evidently excelled himself. Beckford afterwards said that Wolcot was the most delightful company he ever knew and the best story-teller he had ever heard, that he knew the two worlds well—men and books—and was a shrewd observer of life. He could only remain a week at Fonthill where his humour and his play upon human follies much entertained the company. 'He charmed my visitors with his wit and story-telling.'

Nor was this impression merely of the moment. Wolcot thereafter was one of those for whom at Merton Nelson and Emma Hamilton kept open house.

*   *   *   *   *

To old drinking companions such as Morland, Rowlandson and J. R. Smith he was also as welcome a visitor as ever he had been. On one occasion Morland was painting a portrait of Smith and during the sitting the artist asked Smith to lend him some money. Knowing Morland's reputation Smith refused. An argument followed with Morland getting more insistent the more drunken he became. Eventually, as Smith was leaving, Morland shouted:

---

[1] 'Sweet is her song—divine like Banti's breath' Wolcot had written of Fame in *One Thousand Seven Hundred and Ninety Six*.

'So you won't cash up, hey? Then go to the devil, you drapery-faced hound.' It was a piece of imagery which particularly delighted Peter Pindar: 'The pith of the exclamation consisted in the truth of the picture. Smith had recently recovered from a long fit of illness and his fat cheeks had really sunk into folds.'

Much of Smith's money was, in fact, tied up in wine for his clients the French print-sellers often paid him in bottles of Burgundy. When, in the first great exodus that took place from England to the Continent upon the signing of the Treaty of Amiens, J. R. Smith decided like so many English artists to settle in Paris with Rowlandson and Chasemore, a farewell party was held at Smith's house to dispose of the surplus wine. Wolcot was, of course, invited and so was Henry Angelo. It was a hot sultry day in July and Angelo was placed in charge of cooling the Burgundy with wet towels which chilled it so effectively and brought out (so he considered) the bouquet so well that he kept tasting and cooling and tasting until he was far gone before the party had even begun. And when the party did at last get under way it is safe in such company to assume that the rest of them were not long in reaching the same stage—a stage in which the sorrows of parting and the threat of a declining career were mercifully forgotten.

*   *   *   *   *

It was on the last day of February, 1801, that Charles Giddy, described as Wolcot's nephew, but probably his cousin, met him for the first time and reported on the general state of his life at the age of sixty-three at 1 Chapel Street.

'The drawing-room which was handsome, with three windows in front, had a painted ceiling and was adorned with pictures. These were few but choice and consisted of the celebrated Sleeping Girl by Sir Joshua; an excellent Beggar by Opie, in which the foreshortening of the arm was effected with great skill; and a landscape by Wilson. In addition to these was one of his own efforts, in crayons, together with a drawing, I believe by Kosciusko.'

Giddy, seeing his distinguished relative for the first time, commented on the fact that he was physically very like the late

215

Dr William Thomson, the writer, who had completed Watson's History of Philip II, and Wolcot admitted that others had also remarked on the likeness.

'Soon after my arrival,' said Giddy, 'he seized on what he termed "a dumb fiddle" by means of which he attempted to play me a Welch tune. He then pointed to a pianoforte placed there for the accommodation of his friend Shield "whose veins run milk", said he, "until once affronted when the lamb is turned into the lion".

'While talking of medicine, notwithstanding that he was a physician himself yet he very candidly confessed "that although the sons of Aesculapius might alleviate acute disorders, yet it was seldom they could cure them".

'Being in a convivial humour, with plenty of wine &c before us, he soon after exclaimed with much animation that he intended to live until he was a hundred; and then gaily added that while he possessed the free command of three things—brandy, fire and flannel—a man must make interest to die.

'By way of explanation he immediately stirred the fire mingled a very small portion of the right "Nantz", some water and orange-juice together and pointing to his body observed that moisture was the greatest enemy to man; that his trunk and feet were cased in wool and his very shoes stuffed with flannel.

'He was in very good spirits on this occasion for he had just dissolved an injunction in Chancery and got a decree in his own favour against the booksellers both as to costs of the actions and as to the payment of the annuity.

'Life he thought even if accompanied with torture was a blessing; he would willingly live over again his former days and he seemed at this moment eminently possessed of all the pleasures resulting from enjoyment.'

They talked of Jamaica—where Giddy had evidently been—and Wolcot said that he would not go back there even if he were offered the Governorship of the island. He told his cousin about the beautiful Anglo-American and her shipwrecked lover whom he had met in the Caymans. All in all it made a pleasant picture of the old poet happily enjoying without any apparent trace of the literary sluttishness which some visitors had detected the independence that he had so long ago sought and eventually won.

216

Whether it was a result of his reminiscing to Charles Giddy or whether his conversation arose from the fact that he was already at work on the project is not clear, but 1802 saw the production of *The Island of Innocence*, with his old publisher, Walker.

Like all Wolcot's serious verse it has about it an air of unreality and the delights of a Utopian existence for eighteenth-century castaways on the Caymans are perhaps overstated:

> While at thy side thy Julia plants the ground
> With all her little progeny around
> Who study shrubs and flow'rs with eager eyes
> And learn of *simple* nature to be *wise*.

A large part of the poem is, curiously enough, devoted to an anti-blood sports theme:

> No wish is theirs (forbid it Heav'n!) to hurt
> To wound and murder a poor wretch in sport
> To lift the tube of death with hostile eye
> And dash a flutt'ring victim from his sky
> To bait with writhing worms the barb'rous hook
> And drag the finny nation from their brook;
> Justly forbid the cruelty to know
> And gather pleasure from the pangs of woe. . . .
> Oh, when will Britons list to reason's voice
> And, chang'd, no more in cruelty rejoice?
> How nobler thus t'address the harmless hare,
> 'Child of the field, O come beneath my care. . . .'

If he was serious in all this—his principles certainly did not extend to vegetarianism—John Wolcot was very much ahead of his time and almost certainly could not have foreseen the extent to which sentiment on such subjects would change in England. The last part of the poem contrasts, with the idyllic scenes of the island, life in the great city teeming with the wretched victims of civilization.

And into this nostalgia for the simple life John Wolcot introduced a few lines of personal confession: he warns his friends in the Caymans to have nothing to do with Gold:

Own'd be my folly—yes (seduc'd my eye)
I saw the golden mountains with a sigh
Saw with delight the fatal mischief shine
And envied e'en the slave that dug the mine.

Even independence could be too dearly bought.

*   *   *   *   *

He now moved from Chapel Street to 7 Delaney Place, Camden Town, thinking that the country air would be better for the asthma from which he still suffered abominably. His work this year consisted, in addition to *The Island of Innocence*, of *The Horrors of Bribery* (addressed to Addington and imputing a complete political corruption) and *Pitt and His Statue*. The reviews were again bad. 'Peter is generally speaking a merry fellow and often a witty one, but we cannot say we have once smiled during the perusal . . . we are afraid you have almost exhausted your budget.' In both Baltimore and Philadelphia an edition was published of *Tears and Smiles*, but with the literary piracy that existed it is to be doubted if Wolcot received any money for these editions; occasionally one of his works would be printed in London and shipped across the Atlantic to appear under an American imprint and from these copies he may have received payment.

But he was tiresomely involved again in a dispute with Walker over two editions of his work, which is no doubt the reason why *The Horrors of Bribery* appeared under the imprint of J. Dean. Wolcot maintained that Walker had published these editions contrary to their agreement; he filed a bill against the publisher and was granted two injunctions. To one of these injunctions Walker was prepared to submit but the other he fought. The case came before the Chancellor, Lord Eldon of whom Lord Campbell in his *Lives of the Lord Chancellors* commented:

'The decisions of Lord Eldon which I most object to are those by which he erected himself into a Censor of the Press and gave himself the power to protect or to extinguish all literary property at his pleasure.'

218

The case of Wolcot *versus* Walker provided, in fact, one of these unfortunate judgments. It so happened that when Dr Priestley had brought an action at Birmingham for the value of his furniture and books that had been burnt by the mob the Lord Chief Justice had propounded the dictum 'that if any of the books were seditious the plaintiff was not entitled to recover for them'. In Wolcot's case no charge of any kind was made that the works were in any way exceptionable, Lord Eldon had no judicial knowledge of the contents and he was not asked to make any finding upon their merits. Under such circumstances there was a legal presumption of innocence; in other words Lord Eldon should have assumed that he had to try the case on its own merits and not on the merits of the books. But of course Eldon in his private capacity knew perfectly well that Dr John Wolcot was the same Peter Pindar who had so villainously attacked his Lordship's royal employer. Accordingly, relying on the dictum in the case of Dr Priestley, he refused to give an injunction or an order for an account of profits even in the case of the book over which Walker had made no fight.

'The Court', he said, ought not to give an account of unhallowed profits of libellous publications. An author could have no property in a libel. The case was dismissed: 'a very improper judgment', commented Lord Campbell.

It must remain a matter of conjecture whether Lord Eldon also had private knowledge of Peter Pindar's lines in *Pitt and His Statue* about a thief who

> . . . musing rolled his eyes from side to side
> With a most solemn, philosophic case
> Like my Lord Eldon on a crabbed case
> Which often comes into the Court of Chancery;
> Where his *grave* Lordship and *grave* wig
> Both with the first importance *big*
> Are very often puzzled how to answer ye;
> So very *undecisive* in *decision*
> Leaving for future chancery-traps *provision*.

In the case of Wolcot *v*. Walker he was at any rate determined to leave the matter in no doubt whatsoever.

But apart from these tiresome and expensive legal affairs life proceeded peacefully enough for the old poet. His friendships meant much to him. William Godwin and he dined frequently at each other's table. On January 8th, 1802, John Wolcot wrote to him:

'Most willingly would I join your philosophic party at the Polygon but Death on Sunday last sent one of his damned young brats to attack me in bed at Lord Nelson's at Merton.[1] Inspired with a little of his Lordship's courage I fired away at him flannel, brandy, hot-bricks and red-hot coals which by the blessing of God (in whom you *devoutly* believe) overcame him and I am now at Camden Town singing Te Deum for the victory. Though I have not gained the laurels of Aboukir I have (as Marshal Bofflers said of his troops) "performed wonders". To descend from lofty metaphor to humble prose I have been plagued by my asthma for nearly a week past and I have flown to Camden Town to recover. Here I am at Delaney Place, No. 7, with a fiddle and a good fire, the one a balm for the mind and the other for the body. I am truly yours,

J. Wolcot.

P.S. The instant I can with safety crawl forth I will peep in upon you. Report says you are married again. Fortunate man! Forty years I have been trying to get my tail into the trap and have not succeeded. What a monkey!'

Living alone and in lodgings must have become, with increasing years and decreasing health, an evermore lonely existence. Now that there was no longer the same need to be shocking Wolcot who had sneered at morality, who—according to Baring-Gould—was a sensualist and 'flouted at marriage', who had written in *An Apology for Keeping Mistresses*:

Go, Wedlock, to the men of leaden brains
Who hate variety and sigh for chains

---

[1] He had another narrow escape from death at Merton when his night-cap—lent to him by Lord Nelson—caught fire while he was reading in bed by candlelight. His enemies maintained, of course, that at the time he was drunk.

could openly regret that nothing had come of those frustrated courtships of his youth. Where were they, all those golden Cornish girls? Betsy Cranch was still living and the mother of a family; Miss Dickenson had married and gone to Ireland and died there; Susan Nankivell if she was still alive would be fifty-six and a spinster; 'peerless' Miss Coryton. . . . It was no use repining, but undoubtedly as old age drew nearer he was regretting that fatal lack of apparent seriousness that had so often come between him and the marriage which might have spared him the long ultimate years of loneliness. More than ever he must have felt the need to cultivate friendships. Mrs Robinson—Perdita—was dead, but he took the kindly interest of an old friend in her daughter Mary who was preparing a volume of poetry for publication.

The *Anti-Jacobin* commented 'by what obliquity in reasoning has this young lady convinced herself that the reputation of her "sainted parent" will be benefited by boasting of an acquaintance with Peter Pindar? . . .' It was an interest that also horrified Samuel Taylor Coleridge. He dashed off an explosive letter to the girl:

'As to Peter Pindar! By all the Love and Honour I bear to your dear Parent's memory, by the anguish and indignation at my inmost heart I swear to you that my flesh creeps at his name! You have forgotten, dear Miss Robinson! Yes, you have altogether forgotten that in a published Poem he called an infamous and mercenary strumpet "the Mrs Robinson of Greece". Will you permit the world to say her own daughter does not resent it—her own daughter connects the fame of her Mother with that of the man who thus assassinated her reputation! No! No! I am sure you had forgotten it. . . .'

Quite possibly the offending couplet had been forgotten for many years before her death by its subject, and since it had been written by Wolcot in 1783 it may be presumed that if not forgotten the subsequent long years of friendship had certainly caused it to be forgiven.

But to Coleridge, as to many others, Wolcot's carefully cultivated sinister reputation lingered on.

16

WITH the onset of old age the years began to merge swiftly one with the next. Their pattern became distressingly similar. His past works were ephemeral to an extent that certainly affected their continuing sale: out of touch with the new spirit of the times his new works met with increasingly—and often unfairly—antagonistic reviews.

'We have often laughed at and as often deplored the misapplication of the talents of this author but we must now regret that he has not wholly ceased to write for what remains is "stale flat and unprofitable" '

was the total comment of one critic of *Great Cry and Little Wool*. And

'these are the very windfalls of the Parnassian orchard and only so far instructive as they warn the purchaser not to buy any more out of the same basket.' (*Instructive Epistle to J. Perring.*)

Yet even in critical decline such was the power of his name with the reading public that other satirists began to assume the name of Peter Pindar, sometimes (but by no means always) with the addition of some distinguishing qualification such as Junior or Minimus. And as, in age and infirmity, Wolcot's own publications became even fewer, into the gap were thrown works by his imitators, some of whom achieved a considerable success. In particular the poems of C. F. Lawler, writing under the name, *tout court*, of Peter Pindar, ran through almost as many editions, and in as short a space of time as those of Wolcot himself in his heyday.

To add to the gradual breaking up of the old man there was added the slow and pitiful failing of his eyesight. In 1805 he paid one of his fleeting visits to his friends and relatives in Cornwall. Polwhele, still pompous as ever, but not shewing any of the enmity that might have been expected if he had indeed been the author of the hostile account of Peter Pindar in the New York edition of *The Unsex'd Females*, wrote about this visit:

'. . . from my juvenile prejudices in favour of Wolcot it was natural in me to hope that notwithstanding all the storms that had vex'd and darkened the day his evening might have closed in peace. His two sisters at Fowey, Mrs Stephens widow of Mr Stephens, Surgeon Apothecary, and Miss Wolcot a maiden lady, would have been happy, I was informed, to protract the pleasure of his conversation. And, in his old age, blind and ready to drop into the grave, I should have conceived him deriving comfort from the sound sense and religiousness of two such valuable friends. Yet after having fiddled and punned and laughed for a while with all his youthful levity he left his sisters and returned to London. Such was Wolcot! . . .'

Such too, of course, was Polwhele. For the fact that John Wolcot could keep up his friendship with Dr Whitaker, the historian of Manchester, Polwhele adduced as evidence of hypocrisy:

'Whitaker would not have tolerated the slightest approach to scepticism or profaneness. He who had rebuked the Bishop of Derry, who had smitten his Lordship (too light in talk) upon the knee would have indignantly turned Peter Pindar out of doors had Peter lost sight of decorum for a moment.'

The fact that he had not lost sight of decorum must mean that he was a hypocrite. It is a little hard to follow this line of argument: indeed it might be thought that for one who was naturally outspoken and irreverent to control himself in such company might be considered a praiseworthy example of self-restraint. But Wolcot had so successfully created the reputation of being a monster of depravity that only an outrageous solution would solve a simple problem. In an *Epistle to Myself* included in *Tristia, or the Sorrows of Peter*, Wolcot wrote:

> Some paint you a mad bull, wild roaring
> Tossing folks on your horns and goring
> This picture verily provokes my laugh:
> You ar'n't that formidable creature
> Of milder elements your nature
> Your character resembles more the calf.

And certainly when there was no need or temptation to be shocking, even though he was becoming coarser with age, he could still behave as well as anybody else. For, as Mrs John Serres (who had written two operas which attracted Wolcot's attention) told Farington, the doctor was a loose talker, but before her was very guarded in his language. But nobody wanted to believe this. The account of a villainous character made more popular reading than that of a saint.

> '*Tristia* indeed! [wrote a reviewer]. In his former effusions with all their infamy (for who can question the principles of a depraved man) there was not rarely a spark of genius; and even in these *Tristia* there is here and there a glimmering of light; but it is as a few grains of wheat buried in a bushel of chaff . . . Instead of continuing to slander mankind would it not much better become this poor wretched wicked old man to spend the remnant of his days in making peace with heaven?'

The reviewer was clearly overlooking, or choosing to ignore, Wolcot's indication that he was, in fact, achieving some sort of sympathy for the organized religion of so many of his old Cornish friends. In the same *Epistle* to himself he wrote in 1806:

> Of what religion are you pray?
> I think, Sir, I have heard you say
> The Quaker's, void of noise and ostentation
> And to the great, sublime, all-wise
> Creator of ten thousand skies
> That Silence is the *highest* adoration.

224

He was, after all, in his sixty-ninth year—a considerable age by eighteenth-century standards—and if a clergyman of the Established Church were going to patch up any kind of peace with his Maker he must not delay too long.

*　　*　　*　　*　　*

Polwhele noticed that John Wolcot had fiddled and punned and laughed with all his old youthful levity. Levity was not something that commended itself and there is no doubt that the Vicar of Manaccan must have greatly disapproved of the rumbustious style in which Wolcot was only too ready to deal with some of the established idols of the day. Dryden was a poet particularly esteemed and, of all Dryden's works, *Alexander's Feast* still enjoyed a great popularity. To Cyrus Redding Wolcot gave as his opinion that 'Dryden comes into the room like a clown in a drugget jacket with a bludgeon in his hand and in hobnail shoes. Pope enters like a gentleman in full dress with a bag and sword.'

He contested, with Redding, Pope's infinite superiority over Dryden poem by poem.

'But, Doctor,' cried Cyrus Redding, 'what of *Alexander's Feast?*'

'Pooh!' exclaimed Wolcot. 'He was drunk when he wrote that.'

This rather sweeping denunciation he was prepared to justify, point by point. Young Giddy was treated to an exercise of literary criticism in Wolcot's most unbuttoned style:

'The subject is immoral, the catastrophe unjust and the language vulgar and imperfect. Here are a soldier and his trull seated together on a bench which they call an imperial throne. They are evidently surrounded by pimps and parasites, ready to assent to all their freaks; these, ridiculously enough, are denominated "valiant peers". And what is the conclusion of all this? Exactly what ought to be expected— a foreign concubine—an Athenian woman of the town in a state of intoxication—for assuredly there was intoxication of more than one species;—seizes on a burning brand, no matter whether a flambeau or a farthing candle and seconded by her paramour and the drunken crew by whom they are accompanied, basely destroys the noble city of Persepolis to gratify her vile resentments.'

While his nephew listened fascinatedly—and made notes of the conversation—Wolcot attacked the subject of Timotheus' song which shewed, so he said, that Alexander's mother was as great a strumpet as Thais and descended to bestiality with a beast whom she pretended was Jupiter Ammon:

'As to "love and wine" this is mere poetic licentia to endeavour if possible to impress dignity; as for me I can perceive nothing but lust, gin and two-penny. . . .
    And with what bad taste does the whole conclude? We are told that this beastly scene of low desire, drunkenness, music and conflagration
            "raised a mortal to the skies!"
What then in the name of wonder would entitle that same mortal to shame, infamy and punishment?'

No doubt the admirers of Dryden went away in just that sort of outraged condition that gave Wolcot the greatest pleasure in iconoclasm. But in public, in the *Tristia*, to their probable confusion, he included Dryden with Homer, Milton, Otway and Butler—and of course Peter Pindar—as examples of genius grossly neglected by the Crown.

*   *   *   *   *

    To those who believed in the legend that Wolcot was a terrifying example of depravity there now came what must have seemed a startling confirmation of their lively suspicions.
    In August 1806, while still maintaining rooms in London itself, he moved to a new address, to which he had been recommended, in Camden Town, to the house of Mrs Knight in Pratt Place. There were those who maintained that he chose his lodgings according to the accessibility of the landlady, but of this there is certainly no evidence. Here in Pratt Place he at first

occupied for eight shillings a week an attic on the second floor, but he soon moved down to the first floor where he was given a drawing-room and a bedroom opposite the room occupied by the Knights with whom he generally dined *en famille* and waited upon by the maidservant Elizabeth Carter. There were two children in the family and two other lodgers, Mr and Mrs Dyke, who naturally took a considerable interest in their celebrated neighbour who walked daily to and from his rooms in London, and who had just written the Epilogue for Godwin's play *Faulkener* at Drury Lane to which Charles Lamb had written the Prologue. But the Dykes were not to have him as a neighbour for long. Two days before Christmas when Wolcot had been in the house for only four months there was a quarrel between Mr Knight and his lodger. The doctor at once packed and left his lodgings, going to live at 94 Tottenham Court Road. And there in due course a summons was served upon him accusing him of Criminal Conversation—adultery—with Mrs Knight.

In June the case was heard before Lord Ellenborough: the Attorney-General and Mr Garrow represented Mr Knight. The reputation of Peter Pindar was such that news of the case caused a considerable crowd to collect and the Court itself was packed at an early hour. But if the public hoped to see the old writer they were disappointed for Wolcot was represented only by his Counsel, Mr Parke, Mr Jarvis and Mr Marryat.

The Attorney-General, opening the case, observed that the action instituted against the defendant was of a nature that required the most serious attention of the jury, which he was glad to find was composed of gentlemen and men in a respectable line of life. The plaintiff came into court to complain of a most serious injury, aggravated by many circumstances which added to the weight and inflamed the poignancy of his feelings. He had been reduced to that situation which makes a man at once an object of ridicule and compassion. He was what the world in grosser words would call a cuckold—a name of reproach which a man could ill bear who had not deserved it, and which must excite a most bitter acuteness of feeling and the keenest sense of resentment in him who was conscious that he merited the honourable appellation of an affectionate and constant husband.

Mr Knight had married Miss Franks in November 1799,

'a lady extremely young and of a most attractive person. The marriage was what may be strictly called a match of affection. My client was bred to a seafaring life and was in the service of his King and Country. For six years they lived together in the utmost harmony; they had four children two of which are dead; the two youngest are still living to share the disgrace and misery of their father, and to lament the alienation and loss of a parent by the artifice of a seducer.'

The Attorney-General expatiated at some length on the married life of his client. He and his wife had endured many hardships, including shipwreck, together. While the husband was away at sea—he was ship's steward to Captain Rowley—Mrs Knight remained in London earning her living by needlework as a fancy dressmaker. Then, during one shore leave, Knight had bought the small house in Pratt Place and had let out the lodgings to which when Mrs Knight was twenty-six years old Wolcot had come.

'The defendant, I must tell you, is a man in years, old in vice and in the experience of wickedness, but with the passions of youth which we should have thought quelled in one of his age. Being intimate with the plaintiff and his family in the capacity of a lodger he meditated the seduction in the following manner:

'He first practised upon the lady's vanity; he told her that she had powers which were lost in her present obscurity and which if employed in the right direction would bring fame and emolument to herself and her husband. He flattered her into an opinion that she would make an excellent actress—got her to recite to him—corrected her enunciation—shewed her the more graceful attitudes of the stage and taught her much of the gesticulation and manner which we see upon the boards of the theatre.

'He told her that he had taught Mrs Siddons; that he would gladly use his endeavours to make her as good an actress and did not doubt of success. He added that he could readily obtain her an engagement at the theatres, and that her salary would be considerable. The wife believed him; the husband believed him likewise; in short it was a flattering representation and could not be doubted.'

The defendant Wolcot, thundered the Attorney-General, had gone to work and had at length achieved his purpose.

228

'At the same time, which is most to his disgrace, he availed himself of intoxication to put her off her guard and lay her vigilance asleep.'

Witnesses were examined who spoke of the happiness of the little family before the arrival of the doctor, and then the prosecution demanded, 'Call Elizabeth Carter!'

The maid at Pratt Place then went into the witness-box. Her master and mistress, she said, seemed to live very comfortably and affectionately together. Doctor Wolcot came to lodge in a two-pair-of-stairs room when she was there; he taught her mistress to read and speak. Dr Wolcot had behaved rudely to witness; but she did not encourage him. Dr Wolcot had the privilege of the dining-room on the first floor, gratis. She had seen her mistress go into the doctor's room, nice and clean, and come out with her dress disordered and her kerchief unpinned. She had seen Dr Wolcot with his hands round Mrs Knight's neck, when she went in, but not more than once; it was one afternoon at tea-time and her master was not there.

She had seen the doctor and her mistress sitting near the fire-place and the doctor's hand upon Mrs Knight's knee. She had seen the doctor lie on the sofa without his coat, when Mrs Knight was there, near the window, with her hair partly down upon her shoulders. The window-shutters were sometimes partly shut when the doctor and her mistress were together. She left her place and Dr Wolcot remained in his lodgings, two or three weeks before Christmas.

She said the doctor was very old and weak and much troubled with an asthma and pretended he could not see; he seemed very blind; he was very dirty in his person and dress and lay very often on the sofa without his coat. He was very strong when he pulled her about. She used to lead him up and down stairs. She observed him teaching Mrs Knight to put her arms in particular positions and speaking sharply to her when she was in the room. He used to be an hour or two at a time in the room with her when teaching her to act. In answer to the Attorney-General's prompting Elizabeth Carter replied that Mrs Knight usually wore her hair under a bonnet at the back of her head with a velvet bandeau in front, but that there had been occasions when she had appeared 'with her hair down about her shoulders and over her face as if

229

she had been tumbled. Her bosom was bare. Wolcot's hand was around her bosom. . . .'

That was the extent of the maid's evidence and though to some extent damning it was by no means conclusive. But worse was to follow. The next to enter the witness-box was Mrs Dyke, one of the fellow-lodgers. She, too, dwelt on the happy family life that there had been in the house before the arrival of the doctor. Even after his arrival 'great friendship seemingly subsisted between Dr Wolcot and Mr and Mrs Knight and they generally dined together'. The witness understood that Dr Wolcot was to bring Mrs Knight upon the stage; she had heard her frequently reciting and reading passages from plays. Mrs Knight dressed genteely and particularly neat before Dr Wolcot came. One day Mrs Knight had put on a clean white gown, had put her child into Mrs Dyke's arms and had gone up to Dr Wolcot's bedroom where she stayed between dinner and tea. She came down 'looking as if they had been to sleep together' and wearing a green gown. One day, on another occasion, she saw her come downstairs from the doctor's room with her clothes almost off her back and walk into the garden. She appeared intoxicated, but she had not been in liquor when she went into the doctor's room—she appeared tumbled as if she had been in bed or asleep and very much intoxicated. Dr Wolcot used to bring a quantity of rum in pint and half-pint bottles. She never saw Mrs Knight in liquor before, but heard her always exclaim against drinking spirits or liquors.

Mr Knight had gone from home one afternoon, continued Mrs Dyke with relish, and Mrs Knight had been in Dr Wolcot's rooms two hours very quiet, not receiving lessons. The witness slept with her husband in a back room, one pair of stairs, with Dr Wolcot immediately over them on the second floor. And on that same night she heard Mrs Knight go into Dr Wolcot's bedchamber and afterwards heard them laughing and playing together. She then stayed with him about an hour or three-quarters: Mrs Dyke had heard them laughing and playing as if two people were in bed together and she had no doubt of them being either in or on the bed together. This was on the evening when Mrs Knight was supposed to be at Norwood. After this time she became very inattentive to her children and shortly after the doctor had left the house, Mrs Knight, on January 6th, also left Pratt Place.

At this stage the case seemed to be going overwhelmingly against Wolcot. The defence concentrated on discrediting Mrs Dyke. Mr Marryat, for example, asked her:

'When you received the subpoena shilling did you say, "Here goes the subpoena shilling for half a pint of gin"?' The answer was an emphatic denial, but she was forced to admit that:

'I have often fetched gin for my husband but never by a shillingsworth at a time.'

She was also forced to admit that she might have said that she had 'taught the scheme of the sofa and would make the old rascal of a doctor pay £1000'. But she utterly denied having advised Mr Knight to hide himself under the sofa and, in fact, had never acquainted either Mr or Mrs Knight about her suspicions. It was the best that Mr Marryat could do and the Prosecution called their last witness—Mr Dyke. He confirmed his wife's evidence about the couple 'playing together as if in bed'. He had actually remarked to Mrs Dyke:

'The doctor and Mrs Knight are making themselves comfortable!' and had then turned over and gone to sleep leaving Mrs Dyke awake—a piece of complacency that aroused Lord Ellenborough's disgust.

The prosecution had certainly a strong case. And the fact that the defence had no witnesses to call and that Dr Wolcot himself did not put in an appearance cannot have been very helpful.

It was Mr Parke who spoke for the defence. He observed that this was the most impudent conspiracy, the most shallow and trumped-up case that was ever introduced into a court of justice. Dr Wolcot was upwards of seventy (he was, in fact, sixty-nine), blind, asthmatic, and a very antidote to love. He was so helpless that he constantly required the assistance of the female sex in the offices of kindness and attention to his personal wants; and because Mrs Knight, whom he contended to be a mere servant in the lodging-house, performed these offices such as tucking him up when he went to bed and bringing him a bottle of warm water to put to his decrepit feet and sustain a little warmth and vigour in his decaying and enervate frame; because this woman was employed in these purposes and devoted herself with more particular attention to them on account of the doctor's professional kindness to her, the husband availed himself of an opportunity to charge him with the crime of adultery in order to plunder him by the sentence of a court of justice.

'I wish to God, gentlemen,' cried Parke, 'you could see this man—this Peter Pindar! You would soon discover that he had no Pindaric fire or any other *fire* whatsoever. Let him only step into the jury [sic] box and he will infallibly plead his cause better than I can.

'Gentlemen! If the thing were not indelicate in itself I might advert to circumstances which would prove to you that such were the natural infirmities of this man that he was physically incapable of the crime. But it is useless to do this because the plaintiff is out of court. The adultery is proved in no single part or possible case. The maid saw the doctor sometime with his coat on and sometimes off; what then? He had once his hands around her neck; what then? He was instructing her to act. Once he had his hands on her knee; he was blind and knew not where he put them.

'The evidence of the maidservant only instructs you that her mistress was once in a disordered dress; one of her breasts being uncovered and her hair dishevelled! Well! The doctor was teaching her to act. She was perhaps at that moment Euphrasia in *The Grecian Daughter*, employed in the charitable office of administering her breast for suck to the mouth of her exhausted parent.'

As to Mrs Dyke's evidence, it fell little short of perjury! If adultery were proved by this case no old gentleman was safe in similar circumstances.

Mr Parke sat down. He had done all that he could do.

Reading the report of the case at this distance of time the defence seems perhaps just the least bit thin. But in the law report it is often impossible to catch the atmosphere of the court. It is difficult to judge the effect made upon the jury by each witness. Mrs Dyke, for example, was described as a bad witness who equivocated. And, in any case, the impressions of probity aroused by the words of a witness may be offset by his physical appearance in the box. Of Lord Ellenborough's summing up nothing seems to remain other than the reporter's comment that it was 'in an impartial manner. He conceived the adultery not proved.'

The jury conferred momentarily together and without leaving the box found John Wolcot 'Not Guilty'.

★   ★   ★   ★   ★

Though the verdict was, no doubt, just, Wolcot must be accounted fortunate that his carefully nurtured reputation had not this time weighed with the judge and cost him a considerable sum of money.

The lampoonists, of course, rejoiced at the whole circumstances of the trial. A printer named Day, of Fetter Lane, quickly brought out a *Hieroglyphical Advertisement* which appears to read:

> 'Just Published! Embellished with 4 characteristic Plates. The Trial of Dr Wolcot otherwise Peter Pindar for Adultery. This Trial comprehends a great many warm and rakish Courtships which cannot but be pleasing to the Public that are in Town. His Amours, Fancies and Intrigues with the Ladies will have a Place in this Publication, his Productions by his Pen, his Tastes for Music, Poetry and Painting are charmingly portrayed in this Pamphlet.'

Meanwhile 'the very antidote to love' remained in his rooms in Tottenham Court Road. Farington spoke of him in his Diary as being in a breaking-up condition. A Mr and Mrs Carlisle had reported that they had met Wolcot in a house where, still commenting that there were three things would preserve a man— 'Fire, Flannel and Brandy'—he had actually drunk a whole bottle of spirit in a single day. He was nearly blind from a cataract in each eye and this must have contributed to the stemming of the flow of his verse. Yet the state of his decay was exaggerated in these reports: the sheer pleasure that he took from being alive kept the old man fairly active. He managed to produce *The Fall of Portugal: or the Royal Exiles*, a Play in Blank Verse in 5 Acts. He published it himself and it was sold by Longman's but never staged. And in what looks like an attempt to fight his way back into the market with the sort of work which had won him his early fame he produced *One More Peep at the Royal Academy*.

In it he referred to his gradual physical decay, saying, *inter alia*:

> I own that Time to my surprise
> Has done some mischief to my eyes
> And done that mischief much against my will.
> But as the bullfinch, beyond doubt,
> Sings better when his eyes are out
> Why not the songster of th'Aonian Hill?

Of what little he could see his judgment was still sound. As Opie said, he had 'an uncommonly fine eye for harmony effect and colour'. He might be seventy but, unlike some elderly art critics, he could see much that was good among the younger artists. Turner and Wilkie, in particular, he picked out for praise—though he rather sensibly advised the latter to try and break away from his bucolic subjects for a higher sphere of endeavour. But in his old age he had mellowed and softened. The old fire had gone almost out, the acid had lost its searing quality. He was concerned more to praise than to blame—even in an Academy where there were 'few eagles and too many a wren'. Even Benjamin West was now given a word or two of praise, and though the general standard of portraiture received much mockery it was, on the whole, a peaceful farewell that John Wolcot made to the artists. And, in a way that old men are apt suddenly to behave, he reverted momentarily, if *The Satirist* is to be believed, to his earlier calling and was struck by the possibilities of an unlikely enterprise:

> 'if we are not much mistaken he has lately aimed at medical celebrity by declaring himself the inventor of a nostrum for the cure of deafness! Which is, of course, as effective as *other nostrums*. We are sorry to say that for some years past his Pegasus has borne every appearance of a worn-out and jaded hackney.'

*   *   *   *   *

234

But, just for a brief moment, the hack was to be spurred into life again. The scandalous revelations about the place-mongering Mary Anne Clarke, mistress to the Duke of York, which burst upon Parliament and the nation in 1809 were just the sort of subject in which the Peter Pindar of old had delighted. For a moment he almost completely recaptures the gusto of his earlier satires against the Crown:

> Heav'ns what a dire confusion Beauty makes
> The Horse Guards tremble and Old Windsor shakes
> Like Bees the Mob around St Stephens swarms
> And every street and alley feels alarms.
> Men, women, coaches, gigs each other jostle
> And *thou* the cause of all this horrid bustle.
> Hotels and tap-rooms sound with mingled din
> And every coffee-house is on the grin.
> From morn to eve, from eve to midnight dark
> Naught strikes the ear but 'Duke and Mistress Clarke'.
> Nay, too, the Parrot and the simple Starling
> Cry from their cages naught but 'Duke and Darling'.

Many of those in high places were desperately involved in the scandal:

> The mighty Castlereagh himself may fall
> The pompous pillar that supports us all.
> I hear the crack and mourn it most sincerely
> And Ireland too will mourn, who loves him dearly,
> Ireland to Castlereagh that so much owes;
> Her Union—present and her past repose
> And fine fertility the eye that greets
> For docks and grass adorn old Dublin's streets.

In the City of London the Lord Mayor was attacked by the Liverymen for some fancied blame in the matter and this inspired a pleasant simile:

> Regardless of gold chain and pomp and place
> They howl him home in sorrow and disgrace.
> Thus when the Bird of Wisdom leaves his bow'r
> O'er hills and valleys in broad day to tower

The small pert Tenants of the Hedge rush out
To put the solemn Trav'ller to the rout
Magpies and Jays and Ravens, Rooks and Crows
Spit in his face and pull him by the nose
Unheard he hoots; the chattering, croaking train
Tumultuous drive him to his hole again. . . .'

To John Wolcot the whole episode was, of course, Heaven-sent—
and he, it should be noted, of all men appreciated the depth of
devotion to Heaven displayed by his countrymen:

Let Ridicule enjoy with hearty laugh
Commission'd boy and striplings on the Staff.
Ere long may Babes our Army List adorn
And, what may more astonish, babes unborn
Napoleon dares not seize our goods and chattels
We trust our safety to the God of Battles. . . .'

Clearly, even at the age of seventy-one, Wolcot still had flashes
of the old power to illuminate and amuse.

His lodgings were still visited by interesting, lively people
(among them the blind Lord Coventry), who kept his mind
alert and his spirit youthful. Peter Pindar had moved round the
corner from Tottenham Court Road into rooms in Howland
Street and such of his old friends as were still alive—as well as
many younger men—came to him there. He was still invited to
dine in houses where he was regarded as providing the star-turn
of the evening—although not all the guests might equally
approve of him. In May 1811, for instance, Henry Crabb Robinson
dined with Thelwall and afterwards wrote:

'The man whom we went to see and, if we could, admire
was Dr Wolcot, better known as Peter Pindar, . . . though I
felt disgust and all but contempt of him. . . .
He talked about the artists, said that West could paint
neither ideal beauty nor from nature, called Opie the Michael
Angelo of old age, complained of the ingratitude of certain
artists who owed everything to him, spoke contemptuously
of Walter Scott who, he said, owed his popularity to hard

236

names, and called him a miserable creature. He also declared against rhyme in general which he said was only fit for burlesque. Not even Butler would live. At the same time he praised exceedingly the *Heroic Epistle to Sir William Chambers*.

Congreve he considered the greatest miracle of genius and that such a man should early abandon literature was to him unaccountable.

As Peter Pindar was blind a servant cut his meat.

I was requested to help him to his wine which was in a separate pint bottle and was not wine at all but brandy. After dinner he eulogized brandy calling it τὸ πᾶν and said "He who drinks it must make interest to die."

He said he had made a rhyme that morning of which Butler might not have been ashamed:

> Say, would you long the shafts of death deny?
> Pray keep your inside wet your outside dry.

I referred to his own writings. He said he recollected them with no pleasure: "Satire is a bad trade." '

So far, it is clear, John Wolcot was behaving himself at the dinner-party quite unexceptionably. His reference to his distaste for satire is of doubtful seriousness, for it can hardly be doubted that Wolcot had enjoyed a great deal of fun in his attacks. Besides, for one anxious to shock and impress, the trade of satirist must, from his own description, have provided him with much of what he had always sought:

> Dread is the Satirist! A name of fear,
> Beast of a thousand heads! A horrid creature!
> The world's afraid to see him—or come near;
> *Noli me tangere* in every feature. . . .

Then Henry Crabb Robinson continued:

'After the ladies had left the room his conversation became very gross. But it was not on this occasion but one evening at Godwin's that I heard him make a disgusting exhibition of himself—imitating the sounds of a distant organ, belching, squeaking, shouting and making even more offensive sounds. He had a florid coarse look which, added to his sightless eyeballs, rendered his appearance disgusting.

His opinions, I thought, betrayed senility and shewed that he could not in his old age sympathize with the task or recognize the merits of the young age. He suffered intensely from the fear of Death which affected him even to a humiliating degree.'

It has been previously noted that people had a curious habit of seeing in John Wolcot what they wished to see—or perhaps, even, what he wished them to see. Certainly his sympathy and understanding for young artists had already, even in his old age, been made amply manifest. As to his fear of death, at this stage of his life there is no evidence other than that of Crabb Robinson, but it is quite contrary to the peaceful way in which he subsequently faced his end.

And even Coleridge, who as has been seen was by no means a staunch admirer of Peter Pindar, when he went to dinner with Godwin, and found Wolcot also among the company, seems to have observed nothing to complain about in the old man's behaviour.

*　　*　　*　　*　　*

Brandy, flannel and fire, these were the panaceas of his old age. And it was wool that was credited with saving his failing life when the tragedy occurred in Howland Street. He kept two servants there and one day when Nell came into the room to tend to him and to make up the fire her dress caught light and was soon ablaze. Until she screamed Wolcot, in his blindness, knew nothing: then he stumbled towards her and with his hands tried to beat out the flames. As he did so he, too, was dreadfully burned. Fortunately there was a coach-stand opposite the house and one of the hackney drivers rushed in and gave the alarm by which the whole house was saved from destruction. But he was too late to save poor Nell who died of her burns. And it was generally agreed that if John Wolcot's gown had been of linen instead of wool it also would have caught fire and he too would probably have died.

*   *   *   *   *

It was to the lodgings in Howland Street that there came in 1811 a messenger from Wolcot's old admirer the Prince of Wales. Always an avid reader of Peter Pindar's satires against his father he had long been supplied with advance proofs of the works as they appeared. Now with the final madness of the king the Prince of Wales had become Regent. Who knows what hopes of patronage ran through the old man's mind when his visitor was announced.

'How much,' asked the messenger, 'do we owe you for the proofs?' Like many another reformed sinner the Prince Regent had no wish for this embarrassing aspect of his past to catch up with him. Wolcot flushed angrily:

'I thought it sufficient honour that the Prince read my works in that way. I never expected to be insulted by such a demand, so long afterwards.'

'My orders,' said the messenger, 'are peremptory.'

'I have nothing to do with my writings now, nor with money transactions relating to them. You must go to Walker the bookseller.'

The envoy went his way and Wolcot sent a message to Walker telling him to make out a regular tradesman's bill for the Prince Regent shewing in detail the amount owing down to the last farthing. It amounted to forty pounds and a few odd shillings.

In due course the messenger came again to Wolcot with a note for fifty pounds.

'The change,' he said in a princely manner, 'is of no consequence.'

Wolcot waved the money on one side.

'You must take it to my bookseller. This is purely a trade matter and you must deal with the tradesmen. Good day to you.'

'Was not this very pretty?' he asked one of his old friends. 'The Prince had my squibs about his father to read openly at his own table and then fearing that I may blab the fact now he is

239

become Viceroy he thinks if he pays me for the rags all will be right.'

And when he was not invited by his erstwhile admirer to the fête at Carlton House he gave vent to his rancour in *The Carlton House Fête; or The Disappointed Bard*:

> Elate to Carlton House my Rhymes I sent
> Before the poem met the public eye
> Which gain'd applause, the Poet's great intent
> But nought besides, I say it with a sigh. . . .

It wasn't Wolcot's best poem; it was by no means his worst. Its ephemeral interest is heightened only by the fact that it was his last.

17

THE end, it must have been thought, could not now be far away. And as the old poet fell silent so the imitators and plagiarists emerged. In 1812 both John Agg and George Daniel appeared as Peter Pindar Junior. In 1813 C. F. Lawler, the most successful of them, took over without qualification the pseudonym of Peter Pindar. In 1814 Peter Pindar minimus was published together with yet a third Peter Pindar junior. In 1816 came Peter Pindar the Elder. And all these satellites, reflecting the dying rays of their sun, achieved some degree of success.

Meanwhile the Great Man himself was living out a peaceful retirement. In 1814 Sir William Adams, the oculist, performed an operation on one of the cataracts that obscured his eyes.

Cyrus Redding when next he called on Wolcot found him in bed with a bandage across his eyes.

'Why, what has happened?'

'Ah! Since you were here Adams the oculist who goes about blinding everybody persuaded me to submit to the operation of couching.'

'And you consented?'

'Not on both eyes; I only agreed that he should try what he could do with one.'

'And with what success?'

'Oh, of course so famous a practitioner *could* not fail and he has succeeded in curing my eye for ever . . . of seeing. I could before distinguish the figure of anyone between my eye and the light. I have just escaped an inflammation that might have reached the other eye, besides enduring three or four weeks of confinement. I outwitted him however.'

'How?'

'I gave him the worse eye to block up. He had persuaded me

into it, but at my age it was folly; he only wanted my name to puff a cure with.'

After this lapse into even deeper darkness he was led about by a young man and thus managed to visit such of his old friends as lived near by.

He had moved into lodgings in a house in Somers Town, near what is now Euston Square. The house stood alone in a market garden called 'Montgomery's Nursery'. Beyond the garden were the open fields, and Wolcot chose the place for its fresh air and for its smell of flowers. He sat always in a room which faced the south. Behind the door was a square piano on the top of which was generally kept his favourite Cremona violin: music was the one accomplishment with which his blindness did not interfere. He had always greatly enjoyed Italian music and when, one day, a visitor said to him:

'I think, sir, the Germans excel—at least in execution,' Wolcot replied tartly, 'Yes, sir, they *execute* everything—they strangle melody.'

Now, even in blindness, he could, as he himself said, 'strum the piano and play the fiddle'. He even composed light airs for his own amusement and he was grateful that he had these resources, which were lacking to many other blind people, to fall back upon; they were a great comfort to him.

On the left of the room there was a mahogany table with writing things upon it even though, except for a few scrawled lines, he had to employ a secretary to write for him. Everything was in perfect order and the doctor knew instantly where to place his hand on anything that he wanted. Over the mantelpiece there hung a fine landscape by Richard Wilson and two of Bone's enamels which were presents from the artist in gratitude for Wolcot's introductions to influential people when Bone had first come to London from Truro. And there were also, around the sunny room, some of his own framed and glazed crayons—mostly of scenes at Fowey.

To Cyrus Redding Wolcot, as he fingered his violin, said:

'You have seen something of life in your time. See and learn all you can more. You will fall back upon it when you grow old—an old fool is an inexcusable fool to himself and others—

242

store up all; our acquirements are perhaps most useful when we become old.'

Although he was now nearly eighty his stories and tales of his past were as racily told as ever before. His faculties were unclouded, his memory only failing to the extent that if he forgot the name of a person or a place he would begin to repeat the alphabet until he came to the first letter of the word he sought.

And to this pleasant room, standing among the flowers and fields there came a stream of visitors. There was the mildly eccentric George Hanger—afterwards Lord Coleraine, though he would never be called anything but 'plain George Hanger, Sir, if you please'—who carried a short thick shillelagh and enjoyed a quid of tobacco. There were musicians like Shield, Mazzinghi and Mike Kelly. There were booksellers like Philips, who used to come and pester old Peter Pindar for verses for the *Monthly Magazine*. These Wolcot used to give him, asking nothing in return but a copy of the number of the magazine in which they appeared. Then one day the doctor wished to have for his own use a second copy of a particular issue: Philips sent back a message that he 'should have it at the Trade price'.

'The scoundrel shall never have another line of mine,' exclaimed Wolcot. 'He would suck the knowledge out of authors' skulls and fling their carcases on the dunghill afterwards.'

There were fellow writers like Godwin and Hazlitt, C. R. Leslie and Leigh Hunt. The latter reported that Wolcot 'had a fine skull which he was not displeased to be called upon to exhibit, taking his wig off and saying "There!" with a lusty voice; which formed a singular contrast with the pathos of blind eyes'.

This was, in fact, one of his harmless little vanities. He whipped off his wig for Cyrus Redding's inspection and the latter remarked that 'his head might have well served Gall and Spurzheim for the study of their whimsicalities. When young he must have been very handsome. One of his sisters whom I well remember had the same fine features; both were of dark complexion.'

And Hazlitt, too, describing one of his visits to Somers Town, said that Wolcot

'sat and talked familiarly and cheerfully, asking you whether you thought his head would not make a fine bust. He had a decanter of rum placed on the table before him from which I poured out a glassful as he wanted it and drank it pure, taking no other beverage but not exceeding in this. His infirmities had made no alteration in his conversation except, perhaps, a little more timidity and hesitation; for blindness is the *lameness* of the mind. He could not see the effect of what he said lighting up the countenance of others; and in this case the tongue may run on the faster but hardly so well. After the coffee which he accompanied with the due quantity of *merum sal* he would ask to be led down into the little parlour below which was hung around with some early efforts of his own in landscape painting and with some of Wilson's unfinished sketches. Though he could no longer see them other than in his mind's eye he was evidently pleased to be in the room with them as they brought back former associations....'

Such welcome guests at Somers Town make it clear that when his hostile Obituarists wrote that Wolcot had died alone and forgotten they were saying what they considered ought to have happened; a man who had been famous and had made so many enemies and had grown old and unsuccessful ought to die obscurely and forgotten. It was poetic justice. But there was no such justice in this case. It would have pointed a useful moral if Wolcot having lived by attacking society should die miserably and alone, ignored even by his victims. But life, as so often happens, was quite unfeeling for art; Wolcot died with less loneliness and neglect than may reasonably be expected by any normal person who has outlived his friends and his Age.

Not all those, of course, who came to Somers Town were quite as welcome as those who have been mentioned. There was, for example, Colonel Thornton. He was a man for whom Wolcot had little liking, but having spent several days at his place, Thornville Royal in Yorkshire, he felt bound to be civil to him. The colonel was a very rich sporting man, who, wishing also to cut some sort of literary figure, got a parson to 'ghost' for him a Sporting Tour. According to Redding he was mean, a monumental liar and of no integrity.

When he was in London he was in the habit of sending the doctor 'an insignificant present' of game from his estates, either in Yorkshire or Devonshire, with the message that he would be pleased to call and take a chop with him. The gift was delivered to Somers Town by Thornton's own servant who would demand porterage on the game. In this way 'by presenting a little of the worst here and there' the colonel paid himself for the carriage of all his game to London.

One day when Redding called on John Wolcot he found the old man in a terrible temper.

'What do you think, Redding? Thornton has sent game and will dine with me today. His servant has asked for the porterage again. Pray ring the bell.'

While they were waiting for one of the doctor's two servants, Mary and Nance, to answer the bell, Wolcot continued:

'He is the greatest miser and liar alive. He has asked some friends to dinner today in Lincoln's Inn Fields. He repents it, has put them off and comes to me that he may say he was not able to be at home.'

Mary came into the room.

'Did you or Nance pay Colonel Thornton's servant anything for the carriage of the game today?'

'Yes, sir, two and sixpence.'

'Why, Mary, that is nearly as much as it is worth!'

'Not much short of it, I believe, sir.'

'What was it?'

'Two partridges and a rabbit.'

'A shilling apiece for the carriage of the partridges and sixpence for the rabbit—the last may cost the powder and shot, say one charge. Thornton has calculated that to a nicety!'

He gave Mary orders that in future the colonel's gifts were not to be accepted—but Thornton was not in the least offended; he had a way of being not in the least discomfited when one of his tricks misfired.

One day, when Thornton and Redding met at Wolcot's house, the colonel, who also pretended that he owned vast estates and titles in France, invited Redding to visit his collection of game pictures which he kept in his house in Lincoln's Inn Fields. They were, he maintained, by Rubens, and quite the best works that the artist ever painted.

'You haven't got one,' snapped Wolcot, 'and you know it, Thornton. You only think they are so.'

Cyrus Redding was still in two minds about accepting the invitation, but Wolcot advised him not to waste his time.

'Besides,' he added, 'Thornton is no desirable acquaintance for any man who respects himself.'

It was, as it happened, Cyrus Redding who was responsible for relieving the doctor for ever of the society of his unwelcome guest. Colonel Thornton, who was seventy 'and ill-looking into the bargain', was often accompanied to the house by a young girl of twenty-four or twenty-five. One day Redding called on the doctor, after dinner when the wine was on the table, and the young lady was introduced to him as Miss Dormer. By a most curious coincidence Redding recognized her instantly as a schoolgirl he had known in Devonshire. Her name was certainly not Dormer: 'she was Harriet D——' wrote Redding discreetly. The recognition was mutual and the girl at once left the table. She did not return, and after an hour Mary came in to tell the colonel that Miss Dormer had her things on and was waiting for him—she was feeling unwell.

Thornton, who was fond of conversation, plainly disliked leaving the table, and the company were surprised that Miss Dormer did not return to say 'Goodbye' to her host.

When Redding suggested the reason for this omission Wolcot exclaimed:

'The scoundrel has been playing me more of his tricks: he told me she was one of his nieces!'

That was the last time that Thornton came to Somers Town.

*   *   *   *   *

His place in the ranks was most pleasantly filled. One Monday morning, having heard that the old man was blind, infirm, lame and asthmatical, his oldest and once closest friend John Taylor suddenly resolved 'to begin the week with an extinction of all enmity between us'. He went immediately to the lodgings in Somers Town:

'I addressed him in the most friendly tone but he did not recollect my voice; when he understood who I was he appeared delighted, pressed me to have a glass of brandy and

246

water though it was morning, and said that if I would stay I should have a beef-steak or anything else I could desire. In short we were reconciled in a moment and I repeated my visits as often as convenient to me, promising that I would positively drink tea with him every Saturday. I found his faculties as good as ever and his poetical talents in full vigour. . . .'

It is impossible to overestimate the happiness that this reunion must have brought to the old man as they sat comfortably together warmly reunited and reminiscing. Now that it was impossible for him to go to the theatre he must relive those pleasures in conversation. He and John Taylor had once gone together to *Love for Love* and Wolcot had considered Moody's Sir Sampson Legend the most perfect piece of character acting he had ever seen. They had been together in the Rainbow Coffee-house in Covent Garden when Macklin had come into one of the boxes and they had joined the veteran actor at supper. They had laughed together at Kemble's attempts to achieve a particular style of enunciation which had resulted in his mouthing at the words 'like a dog catching flies'; they had agreed in admiring Mrs Jordan; they had agreed, too, that in tragic rôles Garrick's performance was greatly hindered by the unnatural style in which tragedies were always written. There were so many things to talk about. And when Taylor missed his visit one week Wolcot anxiously sent him a rhymed invitation which read in part:

> Ah! Taylor, 'non sum qualis eram'
> For to the tomb I fear I near am
> But who can hope to live for ever?
> One foot is in the grave no doubt
> Then come and try to help it out
> An Ode shall praise thy kind endeavour.

There were other memories awakened in those last tranquil years when, in March, 1816, the news came that Betsy Cranch, at the age of sixty, was dead.

'Did you know Betsy Cranch?' he suddenly asked Redding. 'She was an old sweetheart of mine who dismissed me with the most comfortable assurance that a man in love ever received. Ah! you were not born then. I forgot. She married John Vivian. She was a sweet creature. . . .' And out came the story of that refusal forty years earlier that he had never forgotten.

*　　*　　*　　*　　*

John Wolcot was rapidly becoming a living memory for others. His reputation was still something with which to impress aspiring young men. In 1818 when Wolcot was eighty John Keats wrote excitedly to his brothers:

'I am in the highway of being introduced to a squad of people —Peter Pindar, Mrs Opie . . . Mr Robinson. Honours rush so thickly upon me that I shall not be able to bear up against them.' And at a dinner party with Wells and Severn, after Keats had proposed the healths of his brothers, Severn had risen and proposed that of Peter Pindar.

Even in the coffee-houses the old man was still remembered: in June, 1818, a man in the London coffee-house was overheard by John Keats talking of the sympathy of inanimate objects and saying, by way of example:

'As we were once debating in Common Hall, Mr Waithouse in illustration of some point quoted Peter Pindar at which the head of George the Third, although in hard marble, squinted over the Mayor's head at the Speaker so oddly that he was obliged to sit down.'

There were others who objected to Peter Pindar being quoted in public, as Alderman Scales had found to his cost. A wholesale butcher's salesman of Aldgate, Scales was a stump-orator and a violent democrat, 'but of good education and gentlemanly manners', who was three times elected Alderman by a City Ward and as many times rejected by the Court of Aldermen. On one occasion the grounds of his rejection were that he had publicly related an immoral poem *The Fleas* by Wolcot. But in the expensive and extensive litigation that ensued this was eventually held to be insufficient grounds for disqualification.

Whether this poem was the same as that addressed to *The Fleas of Teneriffe* (in which early exercise there seems to be very little that could be construed as immoral) is not known; it may well

248

have been part of the great body of material that fell, so Taylor reported, 'into the hands of his worthless executor'.

This shadowy, rather sinister, figure remains nameless. Taylor refers to him as 'a very vulgar man, but very cunning and well acquainted with the world. The doctor was disgusted with him and only endured him because he hated solitude after he was blind'.

In spite of his failings Wolcot thought him an honest man and told Taylor that it was he who had the will in his possession—a statement that the executor hotly denied when Taylor mentioned the matter to him.

'After Wolcot's death however he said he had found the will among some copper-plates, from drawings by the doctor, from which prints had been published. A very respectable person ... a clerk in one of the offices in Somerset House who was entrusted by Wolcot and used to receive dividends for him at the Bank assured me that it was impossible a will could be found in the alleged situation as he had looked over the copper-plates a short time before; that no paper was amongst them and that it was likewise impossible for the doctor, blind as he was, to have placed any paper there at a subsequent period or to have found his way to the place where the copper-plates were deposited.'

The suspicion that the will was not genuine was strengthened by the fact that it was witnessed by two persons whose names were quite unknown to the two servants and who, so far as they knew, had never been to the house. These servants, Mary and Nance, were sisters and the elder was described as 'a shrewd, intelligent and attentive young woman'. They had often been told by the doctor what he intended to leave to them—and these sums of £100 to one and £80 to the other the executor eventually paid together with a specified £50 each to the clerk in Somerset House and to Taylor. But for Wolcot's surviving sister, who had been told by her brother that she would be left 'a few hundreds', there was nothing.

Fortunately for John Wolcot's peace of mind in those last days he suspected nothing of all this.

*   *   *   *   *

Towards the end of 1818 it was clear that his body was failing faster than his mind. He was confined almost continually to his house and, according to one rather hypercritical observer, 'he seemed to lie in bed either from indolence or whim'.

To Giddy, arriving from the country and going to see him some three months before he died, he gave an explanation.

'What is the matter with you?' Giddy asked him. 'You lie here, apparently from choice, with your face to the wall and your body enveloped in wool and calico.'

'It signifies but little,' answered the old man, 'in what position a blind man takes his departure; and what should I rise for? It would be folly for me to be groping around my drawing-room; and with what uneasiness would it not be attended, to one now become so weak? When up and in motion I am obliged to carry a load of eleven or twelve stone; but while here I have only a few ounces of blankets to support.'

In those last months there was one thing, apart from the constant visit of his old friends, that evidently gave him great pleasure. Abraham Hawkins who had written from his beloved South Hams asking Wolcot if he would accept the dedication of his book *Kingsbridge and Salcombe* now sent a copy of the work:

> *To John Wolcot long accredited at the Court of Apollo as Peter Pindar Esqre these Pages commemorative of the History and Topography of the Vicinity of his native Earth are (by his Permission) dedicated as a Mark of sincere Respect for his superior Genius amd Talents by his Friend the Author.*

On September 2nd, 1818, Wolcot replied:

My dear Sir,

Your letter found me on the verge of the tomb, overcome by old age and an asthma, but still labouring for a little longer existence which is hardly worth acceptance.

Many thanks for your valuable present but surely you ought to dedicate it to a man of much superior talent. It pleases me much to think our literary studies began under the same worthy master John Morris whose life merits every eulogium and sets even malignity at defiance. If I have any objection to any part of your letter it is to that which contains your flattery. I like your plan of rescuing Kingsbridge and its environs from the pool of oblivion and doubt not of the public approbation. To meet hereafter in the Elysian Fields forms one of the highest wishes of

Sir, Your most humble servant,
J. Wolcot.

Amidst all his other memories those of his far-off, happy childhood beside the sunset-reflecting waters of the Kingsbridge estuary must have been by this gift greatly strengthened.

★   ★   ★   ★   ★

His 'last painless indisposition' continued all that October, November and December. Friends came and went and reported what they saw. To none was there anything distressing in the peacefulness of his slow slipping away from them. On 5th January 1819, only nine days before John Wolcot died, Hazlitt could comment that he looked, with his shaven crown, 'like a fine old Monk. . . . Not repenting the Mirth he had given . . . but like his own Expiring Taper bright and fitful to the last; tagging a line or conning his own epitaph and waiting for the last summons grateful and contented.'

A week before the end Cyrus Redding called and found him dressed but in his bedroom. He had flung himself on the bed, tired by the effort of having sat up for a few hours. His conversation was as bright and sensible as ever it had been. On the table there was a bottle of red wine.

'You ought not to take Port wine,' said Redding, 'it may become acid on your stomach.'

The old doctor reflected. Then he who in his time had prescribed so many extraordinary dishes for no other reason than that the patient had a desire for them said: 'Yes, yes, you are right, but the doctor who has called to see me advised it. I did not think about that effect.'

Redding rang the bell and told the servant to replace the wine by the favourite old rum of which it was his custom to take a wineglassful every day after dinner. 'That will suit your stomach better and you will soon be downstairs again.'

'No, no! I am an old fellow and I must go. I should like to lie as near as possible to the bones of old *Hudibras* Butler. I shan't live. I'm an old man. Nothing will do unless you bring me back my youth.'

A few days later he sent to the faithful John Taylor two Old Master landscapes. Taylor recognized them at once. Many years earlier he had tried to buy one of them from Wolcot and had offered him five guineas for it, but the doctor had refused, saying:

'No, I won't sell pleasure.'

Now the pictures were both so damaged by neglect that they were worth accepting only as memorials of friendship.

From the one that Taylor had originally offered to buy his 'excellent friend Mr Westall, R.A., kindly cut off the injured parts and reduced it into a pleasing moonlight scene. . . .'

Then on January 13th one of John Wolcot's servants came in haste to Taylor's house. She wept—for the doctor had been a kind and considerate master—all the time as she told him that the old man was sinking fast.

As soon as he could do so Taylor hurried out that afternoon to Somers Town. He was told that Wolcot had recovered his faculties but was now asleep. John Taylor sat by his bedside until ten o'clock. It was then that the dying man awoke and recognized the friend by his side. Taylor gently told him how long he had been sitting there and that he must now go for the way home was long and, perhaps, unsafe.

'Is there anything on earth that I can do for you?' he added.

The answer came back in a deep and strong voice:

'Bring me back my youth.'

John Wolcot went peacefully to sleep again and in the morning, without waking more, he was dead.

EPILOGUE

A week later, attended by a band of friends chosen by himself, John Wolcot was buried by the Reverend F. W. Vickery in the vestry vault of St Paul's, Covent Garden. It was the vault in which, 139 years earlier, the remains of Samuel Butler had also been deposited. Now, in accordance with his wishes, Peter Pindar's coffin was placed touching that of the author of *Hudibras*.

And when, the next year, poor mad George III followed his tormentor, Keats wrote to Fanny: 'What will the old king and he say to each other? Perhaps the king may confess that Peter was in the right and Peter maintain himself to have been wrong.'

Wolcot left behind him many boxes of unpublished manuscripts of his own writing for which, it was said, the booksellers offered a thousand pounds, but for which the executor demanded double and which when he, too, died disappeared.

'They will probably be disposed of as waste-paper,' said Taylor ruefully, 'though perhaps, if properly selected they might prove a valuable addition to the poetical treasures of the country.'

Taylor himself, loyal friend that he was, was kept busy writing indignant letters to the Press refuting statements by the hostile obituarists who gleefully flapped down and settled to gorge upon the remains of old John Wolcot's reputation. In the *Quarterly Magazine*, for example, either Gifford or Southey had leaped eagerly to the attack with an account that was as untrue of Peter Pindar's life as it was of his death. And by all his enemies the old scandals were rehashed, all the old allegations repeated with a fine disregard for their accuracy. As the editor of *Dutton's Dramatic and Literary Censor* had remarked, during Wolcot's lifetime:

'Few writers have more daringly approached aggression on the one hand or been more grossly attacked, vilified and misrepresented in return. . . . Various, we might almost say innumerable, are the slanderous anecdotes circulated against him by his enemies, a great part of which for want of opportune detection and timely refutation have obtained general credit. Few on the other hand are his apologists. . . .'

Such apologists as there had been, added the editor, had but feebly touched the outline of their subject and they had been inclined, too, in their efforts to defend Wolcot, to overcolour their portraits almost as crudely as his detractors.

Even Taylor, in his frequent returns to the defence, was at times guilty of spoiling his case by over-emphasis.

Wolcot, with his glee at being an *enfant terrible*, never expressed regret at the shocking picture of himself he had deliberately conjured up. What he might well have regretted was the fact that his legendary self eventually caused his memory to be for an entire century altogether neglected.

Just at first there were still those who were sufficiently near to, or part of, the eighteenth century to carry his poetical reputation forward for a while. Thackeray writing in 1831 to Edward Fitzgerald said, 'When I come to London to make my fortune . . . I shall read Young and Peter Pindar.' Shelley read Peter Pindar aloud to Mary Shelley; William Blake had a copy of the *Collected Works* in his library; Leigh Hunt writing of 'this pleasant reprobate' spoke of his 'most original vein of humour—such a mixture of simplicity, archness and power of language with an air of Irish helplessness running through as is irresistibly amusing. He is the Fontaine of lampooners.'

But then the disapproval of the Victorian moralists threw a soggy grey woollen blanket around John Wolcot's memory. He was a disreputable and profligate character not to be mentioned in polite society. His verse was in any case ephemeral, too near to be anything but out of date and not yet of historic interest. Objections to his fancied immorality and to the unethical subject matter of much of his satire gradually surrounded him with an icy and all-obscuring crust through which the real Wolcot could not penetrate.

The first signs of thaw did not set in until George Saintsbury read the *Collected Works* (more than 2000 pages of them) three times and reported that 'each time I have been more convinced that if only he had been a little more of a scholar and a great deal more of a gentleman he would have been a very great man indeed. As it is his mere cleverness is something prodigious. . . .'

Yet there was one mid-Victorian at least who did not allow himself to be deceived by the legend that John Wolcot had succeeded in creating. A writer in *Blackwood's Magazine* for July, 1868, examined that legend with great care. He investigated John Wolcot's private correspondence. It shewed him to be the reverse of indecorous and licentious. He found 'no ribaldry, no profanity, no impure suggestion'. Wolcot was one, he maintained, who libelled himself in his public manners; now he was 'unmasked as a pretended reprobate'.

'Here then we have a hypocrite of a peculiar kind—one who would have persuaded himself that he was ten times worse than other men were.'

And here, then, he might well have added, we have a doctor with two aunts.

APPENDIX

Wolcot on Richard Wilson

'What a pity that the world should be so fascinated by high finishing, fan painting, the smooth Birmingham-waiter glare, the pigmy efforts of the art as to be totally unaffected by the powers of the giant Wilson, as to proscribe the broad and vivid efforts of his pencil and forbid his works and entrance into its palaces.

What a triumph for the shade of the Medicis, the patrons and idolators of Michael Angelo and Raphael! What a pity that the patronage which might have fostered the breed of eagles should have perverted the blessing to the support of hedge-sparrows and tom-tits!'

The foregoing was written by John Wolcot as the direct result of George III refusing to buy Wilson's *Kew Gardens; Pagoda and Bridge* which according to Thomas Wright was painted 'expressly for the King . . . but which, though exquisite in colour and simplicity of design, was by some mismanagement returned upon the hands of the painter'. The picture eventually became one of Wolcot's own possessions. Always a devotee of 'old red-nos'd Wilson's art' he perpetuated his opinion in a Supplement to Pilkington's *Dictionary of Painters*:

'It may be said of this artist *nil molitur inepte*. His taste was so exquisite and his eye so chaste that whatever came from his easel bore the stamp of elegance and truth. The subjects he chose were such as did a credit to his judgment. They were the selections of taste; and whether of the simple, the elegant or the sublime they were treated with equal felicity. Indeed he possessed that versatility of power as to be one minute an eagle, sweeping the heavens, and the next a wren, twittering on the humble thorn.

His colouring was in general vivid and natural; his touch spirited and free; his composition simple and elegant; his lights and shadows broad and well distributed; his middle tints in perfect harmony, while his forms in general produced a pleasing expression.

Wilson has been called the English Claude; but how unjustly, so totally different their style! To draw a parallel between the two artists, we should say that the Frenchman too often fatigues by the detail; he enters too far into the minutiae of nature;—he painted her littlenesses. Wilson on the contrary gives a breadth to nature, and adopts only those features that more eminently attract attention. Claude, proud of shewing to the world the truth of his eye, in regard to aerial perspective, produces a number of petty parts, paltry projections, such as hedges, banks, hillocks &c to prove his power in a certain department of painting, which though far from contemptible is very distant from the higher order of the art. Claude introduces at times groups of unmeaning and uninteresting figures, while Wilson introduces a paucity, but such as are not only appropriate to the scene, but form part of the composition. The mind of Wilson was that of a classic; the mind of Claude of a mechanic, dead to the energies of classic sensibility.

The pencil of Claude was capable only of describing the general appearances of nature; that of Wilson to clothe them with elegance and grandeur. Claude, possessing no abstract idea of beauty, was confined to the individual merit of the scene; Wilson on the contrary, gifted with the charming *ideal*, could fascinate by combination. Claude was a pretty simple country girl; Wilson was a beauty of a higher order, commanding the graces and uniting them to simplicity. Claude sometimes painted grand scenes, but without a mind of grandeur; Wilson on the contrary could infuse a grandeur into the meanest objects; Claude, when he drew on the bank of his ideas, was a mere *castrato* in the art; witness his landing of Aeneas in Italy. How poverty-struck the scene!—an enterprise destitute of motion—a few clumsy vessels, with a few figures, more resembling Dutch boys, unlading at a London wharf, than ships arriving with an army to form the Roman empire and give a race to immortality. Wilson on the contrary was a *Hercules*. When his subject was grand, he clothed it with thunder; witness his Celadon and Amelia, his Niobe &c. To compare their works that demanded imagination were to draw a parallel between strength and imbecility; the two miserable statutes of Johnson and Howard in St Paul's Cathedral with the labours of Praxiteles. Claude was rather the plain and minute *historian of landscape*; Wilson was the *poet*.'

And, on another occasion, talking to a Mr Field about his hero's influence on British art, John Wolcot is reported to have said:

'It is worthy of observation that none of Wilson's pupils caught the manner of the master and yet a school has arisen which strongly partakes of it, of which the drawings of my early acquaintance, the generous and giddy Tom Girtin, is an eminent instance.'

BIBLIOGRAPHY

Allen, John: *Liskeard*
Angelo, H.: *Reminiscences*
Annual Biography and Obituary, 1820
Annual Register, 1773, 1799, 1819
Anti-Jacobin
Athenaeum, 1852
Autographic Mirror, Vol. iii

Baring Gould, S.: *A Book of the West*
Baring Gould, S.: *Devonshire Characters*
Beaden, J.: *Life of Mrs Jordan*
Bennett, Charles: *Twelve Songs and a Cantata*. The words by Mr
    Wolcot
Blackwood's Magazine: July 1868
Boase: *Collecteanea Cornubiensis 1878–82*
Boase: *Devonshire Biography 1883*
Boase and Courtenay: *Bibliotheca Cornubiensis*
Bolton, A. T.: *Portrait of Sir John Soane*
Bottrell, W.: *Traditions and Hearthside Stories of West Cornwall*
Bowring, Sir John: *Autobiographical Recollections*
Brenet, Michel: *Haydn* (translated by C. L. Leese)
Brightwell: *Memorials of Amelia Opie*
British Critic: Vol. xvi
British Stage and Literary Cabinet, 1820
Brown, Ford K.: *William Godwin*
Byrne, W. P.: *Gossip of the Century*

Cambridge Bibliography of English Literature
Cameron, K. N.: *The Young Shelley*
Campbell: *Lives of the Lord Chancellors*
Cardew, Sir A.: *Cornelius Cardew*
Carlyle, E. I.: *William Cobbett*
Carr, W.: Article on Wolcot in *D.N.B.*
Catalog of Printed Cards in the Library of Congress
Chambers, R. (ed.) : *Life and Work of Robert Burns*

Chambers Cyclopaedia of English Literature
Chancellor, Beresford: *Literary Ghosts of London*
Clark, Benjamin: *William Gifford*
Cole, G. D. H. (ed.): *Letters from William Cobbett to Edward Thornton*
Colson, Percy: *Their Ruling Passions*
Compton, Theodore: *William Cookworthy*
Constable, W. G.: *Life of Richard Wilson*
Cookworthy, W.: *Memoirs*
Cornish Banner, The
Courthope, J. J.: *History of English Poetry*
Cundall, Frank: *Historic Jamaica*
Cunningham, A.: *Pilkington's Dictionary of Painters*
Cunningham, C. G.: *Lives of Eminent Englishmen*
Cunningham, C. G.: *The British Painters*
Currycomb, Carnaby: *Peter Provided For*

Devon and Cornwall Notes and Queries, XXIV, i, vi
Devonshire Association: *Transactions*
Dutton, T. (ed.): *Dramatic Censor*

Earland, A.: *John Opie and his Circle*
European Magazine

Fact, Tom: *History of Peter Pindar from that Memorable Aera when he received a sound Thrashing*
Falk, Bernard: *Turner the Painter*
Family Library: Article on John Opie
Farington, J.: Diary edited by Jas Greig
Ferguson, J. de L. (ed.): *Letters of Robert Burns*
Forman, M. B. (ed.): *Letters of John Keats*
Frankau, Julia: *Life of J. R. Smith*

Gardner, W. J.: *History of Jamaica*
Gentleman's Magazine
Gerard, F. A.: *Angelica Kauffman*
Giddy, E. C.: *MS. Life of John Wolcot*
Gifford, W.: *Epistle to Peter Pindar*
Griggs, E. L. (ed.): *Letters of S. T. Coleridge*
Grylls, Rosalie Glynn: *William Godwin and His World*
Gwynn, S.: *Memorials of James Northcote*

Hamilton, Walter: *The Poets Laureate*
Hamilton, W. H.: *West Country Stories and Sketches*

Hannay: J.: *Satire and Satirists*
Harland, Marion: *Hannah More*
Hawkins, Abraham: *Kingsbridge and Salcombe*
Hazlitt, W.: 8th Lecture on English Comic Writers
Hazlitt, W. (ed.): *Conversations of James Northcote, R.A.*
Hazlitt, W. C.: *The Hazlitts*
Hewlett, Dorothy: *Adonais*
Hodgson and Eaton: *The Royal Academy and its Members*
Hopkins, Mary A.: *Hannah More and Her Circle*
Howard, R. M.: *The Longs of Jamaica and Hamilton Lodge*
Hunt, J. H. P.: *Selections with Critical Notice*
Hunt, Leigh: *Feast of the Poets*
Hunt, Leigh: *Life of Lord Byron*

Jerdan: *Autobiography*

Keats, John: *The Story of Fowey*

Lady's Magazine: Biography by John Taylor
Leslie, C. R.: *Memoirs*
Leslie, C. R., and Taylor, T.: *Life and Times of Sir J. Reynolds*
Lewis, C. T. Courtenay: *George Baxter, the Picture Painter*
Liber Facetiarum, 1809
Library of the Fine Arts, Vol. iv
Lockhart: *Diary*
Lockhart: *Life of Sir Walter Scott*
Long, Edward: *History of Jamaica*
Lowell, Amy: *John Keats*
Lowndes: *Biographers' Manual*
Luscombe, Ellen: *Myrtles and Aloes*

Maclean, C. M.: *Born Under Saturn*
Macready, William Charles: *Diaries*
Mauritius Moonshine: Battle of the Bards
Mayne, E. C.: *Byron*
Melville, L.: *Life and Letters of Wm. Beckford*
Monthly Magazine
Monthly Review
Morning Chronicle

Nangle, B. C.: Index to *Monthly Review*
New Monthly Magazine
Nicholls, J.: *Illustrations of the Literature of the XVIII Century*

262

Nicholls, J.: *Literary Anecdotes*
Northcote, James: *Conversations with James Ward* (ed. E. Fletcher)
Northcote, James: *Memoirs of Sir Joshua Reynolds*
Notes and Queries

One and All: 1868
Opie, Mrs: Memoir in *Lectures on Painting* by John Opie
Oracle, The

Paul, C. Kegan: *William Godwin*
Percy Anecdotes
Physic and Physicians, 1839
Pindar, Peter: see *Wolcot*
Poems chiefly by Gentlemen of Devonshire and Cornwall
Pohl, C. F.: *Mozart und Haydn in London*
Political and Personal Satires, B.M. Catalogue of
Polwhele, R.: *Biographical Sketches*
Polwhele, R.: *Essays*
Polwhele, R.: *Reminiscences in Prose and Verse*
Polwhele, R.: *Traditions and Recollections*
Polwhele, R.: *Unsex'd Females* (1800, American edition)
Public Characters, 1798, 1799

Redding, Cyrus: *Fifty Years' Recollections*
Redding, Cyrus: *Past Celebrities*
Redding, Cyrus: *Recollections Literary and Personal*
Redding, Cyrus: *Reminiscences of Eminent Men*
Redgrave, S.: *Century of Painters*
Redgrave, S.: *Dictionary of Artists*
Reitterer, Theodore: *Leben und Werke P. Pindars*
Robinson, H. Crabbe: *Diary*
Robinson, Mrs (Perdita): *Memoirs*
Rogers, J. Jope: *Life of Opie*
Rogers, Samuel: *Table Talk* (ed. Dyce)
Royal Cornwall Gazette
Royal Institute of Cornwall Journal
Russell, W. Clarke: *The Book of Authors*

Saintsbury, George: *Twenty Years of Political Satire*
Satirist, The, 1808
Scott, Sir Walter: *Journal* (ed. D. Douglas)
Seward, Anne: *Letters*
Shelley, Mary W.: *Journal*

Shelley, Mary W.: *Letters*
Sichel, W.: *Emma, Lady Hamilton*
Smiles, Samuel: *Memoir and Correspondence of John Murray*
Smith, J. T.: *Nollekens and his Time*
Somerville, T., D.D.: *My Own Life and Times*
Sun, The

Taylor, John: *Records of My Life*
Thackeray, W. M.: *Letters*
Thomson, George: *A Select Collection of Original Scottish Airs*
Thornbury: *Haunted London*
Touchstone: *The Analysis of Peter Pindar*, 1795
Town and Country Magazine, 1791
Tregellas, W. H.: *Some Cornish Worthies*
Truro Town Council: *MS. Book of Orders*

Walford, E.: *Old and New London*
Walker, H.: *English Satire and Satirists*
Walling, R. A. J.: *The West Country*
Warner, R.: *Literary Recollections*
Warner, R.: *Literary Remains of Living Authors*
Whalley, Dr: *Memoirs*
Wheatley and Cunningham: *London, Past and Present*
Whitley: *Art in England 1800–1820*
Whitley: *Artists and Their Friends in England*
Whitney, Janet: *Elizabeth Fry*
Wild, John: Unpublished Letters from the Collection of
Williamson, G. C.: *Life and Works of Ozias Humphry*
Wilson, Menzies, and Lloyd: *Amelia—the Story of a Plain Friend*
Wilson, Mona: *William Blake*
Wolcot, John: MS Volume of Letters to Thomas Giddy, London,
              1794
Wolcot, John: *Collected Works of P. Pindar*, Dublin, 1812
Wolcot, John: *Collected Works of P. Pindar*, London, 1816
Wright, T.: (ed.) *Letters of William Cowper*
Wright, T.: *Some Account of the Life of Richard Wilson*

INDEX

A

Aberdeen, University of, 31
Adams, Sir Wm., oculist, 241–2
Alken, Samuel, 183
Andrew, Archdeacon and Mrs, 134
Angelo, Henry, 122, 215
Austen, Mrs, of Fowey, 134

B

Banks, Sir J., P.R.S., 128, 129, 130, 185
Bassett, Sir F., of Tehiddy, 134
Beckford, William, 212–14
Billington, Mrs, singer, 119, 123–4, 160
Bodmin, Cornwall, 19, 22
Bone, Henry, 242
Boscawen, Admiral, 23
Boscawen, Mrs, 87
Boscawen, William G., 39, 40, 42, 44, 45, 54, 87
Boswell, Sir Alexander, is amused, 113–14
Boswell, James, 98–9; is not amused, 113
Buckland, John, overseer of Truro, 79, 81
Bunn, Mary, 93
Burns, Robert, 149–53

C

Campbell, Colonel, 36th Regiment of Foot, 53

Cardew, Mr, headmaster of Truro, 60–1, 71
Carter, Elizabeth, 227–33
Cartrett, Capt., of H.M.S. *Lowestoft*, 54
Charlotte, Queen, wife of Geo. III (*q.v.*), 88
Chasemore, M, 215
Ching, John, his vermifuge, 178
Coleridge, S. T., 13, 221, 238
Colman, George, the elder, 119
Commons, House of, disesteemed, 102, 166
Cookesley, William, 34, 47, 78
Cookworthy, William, Quaker, 28–9
Coryton, Miss, peerless, 23; loves another, 24–5; 221
Cosway, Mrs, 91, 105, 113, 157
Cosway, Richard, 91, 105, 113
Coventry, Lord, 236
Cranch, Betsy, nonpareil, 25; loves another, 70–1; 221, 247–8
Crews, Nicholas, 36–7
Crispin, Thomas, Free School of, 15
Croker, Captain, of Truro, dances, 76
Crosdill, John, cellist, 143
Cumberland, Duke of, 132–3
Curran, J. P., Irish orator, 123–4

D

Daniell, Mr, of Truro, 57
Daniell, Miss, drastic cure of, 59
Delany, Mary Granville, 87, 88
Devonshire, Duchess of, 102

Somerville, Revd Dr Thomas, 121
Spencer, Nancy, importunity of, 74
Stephens, Robert, 134
Swete, Prebendary and Mrs, 134, 135

T

Taylor, John, editor, 21, 66, 93, 100, 113, 123–4, 126, 130, 131, 132, 133, 138–40, 143, 144, 151, 155, 160–2, 166, 172, 174–5, 178, 202, 205, 207, 246–54
Teneriffe, pleasures of, 40–1
Terry, Richard, Bp. of London, 46; invokes divine aid, 47
Thelwall, John, 236
Thomson, George, of Edinburgh, 149–53
Thornton, Colonel, 244–6
Thunderbolts, boiled, as cure, 84
Trelawney, Anne, 42, 52
Trelawney, Lady Letitia, 39, 52, 53, 54, 56
Trelawney, Sir William, 32, 33, 42–6, 47–8, 52–4
Truro, Cornwall, life in, 30, 57–82; Corporation of, revenge by, 81, 87
Turk's Head, coffee house, 135–6
Tyler, Royall, 142

U

Upcott, William, 202

V

Vivian, John, marries Miss Cranch, 71

W

Walker, Mr, bookseller, 153–5, 187, 218–19
Walker, Revd Samuel, of Truro, 82
Wallis, Captain, of Truro, 87
Warner, Revd Richard, 158–9
Warrick, Alderman, of Truro, 72, 78
Wells, Revd Nathaniel, of Kingsbridge, 176
West, Benjamin, 90–1, 100, 105, 106, 109–10, 212, 234
Whitaker, Dr, 223
Whitbread, Samuel, brewer, 115–18
White, Atty, Town-crier of Truro, 80
Wigstead, Henry, 122
Wilson, Richard, 63, 67, 92, 186, 257–9
Wolcot, John (Peter Pindar), family of: Alexander (father), 13, 18; Amy (sister), 17, 18, 223; Amy (aunt, see Roberts); Anna (cousin), 26 (see also Nankivell); Anne (sister,) 17, 18, 134, 223; John (uncle), 18–19, 22, 26, 31, 32, 48; Mary (née Ryder, mother), 13, 18, 101; Mary (aunt), 20–1, 25, 31, 48, 57, 83; William (uncle), 101
Wright, Mr, bookseller, 202–6
Wyatt, James, 212

ALSO MENTIONED BY, OR IN CONNECTION WITH, PETER PINDAR

Actors: Barry, 35; Cibber, Mrs, 35; Dancer, Mrs, 35; Garrick, 35, 123, 247; Johnstone, 97; Jordan, Mrs, 247; Katterfelto, 100; Kemble, 247; Moody, 247; Pope, 123; Powell, 36; Siddons, Mrs, 114, 119, 228; Yates, Mrs, 35

Artists: Blake, 254; Caravaggio, 100; Chamberlain, 91; Chambers, Sir W., 92; Dance, N., 97; de Loutherbourg, 91; Gainsborough, 100; Hone, 106; Kauffman, Miss, 91; Ramsay, 106; Rigaud, 105; Serres, 91; Wright, 106; Zincke, 97; Zoffany, 91

Composers: Abel, 103; Arne, 144; Clementi, 103, 144; Delayrac, 119; Dibden, C., 103; Gossec, 119; Gyrowetz, 144; Handel, 103, 144; Jommelli, 120; Koswarra, 103; Kozebuch, 151; Serres, Mrs, 224; Stamitz, 224

Lawyers: Erskine, 165; Garrow, 227–33; Jarvis, *ibid.*; Mansfield, Lord, 105

Musicians: Bennet, 70; Cervetti, 143; Cramer, 103; Crescentini, 120; Damen, 144; Fischer, 103; Giardini, 143; Hindmarsh, 144; Jarnowich, 143; Kampferr, 103; Menel, 144; Nicolai, 103; Schroeter, 103; Solli, 120

Politicians: Auckland, 196–7; Chatham, 23; Fox, 102, 182; Grey, 182; Hood, 102; Jenkinson, 130; Lansdowne, 114; Osborne, 130; Thurlow, 114, 130; Wray, 102

Printers: Day, 233; Nichols, 138; Spilsberry, 195; Thompson, of Jamaica, 52; Trewman, 137

Singers: Men: Bellamy, 144; Garducci, 36; Manzoli, 36; Nield, 144; Tenducci, 36. *Women:* Banti, 214, 214*n.*; Campolini, 36; Corri, 144; Poole, 144

Writers: Agg, 62, 241; Burrell, Lady, 155; Butler, S., 237, 253; Canning, 191; Cobbett, W., 205; Cole, Revd T., 156; Cumberland, 155–6; Daniel, 241; Dennis, Miss, 182–3; Dermody, 205; Dryden, 225–6; Edwards, 54; Goodridge, 82; Kendall, 156; Lawler, 222, 241; Saintsbury, 255; Scott, Sir W., 202, 236; Shelley, 254; Southey, 253; Thackeray, 254; Walpole, 46; Warton, 61, 114; Warwick, Revd T., 135; Wollstonecraft, Mary, 182, 209